VERNACULAR ENGLISH

translation
TRANSNATION
SERIES EDITOR EMILY APTER

A list of titles in the series appears at the back of the book.

Vernacular English

READING THE ANGLOPHONE
IN POSTCOLONIAL INDIA

Akshya Saxena

PRINCETON UNIVERSITY PRESS
PRINCETON & OXFORD

Copyright © 2022 by Princeton University Press

Princeton University Press is committed to the protection of copyright and the intellectual property our authors entrust to us. Copyright promotes the progress and integrity of knowledge. Thank you for supporting free speech and the global exchange of ideas by purchasing an authorized edition of this book. If you wish to reproduce or distribute any part of it in any form, please obtain permission.

Requests for permission to reproduce material from this work should be sent to permissions@press.princeton.edu

Published by Princeton University Press
41 William Street, Princeton, New Jersey 08540
99 Banbury Road, Oxford OX2 6JX

press.princeton.edu

All Rights Reserved

Library of Congress Cataloging-in-Publication Data

Names: Saxena, Akshya, 1986- author.
Title: Vernacular English : reading the Anglophone in postcolonial India / Akshya Saxena.
Description: Princeton : Princeton University Press, 2022. | Series: Translation / transnation | Includes bibliographical references and index.
Identifiers: LCCN 2021032214 (print) | LCCN 2021032215 (ebook) | ISBN 9780691223131 (paperback) | ISBN 9780691219981 (hardback) | ISBN 9780691223148 (ebook)
Subjects: LCSH: English language—Social aspects—India. | Language policy—India—History—20th century. | Indic literature (English)—20th century—History and criticism.
Classification: LCC PE3502.I6 S39 2021 (print) | LCC PE3502.I6 (ebook) | DDC 427/.954—dc23
LC record available at https://lccn.loc.gov/2021032214
LC ebook record available at https://lccn.loc.gov/2021032215

British Library Cataloging-in-Publication Data is available

Editorial: Anne Savarese and James Collier
Production Editorial: Sara Lerner
Cover Design: Layla MacRory
Production: Erin Suydam
Publicity: Alyssa Sanford and Charlotte Coyne
Copyeditor: Aviva Arad

Cover art: Dhruvi Acharya, *Words, Words, Words*, 2016. Synthetic polymer paint on unprimed linen, 18 × 18 in.

This book has been composed in Miller

मेरी प्यारी माँ के लिए

CONTENTS

Acknowledgments · ix
Preface. On the Grounds · xiii

Introduction. Vernacular English: Reading the Anglophone   1

Elsewhere, or The Problem of English   1

Vernacular Resolutions   7

The Promise of the Common: Historical Routes of English in India   15

The Anglophone, or To Read What Is Not Written   20

Chapter Descriptions, or Anglophone in Five Speech Acts   25

CHAPTER 1   Law: Democratic Objects in Postcolonial India, or India Demands English   29

A Language of Paper   29

Administrative Anxieties of the Postcolonial State   32

The Alliance between Hindi and English   36

India Demands English (Anxiously)   40

Satire, or The View from Below   45

Language Ex Machina: English as an Instrument   56

CHAPTER 2   Touch: Dalit Anglophone Writers and a Language Shared   60

The Dalit Writer and the English Language   60

Ambedkar, Phule, and the Goddess English of the Bloodless Revolution   69

Dalit Anglophone Poets   80

	Hindi Dalit Writing and the Sensation of Touch	87
	Reading English after Touch	96
CHAPTER 3	Text: A Desire Called English in Indian Anglophone Literature	98
	Caste and Representation in Indian Anglophone Literature	98
	How Does a Dalit Character Sound? Reading Anand's Untouchable	103
	Performing English in Adiga's The White Tiger	113
	Fugitive Fictions	121
CHAPTER 4	Sound: The Mother's Voice and Anglophonic Soundscapes in Northeast India	124
	Orality, or English as a Mother Tongue	124
	"Indian Army Rape Us": Political Mothers and the Indian State	130
	A Language of Protest: Mahasweta Devi and Arundhati Roy	136
	Sonic English and the Aesthetics of Witness in Literature from Northeast India	140
CHAPTER 5	Sight: Cinematic English and the Pleasures of Not Reading	148
	Seeing, Not Reading	148
	Montage, or Meaning Deferred in Slumdog Millionaire	155
	The Ordinariness of English in Gully Boy	164
	Materiality of English in Hindi-Urdu Cinema	170
	Coda. Radical Anglophony, or The Ethics of Attunement	178

Notes · 181

Index · 199

ACKNOWLEDGMENTS

VERNACULAR ENGLISH IS A book about learning to know again what we thought we knew well. Writing it, I have often paused with curiosity at my experiences of learning and unlearning, and felt renewed gratitude for everyone who held my hand. I was particularly struck by how much of this book took shape even before I knew I wanted to write it. More than I can know—much less acknowledge—mentors, friends, and conversations from the University of Delhi and Jawaharlal Nehru University have left an indelible imprint on it.

Most recognizably, *Vernacular English* began as a doctoral dissertation at the University of Minnesota, where I arrived with a seed of an idea. Shaden Tageldin, the most extraordinary graduate adviser and mentor, helped me nurture that idea into the book it is today. Her personal and intellectual generosity will forever be an inspiration for my work. John Mowitt met all my ideas, especially my interest in sound, with the most supportive combination of excitement and insight. He has read several drafts beyond the dissertation stage, responding to each with precision, possibilities, and puns. Ajay Skaria has modeled the kindness of clarity in scholarship and Simona Sawhney the solidity of political convictions. For all this and more, they will always have my gratitude.

Vanderbilt University welcomed me and this book with warm enthusiasm. Colleagues in the English Department, Asian Studies, and Cinema and Media Arts have provided a hospitable environment for me to complete the manuscript. I am grateful to Dana Nelson and Lorraine Lopez for their support as chairs of the English Department. Vera Kutzinski, Jonathan Lamb, Leah Marcus, Bridget Orr, Allison Schachter, Samira Sheikh, Ben Tran, Rachel Tuekolsky, and Mark Wollaeger have been supportive mentors and readers of my work. Allison, Ben, and Vera especially have thought with me about some of the smallest—indeed the most important—details of the book. Jen Fay invited me to share a part of the book at the Cinema and Visual Culture Seminar. The wonderful discussion from that day guided me through the thickets of revision.

Ulka Anjaria, Laura Brueck, and Debjani Ganguly read drafts of the entire manuscript. My shortcomings aside, their ability to see what I could not has made all the difference. Iftikhar Dadi, Susan Snow Wadley, and Anand Yang steered the American Institute of India Studies' Book

Workshop in 2017 that distilled for me the shape of the project. Jahan Ramazani planted the idea that I should write about Anglophone poetry. His reflections on poetry and sound came alive when I encountered the writings of Yogesh Maitreya and Chandramohan Sathyanathan. Both Yogesh and Chandra have shared their world and time with me with an open heart. Anita Dube, Aruni Kashyap, Chandrabhan Prasad, and Snigdha Poonam gave me transformative opportunities to see the English language anew through their art and activism.

Big thanks to friends who read drafts of chapters, offered references, and gently loosened the knots of my argument. They give me the community I write for—an honor and a gift. I am especially grateful to Isabel Huacuja Alonso, Candice Amich, Nasia Anam, Pavneet Aulakh, Amit Baishya, Hongwei Thorn Chen, Daniel DeWispelare, Rosalyn D'mello, Alex Dubilet, Vebhuti Duggal, Daniel Elam, Jessie Hock, Sucheta Kanjilal, Roanne Kantor, Monika Bhagat-Kennedy, Marzia Milazzo, Kalyan Nadiminti, Pooja Rangan, Helen Shin, Ragini Tharoor Srinivasan, Pavitra Sundar, and Anand Vivek Taneja. A special shout out to Monika, who has organized the monthly meetings of our yet-nameless writing group with Kalyan, Nasia, Ragini, and Roanne, as well as to Ragini for inviting us to reflect on the Anglophone in the first place. Sucheta and her students at the University of Tampa read a draft of chapter 5 in their class, buoying me with their sharp observations and heart-warming notes.

At Princeton University Press, thanks to Anne Savarese for her trust and guidance as well as to James Collier and Sara Lerner for their care and attention to this project. Jennifer Gutman assisted me with research in 2019 and Ellen Tilton-Cantrell helped me with editing. They played a valuable role in keeping me organized through the process of research and writing.

Several postdoctoral and predoctoral grants and fellowships provided tangible support to complete research and writing. I am grateful to the Office of the Provost at Vanderbilt for a 2017 Provost Research Studio Award and a 2019–20 Research Scholar Grant. I would also like to thank the College of Arts and Sciences at Vanderbilt University for a 2021–23 Dean's Faculty Fellowship. At the University of Minnesota, I was able to travel to New Delhi and Pune for research with the support of a 2013–14 Interdisciplinary Doctoral Fellowship funded by the Interdisciplinary Center for the Study of Global Change and a 2014–15 Global Spotlight Doctoral Dissertation International Research Grant funded by the Global Policy and Strategy Alliance. A 2014–15 International Dissertation Research Fellowship from the Mellon-Social Science Research Council and a Mellon/American Council of Learned Societies Dissertation Completion Fellowship in 2015–16 supported the dissertation on which this book is based.

Excerpts from chapters 1 and 3 appeared in Akshya Saxena, "Language Ex Machina: Private Desires, Public Demands, and the English Language in Twentieth-Century India," *Cultural Critique* 110 (Winter 2020): 110–39 (copyright 2020 Regents of Minnesota), as well as in Akshya Saxena, "The English Language and the Indian State: From *Raag Darbari* to *The White Tiger*," *South Asian Review* 35, no. 3 (2014): 149–65. I thank the Regents of Minnesota and *South Asian Review* for their permission to publish this material here.

Equally tangibly, I could not have finished this book without friends cheering me on with wise gifs and timely distractions. Sunayani Bhattacharya, Hongwei Thorn Chen, Vedita Cowaloosur, Courtney Gildersleeve, Sucheta Kanjilal, Sravanthi Kollu, Saklendra Sikka, and Heeryoon Shin—you have my heart.

Finally, not that there are words, but I'll try. I owe everything to my family, who have been the wind at my back. To Uncle and Aunty for their rock-solid support. To Badi Di and Anindya for all the laughs. To Harsha for his exhilarating idealism. And to my mother for teaching me the most important lesson of all: trust the hours.

PREFACE. ON THE GROUNDS

OVER THE COURSE of the 2010s, two English speakers have transformed the political landscape of India. In turn, they have also transformed the meanings of the English language. These figures are Narendra Modi, India's fourteenth and current prime minister, and Rohith Vemula, a Dalit (formerly, "untouchable") PhD scholar who took his own life.[1] They share a few similarities—their marginalized class and caste positions, for instance. But for the most part, Modi and Vemula stand at opposite ends of the ideological spectrum. Their political positions make them enemies, and it is said that Modi's government has Vemula's blood on its hands.

But, together, Modi and Vemula exemplify the life of the English language in postcolonial India, and reframe the grounds of postcolonial comparativism. Modi epitomizes the hustle and humiliation of many English neoliterates in India. As a tentative speaker of English, he draws on it as a symbol to entrench a neoliberal and Hindu nationalist conservatism. Vemula, on the other hand, turned to English as the language of scientific rationalism to challenge the centuries-old practice of caste in India. In his English-language suicide note, which has become the symbol of anticaste struggle today, he saw English as the language of Dalit leaders like B. R. Ambedkar and not of British colonialism. For both Modi and Vemula, English is the language of aspiration, global affiliation, and the future. Steeped in the asymmetries it offers to erase, English holds the promise of democracy and equality. In the name of these political aspirations, Modi turns to English to uphold a neoliberal and casteist Hindu Indian state, whereas Vemula used English precisely to resist this vision.

Modi has cultivated a larger-than-life image by presenting himself as an everyman. Equivocating about his low caste identity, Modi has claimed that he belongs to "the caste of the poor" and never ceases to remind his audience that he used to be a tea vendor in the early years of his life.[2] Modi's humble-origin narrative, writes Praseeda Gopinath, is distinctly lower class, local, and divorced from the elitism of English as well as upper-caste culture.[3] It is a welcome contrast to his political opponents and upper-class pedigreed predecessors, all of whom have been fluent in English. While Modi gives inflammatory public speeches in Hindi and Gujarati to rally Hindus against Muslims, his poor English language skills have been mocked. He has been farcically "challenged" to speak in English by his political rivals. On his visit to India in 2020, even Donald Trump teased Modi by saying to the press that "his English is actually very good, you don't wanna hear about it!"[4] Modi's rise to the prime ministerial position has represented to his supporters the victory of many things: the victory of Hindu nationalism, of exclusionary economic policies, and of the economically marginalized underdog.

In the international arena, Modi falsely naturalizes Hindi as India's national language, boosts his Hindu nationalist stance, and intensifies his brazen attempt to alienate non-Hindi speakers within India. He has addressed the United Nations in Hindi. He converses in Hindi with world leaders and audiences in non-Hindi-speaking parts of India. Modi's proud embrace of Hindi only further emboldens other Hindi-speaking and Hindu resident and diasporic Indians. The equation is almost mathematical—Hindu nationalism = Hindi. But in the figure of Modi, it has constellated seductive associations with Hindu virility, economic development, and social mobility as well.

Still, even (especially?) Modi cannot resist the allure of English, and he regularly appeals to its symbolic power. As he uses it, English is both the ally and the foe of Hindu nationalism. For instance, in an address to the Indian Parliament, Modi used English and Sanskrit to proclaim what he and his party saw as the essence of India. In an aggressive vocal performance, Modi repeated the English phrase "idea of India" like a chant, and followed it with Sanskrit verses and Hindi aphorisms that translated to "victory of truth," "the world is a family," "god lives in a plant," et cetera. By glossing the idea of India in Sanskrit without translation he created the parliament as an upper-caste Hindu space where everyone understood Hindi and Sanskrit, and welcomed English into this space. The English phrase called to mind a popular Indian advertisement for cellular service and sounded like an advertisement itself. His performance left out millions of Indians who knew neither English nor the classical caste-marked language of Sanskrit. Modi's translation erased India's linguistic and religious diversity, and yoked English to a Hindu idea of India.

Still, Modi does not often speak in English. In contrast to his aggressive posturing in the parliamentary address through an English phrase, the few times he has *spoken* at length in English, his speeches have lacked luster. Critics and commentators have pooh-poohed him for sounding self-conscious, slow, and strained. But he has used English—not as a language to speak in—but as a language to wear, as a symbol to invoke, and as an object to fetishize. For instance, in 2015, when Modi wore a pinstripe suit to meet his guest, Barack Obama, the stripes were really his own name embroidered in gold thread in the Roman script across the length of his outfit like a brand name. In his meeting with Obama, Modi maintained his pro-Hindi stance by conversing in Hindi, but he literally *wore* the English language to make up for its absence and to accrue transnational recognition of his own person. Using an interpreter in his meeting with Obama freed Modi from the burden of speaking in English. Modi's sartorial choice was criticized by national and international press that saw in it the most indefensible act of a megalomaniac and a "narcissistic parvenu."[5] Contrary to a worldview where the affiliation with English elevates one into the upper echelons of society, Modi found himself to be the laughingstock of the nation. His exhibitionist performance of the English language showed him to be lacking in sophistication. Instead of uplifting him, Modi's appropriation of English as a brand offered the surest characterization of him as an upstart.

Now six years in power (as I write this book in 2021), Modi has continued to rely on the English language as a brand to make him and his politics seem progressive, popular, and palatable. Over his two terms, Modi has launched a number of campaigns that include: #IndiaSupportsCAA, #SheInspiresUs, Digital India, Make in India, and #selfiewithdaughter. These initiatives have been widely criticized for manipulating public consent and for ignoring the structural issues of governance that need to be addressed. For instance, #selfiewithdaughter was supposed to raise awareness about the deteriorating gender ratio and growing cases of female infanticide in India. As a solution to entrenched gender discrimination, it asked fathers to take selfies with their daughters and post them on social media. In another campaign, Modi asked people to use the hashtag #IndiaSupportsCAA to express (only) support for an unconstitutional act that proposed to strip many Muslims of their citizenship. Modi has called technology a catalytic agent that connects him with his country and with other global leaders. In such initiatives, Modi leverages the symbolic power and sociotechnical effects of English along with the infrastructural power of social media to reach (only those who have access to the Internet). While he favors Hindi as a political gesture, Modi instrumentalizes English for its metonymic association with global capitalist modernity.

The earliest text to justify the Hindu caste system—*Manusmriti* (*the remembered laws of Manu*)—mandates that a low-caste person who intentionally listens to the *veda*s to memorize them must have his ears filled with molten lead and lac, and that one who dares to utter the knowledge denied him must have his tongue cut off. In contemporary times, this proscription takes the institutional form of expulsion and social alienation. Reports claim that a number of Dalit students die by suicide, especially in institutions of higher education, as they are unable to keep up with the constant harassment and the pressure of functioning in an Anglicized society.[6] On January 17, 2016, Rohith Vemula died by suicide in the hostel of Hyderabad Central University. Vemula was a PhD student in life sciences, an active member of the Ambedkar Students' Association, and a Dalit. In July 2015, he and a group of other students had clashed with the student wing of Modi's political party. University administrators then barred the students from public spaces on campus and withheld their fellowship stipend. The mental toll of having no money and nowhere to go was too much for Vemula to bear. In the campus where Vemula ended his life, "eight other Dalit students [had] committed suicide" before him.[7]

However, unlike the other Dalit students, Vemula left a suicide note. This note is both an autobiographical life narrative in the English language as well as a witness to its traumatic end. Vemula's death has sparked a strong wave of anticaste activism in India. The clarity of the note—heartbreaking and inspiring—has become a symbol of that agitation. The note has been excerpted on posters, woven into poems, adapted into plays, and read at protests. It has achieved a textual and material afterlife. The English of Vemula's letter—now visible in public spaces—draws attention to the educated Dalit subject. It stands for Ambedkarite Dalit politics, a branch of politics inspired by activist B. R. Ambedkar that rejects religious and patriarchal Hindu nationalism with rational humanism and universal liberation. This radical Dalit discourse has questioned the very existence of a Hindu society, and highlighted the brutality and inhumanity of the caste system.

Vemula presented his life-narrative as a rejection of the casteist bias of the modern Indian state. The letter describes his alienation by calling his "birth his fatal accident."[8] Vemula's death reveals the possibility and the limits that the English language signifies for the educated Dalit. Vemula wanted to be a writer like Carl Sagan, but finds himself hopelessly condemned by and to his caste identity. He wished to imagine the human as "a mind" and "a glorious thing made up of star dust" rather than a body regulated by caste practices. Instead, Vemula finds that the value of a human being is reduced to the caste he is born in, to what he called "the accident of his birth." In the arithmetic of democracy, human life is measured in votes and statistics. The English language appears in the letter as

Vemula's means of accessing a world beyond this one, a realm of what he called "Science, Stars, Nature." The promise of English is highlighted in the Ambedkarite politics Vemula practiced and the letter that has outlived him and sparked a revolutionary fervor. But perhaps, most important of all, it is evident also in the fact that—inspired by the works of Sagan—he believed he could "travel to the stars." Vemula's letter illuminates the role that the English language plays in narratives and experiences of caste. It is an invitation to take seriously the role of English in advancing as well as thwarting a Dalit critique of the casteist state.

The use of English by Modi and Rohith conjures a vernacular English that is belied by and buried under the rather flat narrative of global English. By interrogating the grounds of comparison, this vernacular English uncovers the shame, anxiety, and hope of a language that has long been read only through colonial compulsions as hegemonic and elite.

Modi's English limns the limits of his pro-Hindi stance and the inadequacy of using only Hindi in the democratic address. In Modi's suit, English is materialized as an image that even those unlettered in English can understand. The circulation of English as Roman script—its visual character—transforms the language from something to read to something to *see*. It also imbues English with a different, nonelitist register of power, associated with technological modernity, mass connectivity, and populism. Rohith Vemula's English, on the other hand, brings to us most forcefully the need to reckon with the role of English *in* caste struggles and *as* a site of caste struggle. Together, these two figures stand in testimony to how different English looks in India today—on Modi's suit and in Vemula's crushing note—and to the inadequacy of our conceptual understanding of it as simply a global language. It is the argument of this book that *this* is what the Anglophone looks like, sounds like, and reads like.

VERNACULAR ENGLISH

INTRODUCTION

Vernacular English

READING THE ANGLOPHONE

Elsewhere, or The Problem of English

In the early 2000s, after almost a hundred years of stuffy great books fare, the Department of English at the University of Delhi in India revamped its curriculum. It hoped to undo the damage of colonial education practices and make English literary studies more relevant—less alienating—to the postcolonial Indian student. Accordingly, my peers and I began the degree program in English literature with one course on Victorian literature and another on Indian literature written or translated in English. The two literary traditions charted English between the colonial formations of the English canon at the height of imperialism and its postcolonial rebuttals. The inclusion of literatures from Indian languages in English revealed English in and through other languages, and radically redefined what English literature could mean in India.

This hard-won curriculum was a step worth celebrating, and I am fortunate to have benefited from it. But it also laid bare a problem.[1] In class, we talked about the subversion of colonial paradigms, about how Indian writers negotiated English, and whether it was adequate to India's political and linguistic complexity. But even as we read upper-caste writers, rarely did we discuss how caste and ethnic politics predating colonialism shaped different receptions of English in India. I wondered if the department felt that English literary study in a former British colony could only be a colonial compulsion. By anxiously returning to the colonial origin story, by naming the breach Indian writers and readers were condemned to stitch over, did the new curriculum distance English from India?[2] Did it parse the relevance of English literature to the postcolonial student as her continued resistance to it?

The worlds inside and outside the classroom also felt different. Inside, the tenets of postcolonial studies held sway. We knew to read English suspiciously, against the grain. It was the language of British colonialism, fit only for critiquing the erstwhile empire. Outside, English was the language of Indian bureaucracy, political solidarity, global media, and the most contentious debates around class, caste, and access to education. India had just conducted nuclear tests, its economic growth had been steady, and call centers were mushrooming all over urban centers. English was everywhere, whether one knew it as English or not. What felt jarring—what made an impression on me—was that we read English only as a colonial language when it was also a language that all of us in the classroom lived daily. I often thought of the well-known Derridean aporia—the colonial language that is not mine but not foreign. But I wondered if English was also *our* language, made so with as many compulsory and aspirational encounters as there were speakers. This familiar ordinariness of English loomed menacingly outside the classroom but never made its way inside.

What became intelligible as English, and how? Could the use and presence of English be understood only as the continued operation and success of a former colonial power? English has existed for three hundred years in India. And yet, it continues to be studied only as a problem to be solved. It remains the language of imperial hegemonies from elsewhere. Scales, spaces, and sources located elsewhere are used to explain its everyday affects and politics.

Years later in an art show in New Delhi, I found a visual reference for this problem of English. For one of her works in the show, *Disparately Yours*, Anita Dube, an Indian contemporary artist, covered cheap steel wire with velvet and twisted and tied it to write out one of Franz Kafka's parables in English. Placing one full grate-like parable on top of itself several times, she created thick metal armatures. Looking at these pieces, it was hard to tell if the artist had written something or made a mesh of steely squiggles. Dube's laborious repetitive overlaying of text on top of itself transmuted Kafka's German into something primarily visual and tangible. As a German-language writer of the Jewish diaspora in Prague, Kafka's minority ethnic and religious identity was always at odds with his German. Dube's art practice gave that tension as well as the ambiguity and confusion of the parable a concrete form. The audience could hardly see the individual words to make sense of it; what remained was the uncanny density and materiality of language. Dube's work modeled how profusion

FIGURE 1. *Short Stories by Kafka—An Everyday Occurrence.* Steel wire covered with black velvet. Anita Dube. 2014. (Courtesy of the artist and Nature Morte, New Delhi.)

could make something at once self-evident and unrecognizable. Looking at these artworks, I wondered if perhaps something similar had happened with English in India. The English language itself had become so obvious and ubiquitous to us—in disciplinary debates in literary studies and everyday encounters—that we as scholars were unable to read it.

As I sat in her studio one January morning, Dube variously referred to this opacity of linguistic and textual excess as text becoming "noise," "a thick curtain," and "a jungle." No matter what she wrote in her artwork, the audience noticed only the materials and the techniques: cheap wire, enamel eyes from temple statuary, raw meat, ink-saturated flat color fields, and velvet-clad found objects. These materials and processes were the artist's way of "giving body to language" by asserting its location in the developing world and staging solidarity with its people. In another work, *Strike*, for instance, the titular word was painted in a bloody red and shaped by arranging ceramic eyes from Hindu religious sculptures.

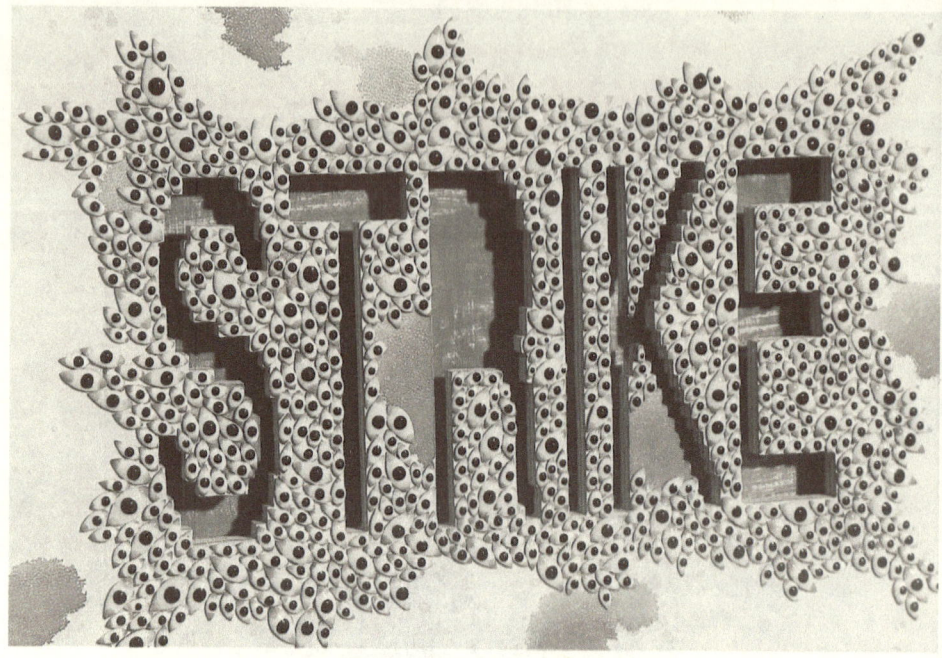

FIGURE 2. *Strike*. Enameled votive eyes on painted board. Anita Dube. 2014. (Courtesy of the artist and Nature Morte, New Delhi.)

The eyes conjured the amoebic masses exhorted to strike and ascribed them divinity. The wrought body of language drew its meanings both from the laboring bodies who traditionally worked with those inexpensive materials and the beady-eyed deities. What was written and how it was written were both political choices that mutually transformed the other. To read the language, one also had to read the many bodies that made it legible.

Today, the English language has achieved a similar excess and opacity. English is the undisputed global language whose reach, visibility, normativizing power, and capacity to assimilate foreign words rival every other language in the world. Ironically, this spread of English has made it a comparative cipher in contemporary scholarship, which is rarely considered a language with history and culture that isn't already global or colonial. As literary scholars, we have mapped newer and newer trajectories to expand our archive. Still, we have seldom probed English, the medium of our study, as it facilitates comparative scholarship. This oversight has contributed as much to the perpetuation of a linguistic exceptionalism as has the institutional neglect of other—especially non-Western European—languages.

This is not to say that scholars have not produced work that refutes the exceptionalism of English. Simon Gikandi, Srinivas Aravamudan, Jonathan Arac, Gaurav Desai, and Rey Chow have repeatedly urged scholars to account for the multiplicity of the very organizing principle of English literary studies.[3] In an ethnography of English literature in India, Rashmi Sadana has persuasively shown how English is no longer a language of the erstwhile British colonizer and has taken on a very different life in postcolonial India, which must be viewed in relation to other Indian languages.[4] Outside India, Moradewun Adejunmobi has shown that English does not spell a negative burden in Nigeria but appears desirably foreign and unintelligible in cultural forms like "World Music" and Nigerian video film.[5]

However, dominant strains in postcolonial studies and comparative literary studies—their forms, methods, archives, and conclusions—remain remarkably unperturbed by such scholarship. In fact, since the 2010s, with the decline of language programs in the United States, we have witnessed vigorous debates on the imperious and Orientalist role of English and what the title of Minae Mizumura's 2015 book has called the "fall" of other languages.[6] Across the Anglophone world, discussions of the relevance, representational possibilities, and authenticity of English have such a long history that they have become, to quote Tobias Warner, "zombie" debates.[7] The verdict is insistent in these discussions: to read or write in English is to always be in the shadow of its colonial pasts and global presents. Both the unmarked neutrality of English as a scholarly medium and its much-remarked-upon expropriations as a global imperialist language perpetuate the absorptive logic of English.

Where India is concerned, numerous scholarly accounts of global literary successes, modernist internationalism, and call centers suggest that English is a language both from and directed elsewhere.[8] The prized neutrality of English in the call-center economy further exaggerates English as a language of nonstop time, no place, and no people. It should come as no surprise that studies of global texts, movements, and industries suggest that English provides a foundation for exploitative global economies and disadvantages local languages.[9] In South Asian studies, English has mostly been written about in opposition to other Indian languages—as a scavenging discourse that manages and metabolizes other languages. Enduring is the dictum that the English language in India—and, possibly, everywhere else—has always done the same work. It advances the same modern imperial and neoimperial logics. English is hegemonic and violent, insufficient and oppressive, elite and exclusive.

Depending on how you read them, the numbers also tell a revealing story about access, education, and what the novelist Aatish Taseer has called "the linguistic color line."[10] At the time of writing, surveys conducted by the 2011 Census of India and the Lok Foundation-Oxford University show that of the approximately 1.3 billion people in India, only about 125 million consider themselves native speakers of English.[11] Of these, most people report English as their second language, often learned through formal institutions of education contingent upon one's caste, class, and gender privilege. This relatively small figure, in a country of about twenty thousand different languages, reinforces English as the language of power, whose exclusivity could only hamper literary and political representational possibilities.

But if over 90 percent of Indians do not speak or understand English, how do they experience its ubiquitous presence? *Vernacular English* shows that numerous stories remain untold: stories that show how and why English in India is never simply an elite language of colonial and global power. Every day the English language accrues and exerts meanings beyond conditions of formal literacy. It courts emotions, feeds obsessions, shores up histories, and conveys ideas even among those who do not know the language. Now more than ever in India, English is seen on bureaucratic documents, billboards, clothing, and storefronts—and heard in political slogans, classes in spoken English, and Bollywood films. It circulates and commands authority not only in literary networks but also in visual and sonic discourses. The variety of (mis)recognitions, accents, and inflections that mark English chart desire and (un)belonging across class, ethnic, gender, and caste differences. This economy of literary, sonic, and visual English across languages and media—its use by people outside of traditional privileges of class, urbanism, and education—diminishes the authority of English as a language of global and colonial power. With such profound ubiquity, English demands newer ways of reading and conceptualizing language and power.

Vernacular English retells the story of English in India as the story of a people's vernacular in a postcolonial democracy. It identifies two broad categories within this "people's vernacular"—a political vernacular, used by the postcolonial state, and a popular vernacular that emerges amid varying degrees of literacy. It returns to disciplinary conversations with the argument that a language imposed from above is always remade in reception. The book highlights the adoption of English as one of India's official languages after independence, its role in public and private political protests against the state, as well as its wide circulation in popular media. Spanning the course of three centuries, this book looks for the English language in local, corporeal, and liberatory experiences. The meanings of a colonial and global English have always been shaped in relations—of alliance or opposition—to other languages, publics, media, and politics in India.[12] *Vernacular English*, literally, stages the proximity between what is considered vernacular and what is considered English—through the traces of one on the other. It follows how English lives in other Indian languages and media, such as Hindi literature, bureaucratic documents, language legislation, Bollywood and international films, and public protests. This book is especially interested in what happens when in its journey around the world, the English language faces those who see or hear it but can neither read nor speak it. By centering such embodied experiences of listening, watching, remembering, and speaking English, *Vernacular English* reimagines what is readable—and thus, knowable—about a language.

Vernacular Resolutions

Both the term "vernacular" and the English language have been the subject of countless monographs, essays, and conferences in postcolonial and comparative literary studies. There is a good chance that seeing the two together in the title led you to reasonable conclusions about my object or arguments. Perhaps you thought of nonstandard uses of the English language. Perhaps the title seemed counterintuitive or even paradoxical given the popularity of "global English" and "global Anglophone." In scholarship on India, English is considered an elite and global language, and vernacular brings to mind a quotidian and local register associated with modern Indian languages or *bhashas*. If there is a contradiction in the book's title, it is intentional. It highlights a tension that makes vernacular a useful framework for the study of the English language.

The global spread of English brings the recognition, the fantasy, and the dread that all across the globe, people may share one language. Vernacular anticipates the coercive and liberatory potential of a shared commonality imagined in and through the English language. It clarifies the profound ways in which English circulates with the potential to make common; it also reveals the different kinds of literacies that encounters with English usher. In my use, the term "vernacular" is not a substantive name for a language. It describes intellectual and affective relations *between* languages, where the vernacular is at least, as Fiona Somerset and Nicholas

Watson write, "notionally in the more embattled position."[13] The critical power of vernacular languages draws from the emotional weight of these relations.[14] No language is always and only a vernacular. To call English a vernacular is a way of historicizing its presence in the Anglophone world as well as a way of reading it. It names the affectively laden representative power of English, its imagined and desired capacity to speak for a people.

Having told you what vernacular English is, let me also clarify what it is not. Vernacular English does not name a special hybrid or dialect or local lower-case english that logs departures from a standard upper-case English in the mode of Enlightenment Orientalism.[15] The moral or physiological assessment of bad or rotten English is questionable, to say the least, and I do not wish to use it. Vernacular English is also not a strategy to provincialize English. It does not exemplify English in the colonies to pluralize (and unwittingly maintain) the standard English of the colonial metropole. Vernacular English is also not simply the suggestion that we consider English another Indian language. Instead, vernacular English is my effort to imagine language from different kinds and levels of literacies. It is a way of gathering the bodies that read, write, speak, and hear English, whether they are supposed to or not, whether they can or not, whether or not we as scholars recognize them as literate in English. Vernacular English is a way of recognizing that what seem nonstandard and hybrid englishes are the English language.

While the English language has had a rich vocabulary to characterize vernacular experiences and politics, literature scholars do not describe English as a vernacular today. Since the fourteenth century, the term "vernacular" has named a common experience of language. Writers and scholars alike have claimed languages and aesthetic forms as vernacular to create shared, demotic, vulgar, and natural experiences. But with the standardization of English as a racialized national language in early modern England, it spread across the colonized world as a language of national, colonial, and global power.[16] Imagining global literary history as a progression of six distinct literary ecologies—epichoric, panchoric, cosmopolitan, vernacular, national, and global—Alexander Beecroft shows that English has been a vernacular and has vernacular doubles. According to him, English was a vernacular language against Latin. But African American English or Haitian Creole, which are often considered vernacular languages, confirm English as a global language.[17] Even though these languages stand testament to the writers and users' creativity, they only confirm the dominance of English. In literary studies and the world alike, English in its "standard" literary form seems to have outgrown the epithet of vernacular.

Particularly in comparative literary studies and postcolonial studies, vernacular has emerged as a veritable antonym of the English language. Common parlance associates the vernacular with a set of discourses of the local, folk, oral, bodily, unstandardized, common, and indigenous—all of which, Shaden Tageldin rightly notes, are "non-synonymous."[18] As a result of these attributes, whether the vernacular describes a language, a sensibility, an aesthetic, or knowledges, it operates as a negative fallacy that is nondominant, adversarial, and oppositional. Postcolonial and comparative scholars often enlist a vernacular language to challenge the racist, colonial, and Eurocentric frameworks produced in English.[19] To borrow a phrase from Susan Koshy, "an unexamined logic of small and large" minoritizes and localizes the vernacular against global and transnational scales of power.[20] As a result, English is associated with colonial modernity, radical mobility, and communicability, while the vernacular is imagined as a language or textuality preceding modernity, local and untranslatable.

In the eighteenth century, the adaptability and copiousness of English—its covetous incorporation of different languages—was a symbol for the British Empire's reach. In his study of eighteenth-century Anglophone culture and the rise of monolingual Standard English, Daniel DeWispelare writes that "both Englishness and the English language [were] singular because plural, multiply formed, and adaptable."[21] The preeminence of English language and culture both lay in encompassing heterogeneity and consolidating wide imperial publics. Scholars of global Anglophone literatures and global English like Aamir Mufti, Rita Raley, Subramanian Shankar, Rebecca Walkowitz, and Ben Tran have noted this constitutive copiousness of English by describing it as a radically translatable and normativizing language.[22] Mufti and Shankar have specifically challenged the entitlement of this translatable and mobile English through vernacular languages that are imagined as more culturally and politically rooted.

Most clearly, in *Flesh and Fish Blood: Postcolonialism, Translation, and the Vernacular* (2012), Shankar has advanced vernacular as a broader category that stands in difference to the transnational, the global, the cosmopolitan, and the national. The vernacular, Shankar writes, resists systematization and abstraction; it remains "untranslatable" as an instance of "extreme cultural difference."[23] Similarly, in *History in the Vernacular* (2008), Raziuddin Aquil and Partha Chatterjee conceptualize vernacular history in terms of its difference "to critique and disturb" authorized forms of colonial and postcolonial modernity. They locate the vernacular as the opposite of colonial modernity when they frame their project as a search for history writing in India before the British intervention. To them and the Subaltern Studies collective at large, vernacular has offered a way to access histories outside institutional frameworks of the colonial and postcolonial state.

However, scholars of vernacular history, aesthetics, and literatures do not only value the vernacular as local, intimate, indigenous, authentic, before modernity. They also use it as shorthand for other Indian languages. It is only by uniting these two unrelated registers that the vernacular—as a language and a position—can contest the dominance of Anglophone postcolonial studies. To name only the most recent publications, several dossiers, like "Literary Sentiments in the Vernacular: Gender and Genre in Modern South Asia" (2020), edited by Charu Gupta et al., "Translating Porn Studies: Lessons from the Vernacular" (2020), edited by Anirban Baishya and Darshana Mini, and "The Vernacular" (2020), edited by Subramanian Shankar, use "vernacular" to mean Indian languages against English.[24] In the introduction to "Literary Sentiments in the Vernacular," the editors use the word "vernacular" to describe many things, like literary spaces and connections. Phrases like "vernacular literary spaces" and "vernacular interconnections," while not explained, imply Indian languages besides English as well as an intimate register of action. The guiding impulse for all of these works is to bring attention to lesser-known and actively marginalized languages, cultures, and narratives.

The English-vernacular divide, at least in recent literary history, has consolidated over numerous debates about the place of English in the postcolonial world. The most famous is the debate between Ngũgĩ wa Thiong'o and Chinua Achebe over the place of English in the postcolonial African literary imagination. Since the fateful Makerere Conference in Uganda in 1962, Ngũgĩ has maintained that English is always implicated in colonial histories and politics. According to him, it is impossible to imagine a decolonial politics in English. He switched to first writing in Gikuyu and translating himself into English. Achebe, on the other hand, held it was possible, nay necessary, to fashion an English which was at once universal and able to carry the peculiar experience of the African writer. He had been given the English language, Achebe wrote, and he intended to use it. In 1997, Salman Rushdie controversially claimed that the most important and strong body of literary work in India was produced in English and not vernacular languages. Rushdie's statements led Amit Chaudhuri to argue that "English is not an Indian language in the way it is an American language; nor is it an Indian language in the way that Bengali or Urdu, for instance, is one."[25] In the year 2000, author Vikram Chandra called out the "cult of authenticity" that made writing about India in English "at best a brave failure, and at worst a betrayal of Indian "realities."[26] In 2001, Amitav Ghosh withdrew his novel *The Glass Palace* (2000) from the Commonwealth Award because the category of "commonwealth literature" only recognized English-language works and not those from other languages. These dispersed moments shaped scholarly debates for years to come. These debates are charged—surfacing questions about choice, visibility, politics—and have led postcolonial comparatists to fix the vernacular as a political and affective locus of, if not authenticity, then immediacy, and pursue English as "global."

The political rationale for distinguishing English from other Indian languages seems clear enough. Still, this accepted and principled opposition between English as modern/colonial and the vernacular as not modern/anticolonial is hard to sustain and counterproductive. The definition of a vernacular as regional, immediate, or native or even anticolonial, writes Tageldin, is "adumbrated by shadows of colonialism and slavery" and is a product of "imperial genesis."[27] As scholars, we associate vernacular with regionalism and lack of power because colonial modernity constructed it as such to hierarchize languages and the people who used them. African American language practices, often described as vernacular, derived from British dialects and West African languages in the wake of the transatlantic slave trade.[28] As a linguistic mode, vernacular encompasses the oral and nontextual because it is the product of colonial modernity, not because it is exempt from it.

In India, "the command of language," as Bernard Cohn showed, was key to the consolidation of colonial power.[29] The imperial quest for efficient governance led Orientalist philologists to standardize native languages that would allow British administrators to speak to the people directly. These languages were standardized in script and grammar so that British civil servants could learn them for administrative purposes. Treatises, textbooks, and dictionaries were produced with the explicit purpose of making these languages knowable by the British Empire. Scholars of vernacular languages and practice who position these against Anglophone forms also show how vernacular language and literature developed by emulating styles and forms made familiar by colonial modernity.[30] Vernacular languages like Hindi or Urdu are an example of the conversion of Indian forms of knowledge into European objects. These languages do not necessarily stand against colonial languages but were often brought into existence by colonial effort.

In fact, this well-established history of vernacularization has also led, in some quarters, to suspicions about the usefulness of the term "vernacular."

It carries the stigma of colonial intervention and the etymological meaning of the "language of the slave." The casteist nature of public language practices predating colonialism has further deepened these derogatory meanings. When I presented early iterations of my argument, I received one consistent feedback: drop the "vernacular"! Indeed, Shankar pointedly notes "vernac" as a classist slur in his youth in India: "To be vernac was to be backward, gauche, naïve. It was the epithet with which, during my teen years in Bombay and Madras, you dismissed the kid from a distant village who, knowing no better, slicked his hair down with coconut oil, tucked in his T-shirt and spoke English with the wrong accent (all our postcolonial accents were wrong but some were wronger than others)."[31] The conception of vernacular as native or nondominant or oral is shaped by colonial and caste dominance, which blunts its power to launch effective anticolonial rebuttals. Vernacular is not a pure site of otherness that can be a seat of radical politics to repudiate and offer refuge from Eurocentric colonial, global, and national paradigms.

Yet, despite (or because of?) the compromised nature of any vernacular, writers' use of vernacular language has also been a reclamation and assertion of power against a dominant tradition. To use vernacular languages is always a way to usher new literacies, readers, and writers in the literary establishment. Writing about colonial Punjab in South Asia, Farina Mir shows that despite the colonial state's imposition of the vernacular of Urdu, the thriving public culture of the Punjabi language—enabled by print technology—contested the colonial vernacularization.[32]

Zooming out of India briefly, we see that manifestoes by figures as diverse as Dante Alighieri, Geoffrey Chaucer, John Gower, Houston Baker, and Henry Louis Gates Jr. all share the common goal of calibrating new power relations between the dominant and the emergent sections of the society. Writers who used the vernacular democratized the potential of literature by creating new readers and writers. For instance, writing in a politically fragmented Italy of the Middle Ages, Dante sought an illustrious vernacular (*Latium vulgare*) both to rival Latin and to elevate Florentine above other Italian dialects. Chaucer and Gower wrote in a Middle English vernacular at a time when the dominant literary languages in England were French and Latin. Through their vernacular English, they transmitted Greco-Roman and European literature into English and shaped the English nation. Responding to the economic discontent of 1381 Peasants' Revolt, these poets used their poetry to disseminate English, the language of the peasants, as cultural capital. At the same time, they also retained enough Latin glosses to give English a veneer of elitism and ensure that not every person who knew English was admitted in the national polity. As a critical term, then, "vernacular" captures the twin dynamics of the assertion of a challenged people and their consolidation of power. Vernacular is not simply a nondominant discourse.

In the twentieth century, the Black vernacular tradition has reframed literary and cultural expression into an assertion of identity beyond geography and indigeneity. Here the etymology of *verna*, the domestic slave, takes on a literal meaning. Houston Baker used the vernacular to name the "living and laboring" conditions—the material conditions of slavery—in the United States. The new modes of creative expression, like the Blues, that resulted from these conditions were vernacular forms. Henry Louis Gates Jr. also drew on vernacular aesthetics "to confound a Eurocentric bias of literary theory" by reading African American literature through an American literary tradition and the Black vernacular tradition.[33] In each case, the claim to the vernacular was supposed to be, as Steve Botterill writes about Dante's vernacular, "a declaration of independence"[34]—rooted in the legitimacy of human experience, its historical reality and geopolitical specificity. But while the Black vernacular tradition is very strong, it is marked by the question of whether, as Audre Lorde wrote, the master's tools can ever dismantle the master's house. One need only think of Frantz Fanon's hostility toward the Blues as a "slave lament" that he said was "offered up for the admiration of the oppressors" to appreciate the political compromise of a vernacular.[35]

With such paradoxical historical entanglements and political overtures—its internalized shame and self-assertion, its weaker position and its bid for power—the vernacular makes it possible to assemble a thick description of language circulation, power struggles, and textuality. It presents a Möbius strip-like continuity from within the dominant system, rather than an objective vantage of neat opposition or unsullied indigeneity. As the common language that is standardized—by force or volition, in resistance or capitulation—the vernacular encompasses several contradictions. It refers both to oral cultures and to the written standards that name them. It refers to the particular experience as well as its abstractions, and can acknowledge aspirations within specific groups to commonality or a unified identity.

This messier modeling of the vernacular as a paradox can provide a greater purchase on English. It alerts us to a deeper history and more intersectional transmediations of English. Doing so illuminates how the meaning of a linguistic sign is socially produced. It pries open the space between *la langue* and *la parole*, between the individual utterance and the signifying system. English often functions as an unmarked medium of literary scholarship, as if it itself is incomparable![36] The discipline of comparative literature has turned to the vernacular to assuage its anxiety of Eurocentrism. Annette Damayanti Leinau writes that the vernacular has "accompanied Comparative Literature as an implicit conceptual frame," where it guides determinations of Europe's others. Vernacular is "an object of comparative promise."[37] Its demotic energies—both common and everyday—have motivated philological comparatism, and its regionalism challenges the imperial expansion of comparative inquiry.[38] But, as a vernacular, English moves from being a comparative cipher to allowing for comparative plentitude.

The association of vernacular languages, aesthetics, and politics with lived experience can bring scholarship closer to a decolonial theory of the English language. By reading English as a vernacular—by noting its colonial and casteist formation as well as its promises of liberation—it is possible to reconstitute horizons of universality through local enunciations of a language. We can name the colonial and global power structures associated with English without re-inscribing them each time we discuss English. By casting globally present English as vernacular English, this book recognizes that the global does not exist in a realm distant and different from the local. *Vernacular English* questions the automatic assignment of values to the global regime associated with a dominant language like English. In doing so, it refuses—in a much-needed critical gesture—to cede power to dominant frames of analysis and study of Anglophone postcolonial literature and culture.

Simon Gikandi and Rey Chow, especially, have exhorted literary scholars to account for the range of English-language experiences. For instance, weighing in on the debate between Ngũgĩ wa Thiong'o and Chinua Achebe, Gikandi argued that "Achebe's endorsement of English as the universal language and Ngũgĩ's critique of it as an agent of linguistic imperialism endowed the language with a singularity and power that it didn't have."[39] English appeared powerful only "because of its association with the compulsory Englishness."[40] Gikandi drew on Dipesh Chakraborty's concept of provincializing as a way to renew European thought from the margins without repudiating it. To provincialize English, Gikandi wrote, was to represent English as one language among many. It was an "effective way of dealing with the anxieties that English generates."[41]

Similarly, in her 1995 essay "In the Name of Comparative Literature," Rey Chow invited scholars to examine the multiple languages and cultural enclaves that already exist within English. The discipline of comparative literature, argued Chow, could no longer conduct "Eurocentrism in the name of the other, the local, and the culturally exceptional."[42] The discipline's embrace of multilingualism and non-Western languages must be accompanied by an implosion of English itself as a singular language. English literary study should not be limited to British and American literature but also include Black English, Indian Anglophone literature, and ethnic American literature. Chow exhorted colleagues in the 1993 Charles Bernheimer Report to grasp the premise of language as power in the spirit of decolonization, not of diversity.

To borrow from Chow, it is in this spirit of "decolonization, not diversity," that I approach English through the lens of the vernacular, as a vernacular. My use of vernacular to emphasize people and places retheorizes English away from its long-standing meanings and towards what Gikandi, drawing on Fanon, called the spaces where "the people dwell." Such spaces stand apart from the metropolitan circulation of postcolonial literature, in "the marketplace where English encounters forms of popular writing that are not imprisoned in its rules, that the former language of empire is creolized."[43] In a similar vein, Ulka Anjaria has made a spirited case for defetishizing the distance between "vernacular" and "English," and reading English as provincial in India.[44] To build on Gikandi's and Anjaria's proposals, English cannot be provincialized until we acknowledge—in scholarly paradigms—that English is already provincial. To read English as a vernacular is to deprive it of its singularity.

The Promise of the Common: Historical Routes of English in India

Despite its overdeterminations as a colonial and global language, English came to India with vernacular ambitions. This is to say that English was a vernacular—not classical—language in Britain at the time, where writers like Samuel Johnson and Daniel Defoe sought to elevate it by strengthening it through borrowings from other languages around the world. Universal grammar was a key feature of eighteenth-century linguistic philosophy that imagined global linguistic diversity as translatable and traceable to one language. British Orientalist philologists translated from different world languages into English to elevate English as this common linguistic source. As a language of administrative control in the colonies, English had numerous encounters with local languages, and it realized these ambitions in consort with Indian vernaculars through their translation into English.

In this quest for universal grammar, one nineteenth-century Orientalist philologist, John Borthwick Gilchrist, upheld Hindustani, a popular north Indian vernacular outside courts, as the most useful language of study. The confluence of industrial, scientific, and imperial expansion in the eighteenth century had led to interest in language itself as something to be standardized and used. Gilchrist's interest in linguistic value in practical terms of trade and governance led him away from classical scholarship of courtly languages like Sanskrit and Persian, and toward Hindustani as a useful site of imperial expansion. As a corollary, this move extended legitimacy to all vernaculars, a category that was distinct from classical literary languages and that now included English. Rita Raley writes that Gilchrist insisted that the phonetic Roman alphabet of the English language could encode "all the sounds of all known languages."[45] By focusing on the Roman alphabet, Gilchrist stripped the English language of racial, geographical, or cultural value, and reimagined its value as utilitarian. Despite the absence (or rather, because of its repackaging) of British cultural values, English still remained useful as a translational and transnational medium that could translate other languages and which could thus travel beyond national borders.

Gilchrist's comparative philology was guided by a rationale similar to that of the famous Orientalist philologist William Jones and Anglicists Thomas Babington Macaulay, Charles Trevelyan, and Charles Wood, all of whom supported the introduction of English education in India to streamline administration and to morally improve the natives. He considered it necessary to transliterate foreign languages into the Roman script of English because their ostensible difficulty impeded rationality and civilization. His approach was also motivated by the quest for the "common" of the common source and universal grammar and to elevate English at home in England. But, through his plan of "Practical Orientalism" Gilchrist showed that only as a vernacular itself could the English language vernacularize Indian languages. His language philosophy valued vernacular as profitable and literary, and exploited the potential of the phonetic Roman alphabet to encode different languages.

As my discussion of the derogatory connotations of vernacular indicated, much has been written by postcolonial scholars about the vernacular as what Geeta Patel called an "etiology of turpitude," or the logic that "the base nature of the vernacular was the reason for the backwardness of the colonized people."[46] But, this simultaneous history of English is also significant not because English is, in fact, a language of universal communicability. Rather, its promise as such a language makes it an affectively and politically charged site. The history of English in India is the history of vernacular English.

From the year 1608, when the British East India Company first arrived on Indian shores with English as the language of trade and governance, the English language swelled with the sounds of the languages with which it came into contact. Missionaries of all denominations followed shortly, making English the language of Christianity across British colonies in Asia. Amitav Ghosh's *Ibis Trilogy* (2008–2012), for instance, dwells beautifully on the promise of linguistic contact, or what B. Venkat Mani, drawing on Jahan Ramazani, calls "code-stitching."[47] In the year 1835, Thomas Babington Macaulay, a British politician, successfully convinced the British Parliament that it should spend money on public education in English in colonial India. His now-infamous "Minute on Indian Education" led to the creation of an elite minority of English-educated Indians who brokered as clerks in the British colonial government and cemented their position within local hierarchies of caste, class, and gender. The "Minute" singularly unleashed English as the language of colonial *and* caste power for centuries to come.

After India won its independence from British rule in 1947, in a historic speech, Jawaharlal Nehru, India's first prime minister, announced the nation's birth in English. Nehru asserted India's sovereignty, reflecting triumphantly on India's resilient past and future. Was it ironic or fitting that what Nehru called the "the soul of a nation, long suppressed" found its "utterance" in the language brought by the former colonizer?[48] Soon after, the Indian Constituent Assembly adopted a bilingual Hindi-English Constitution, naming English its associate official language and Hindi as India's official language. The drafting committee of the Constitution was headed by Bhim Rao Ambedkar, the radical Dalit leader, who had used English to name the violence of casteism at the heart of Indian society and politics. Decades later, in 2010, Chandrabhan Prasad, a Dalit writer and activist, built a temple for the English language. Holding on to the promise of Ambedkar's Constitution, Macaulay, the Internet, and global capitalism, he called English a Dalit Goddess.

Indeed, an oft-overlooked legacy of English as a translational and transnational vernacular is its legislation as one of postcolonial India's official languages. In an echo of Gilchrist's vocabulary, the postcolonial Indian state made the English language its administrative vernacular. In 1949, the Indian state declared Hindi in *devanagari* script as its official language and English as its associate official language, because, as for Gilchrist, it was the "least-inflected dialect of the lettered world."[49] As a translational and transnational vernacular, English belonged to the world, yet remained uninflected by it, neutral, as if all materiality were stripped from it.

India's struggle for independence and postcolonial statehood came with a push to dub its multilingualism into a monolingual national identity. But Hindi—the language favored by the Hindu nationalist elite as a possible "national" language—was spoken only in the northern part of the country. Given the diversity of languages, religions, and ethnicities, the idea of India as an independent and democratic republic could not be anchored in any one Indian language. In a multilingual country that could not agree upon one language to represent itself, English promised a neutral territory. Ambedkar, for instance, held that Hindi—were English not enlisted to secure it—would risk consolidating a hegemony of the northern Hindi-speaking states over the southern states that did not speak it. Jawaharlal Nehru, on the other hand, saw in all regional languages a threat of secessionism from the Indian state. English was deemed necessary for the consolidation of India as an idea and a political unit. It was almost as if, as a language of the erstwhile colonizer, English was similarly foreign to everyone in the colonized land, and thus well positioned to address the nation equidistant from all competing linguistic cultures. English could link the people because all linguistic constituencies were willing to converse in it without having to recognize the authority of any regional language. The alleged foreignness of English, its untranslatability into native categories, was its greatest advantage. Enshrined in the Constitution, English gave language to the postcolonial state's values of secularism, democracy, modernity, and sovereignty.

The promise of the common stemmed from the promise of the foreign. While the nonnative character of English has been key to its political meanings as national and democratic, the advocates of English and the Constituent Assembly at once suppressed and invoked, forgot and celebrated the foreignness of English. As English was recruited to uphold the democratic state, advocates like Nehru and Ambedkar elided its foreignness so that they could use the language in postcolonial nation-building. But that foreignness was also invoked and celebrated to suggest the suitability of English for this role. Without its colonial history, English could be expedient in a variety of situations. It could communicate across wide swaths of people and allow the state to speak in the name of the many who had historically been disadvantaged both by Hindi and English.

But this promise of English was also underwritten by the communalization of Hindus and Muslims, and the politically motivated argument that Urdu was the language of Islam and Muslims in India. As a glorified vernacular, English enjoyed, as Rashmi Sadana has also noted, a translational relationship with Hindi, and never replaced it as India's official language. However, this relation between English and Hindi was one of mutual reliance; English bolstered and supplemented Hindi's religionational aspirations. As the articles of language legislation show, English was chosen as an associate official language to prepare Hindi for its new role as the sole official language in the near future.

In this endeavor, as in every liberal imperial justification, it was hoped that time would be an ally. Hindi, while insufficient now, would become fit with its association with English. With patience, a more nationalist future could be realized. English promised to both buttress and disrupt the Hindu nationalist aspirations founded in the claims of the Hindi language. The government launched numerous lexicographical and translational efforts to modernize Hindi by association with English. The idea was that English would compensate for the insufficiency of Hindi as a language of national and international communication.[50] Its advocates considered English the conduit to ideas of political modernity, democracy, and science and technology. In its supplemental role, English was deemed the most democratic, the most secular, and itself an instrument that could make things happen. Hindi had already assumed the space of the vernacular. Its association with English endorsed the same status for English as well.

In the postcolonial phase of India's history, the political value and cultural power of English has remained specifically functional—at once profoundly objectified and fetishized. English is valued for its potential to foster modernity and to educate citizens in a democratic society. It becomes meaningful as a machinic object, a technology, that can be attached or removed, remembered or forgotten as needed. For advocates of English in India, the association of the language with science made it seem encouragingly pliable. English, as a language that could be taken apart piecemeal and harnessed at will, built on the utilitarian idea of language developed in the eighteenth century. For instance, Maulana Abdul Kalam Azad, independent India's first education minister, remained wary of English. However, in 1947 he floated the idea of teaching Hindi to non-Hindi- or Urdu-speaking Indians through the Roman script. There were millions of Indians who understood Hindi but did not know the script, he reasoned, and suggested using the Roman script as a supplementary script, in addition to the *devanagari* of Hindi and *nastaliq* of Urdu, in educational publications of the Indian government.[51] Azad's proposal did not find supporters at the time but has come to be realized today as the Roman script transcribes Indian languages on social media.

As I began by saying, scholars in comparative or postcolonial literary studies rarely approach English as a vernacular. Instead, vernacular—encoded as other Indian languages—makes it possible to trace national or subnational knowledges. And yet, the conscription of English as a vernacular in India made the postcolonial nation possible, in the first place! The adoption of English bolstered the place of English in India's cultural and political imagination for time to come. No doubt the turn to English was the logical culmination of British rule, and parts of the Constitution of India quoted verbatim from the colonial Government of India Act of 1935. Yet both the Constitution of India and English—its "alien language"—were transformed into what Rohit De calls "talismans" to notionally and literally activate democratic citizenship and equality for millions across caste, class, and language differences.[52]

The Anglophone, or To Read What Is Not Written

As the history of the legislative adoption of English shows above, the meanings of English are produced in an interplay of translatability and untranslatability into other Indian languages, especially Hindi.[53] The practice and metaphor of translation highlights both the original and the translation as *produced* in the act of making meaning. Scholars have been attentive to the translational role of English, primarily in its role in Anglophone literature. In *Forget English!*, Aamir Mufti rightly posits, "in world literature the (South Asian) Anglophone novel as a form marks a sort of *translation* of non-Anglophone and vernacular social and cultural spheres and life-worlds into the novelistic discourse of English and its cultural system more broadly. As such it is subject to a *politics* of translation."[54] Indeed, the global circulation of English as a translational vernacular—as a language of translation from and to languages—requires greater attention to the practice of translation. Similarly, Rebecca Walkowitz has also theorized Anglophone novels as born as and from translations, *born translated*, "pretending to take place in a language other than the one in which they have."[55] In this sense, Anglophone literatures, while written in English, are read as if they were produced in another language and then rendered into English by the author. Walkowitz attributes this quality of "being born translated" to global publishing pressures; if the author did not have to consider the global publishing economy's capitalist pressures, the work would be published in another language.

In this view, translation is always unidirectional (from other languages into English). English, as a translational and transnational language of elsewhere, obfuscates the original language. Because we are convinced that English is not itself—that it must be a different language in which the characters must have spoken—this formulation also obfuscates the moments when English is supposed to be English. Using Dube's artwork as a reference, it seems that, as scholars, we are so drawn by what the twisted wires write that we forget to notice the wires themselves. We are so focused on what English stands for that we do not quite see how, where, with what it stands, and how these details shape its meanings right before us.

The Anglophone world looks very different if we theorize it from the Anglophone. Two overlapping institutional configurations have recently raised suspicions about the English language: world literature and global Anglophone literature. As disciplinary signs for "Literatures Other than British and American," these categories rely on the English language to access this other. But the suspicion has extended not simply to the representative-ness of English or English literature, prompting questions like "Is there a world literature?" and "What is global Anglophone literature?"[56] It has also led to questions about the veracity of the Anglophone world.[57] While arguments about the tyranny of nomenclature, the vagaries of academic job markets, and institutional politics are well taken, such debates should not eclipse that there very much is an Anglophone world. For instance, recently, Madhumita Lahiri has paid attention to new collectivities and alternate geographies that are created through the coinage of new words within the worldwide hegemony of the English language signaled in the phrase "the global Anglophone."[58] That the idea of global Anglophone literatures coheres the ethnonationalist logic of the Anglo-Saxon or the Anglosphere is indeed a warning to heed. But, it is also a missed opportunity that furthers said racialized logic if we are not careful.

English lives in the impossibility and desire for commonality in India. It manifests in ideas like democracy, in brands and bureaucratic documents, as sight and sound. To read English and the Anglophone after the vernacular is also an invitation to think language again—not at its limits but in its proliferation with bodies, media, and languages. The vernacular, as subaltern historiography has shown, is always a question of reading—it is not that the subaltern does not speak but that she demands newer ways of hearing.

Let me give you an example of what I mean. When the first call centers arrived in India in the early 2000s, they taught English as a spoken language, often sundered from rules of writing. English was thus unstandardized in this process. In her book, *Dreamers: How Young Indians Are Changing the World* (2018), journalist Snigdha Poonam shows how the English language itself has transformed under the imperatives to learn it. Poonam attends one of the many English-language-speaking schools that appeared across India to train call-center employees. Known as "The

American," this particular chain of schools prides itself on teaching *anyone* to speak English in a matter of days, no matter their background. Poonam describes the pedagogical method that breaks English down into a formula made of clichés, proverbs, and social pleasantries. This English is known as Spoken English or "Spoken." The strategic elision of script unstandardizes English by writing out the very phonetic script that made it the oxymoronic "international vernacular" since British imperial expansion, up to the contemporary growth of digital media. English, once again, comes apart as the script, while its sound develops an affective charge in a localized regime of power. With immeasurable promises of "life improvement" and "personality development," English becomes the sound of success, aspiration, and confidence in India today.

At "The American" Poonam meets Moin Khan, "The English Man." Born a milkman in a small village in the state of Bihar, Khan became obsessed with learning English when he encountered his first English speaker. Over two months, he raised money for his lessons by milking every cow in his village. Khan's obsessively rehearsed English sentences are cut loose from any grammatical compulsions and perfected over calls to strangers. Poonam writes with tenderness: "Every night when [Moin Khan] came back from the market, he sat in a corner of his house with his notebook and repeated aloud every single word the English teacher had uttered in the day's class. Not only did he try to copy his teacher's pronunciation of words, but also the manner in which they were delivered—whether it was with a pause or a drawl or a chuckle. The teacher used to make his English sound effortless by dropping in words from the local dialect. That's the effect Khan strived for in his private practice sessions."[59] As English promises social mobility outside formal education and paths to freedom hitherto unavailable, its experience in contemporary India is charged with thrill, hope, promise, and shame. After learning English, Khan may well speak with customers outside India. Still, his primary motivation is to achieve social mobility in his own country, in a landscape riven with caste and class barriers. English affords Khan with just such a vector that can bring him closer to the authority and respect that he would not otherwise have. What is more, unlike the dominant languages of the past, English is also within reach for a "cut-price," a fee of five hundred and fifty rupees for six months of classes.[60]

New English speakers in India like Moin Khan do not see English as a language that comes from a particular country. As Poonam told me over the phone from New Delhi, they understand English as vaguely "Western" rather than British or colonial. All that the English aspirants know about the language is that it can create paths for those who are disadvantaged by their social and economic marginality. The attitude is of survival: it doesn't matter where English comes from but it is here now. The imperative to learn and use English is mapped onto changing relations of class, caste, and regional power.

Most readers or writers or listeners of English—across its global life—may not even literally understand the language. This unintelligibility neither blocks access to English nor makes it foreign. It certainly does not make English less English. Walkowitz has argued that English-language literary texts are never only written or read in English, and has made a case for non-comprehension as a way to read global Anglophone literature to account for the fact that the globally circulating novel may or may not be written for the reader. Similarly, we must account for noncomprehension—our own and of others—when considering a globally circulating language; recognizing that not everyone in the world experiences English like we do. In this dialectic of translatability and untranslatability, English appears multiplex. The unintelligibility presents an inventive understanding of English that playfully and persuasively refigures expressive geographies in the Anglophone world in search of aspiration, class ascension, and global affiliation. Across vocal training at call centers and schools that promise instant English-speaking skills, English becomes vernacular through and in translation. Unhinged from its language, the Roman script—as metonymy for English—becomes something figural and hieroglyphic to be apprehended visually. It is no longer the written word but of the order of the image. The accent of English, its sounds and phonemes, become sound objects that gain new meanings by repetition and do not necessarily invoke where they are coming from. As the signified and the signifier split, the symbolic affordance of English multiplies. English becomes both iconic and banal.

These new expressive geographies of English put into crisis both textuality and what is readable. Vernacular English is not a category of texts but a mode of reading that attends to the interplay of sound and script to interrogate the textuality of the work. In a way, this is a process of flipping the gaze and audit, to read English through other eyes and ears.[61] Instead of estranging postcolonial writers of English of all ilk, this reading practice estranges the critics' own process. It demands that we read English like a brand or a bureaucratic document or a filmic image or a formula, paying attention to its lived experience. This also means that, as readers, we notice the indexicality of the English language.[62] In doing so, we attend to what is being made visible and audible. Reading English as a vernacular is not to reduce language, as François Noudelmann has suggested, to a "simple expressive function" but to go on to notice the interplay of sound and silence, orality and writing, whereby written and literary language is estranged. To those not bound by the assumptions of coloniality or globality, the sounds of English speak of new possibilities. We need to be asking different questions: What does it mean to read the Anglophone, the English-speaking world? Who is reading it? Who is listening to it?[63] We need a more, not less, Anglocentric approach.

These questions can bring greater awareness of the different kinds of speakers and different modes of speaking and counter what Noudelmann has called the "voluntary deafness of the users of abstract language."[64] In keeping with the conception of global Anglophone literatures as translations into English, for instance, in studies of world literature, global English has become a metaphor to describe the literary work's presumptive encoding of the heterogeneity and multilingualism of its points of home. In the software and technology industry global English is understood to be "simplified or controlled English" that is universally accessible and comprehensible. It is almost a different language that encodes language and linguistic standard.[65] David Damrosch has called it "nothing more than a minimum competence, a bland, watered-down commercial and touristic language whose use could dampen down the linguistic richness of English even in its original home locales."[66] This definition, bemoaning growing literacy in the absence of an accompanying literariness, is ironic. The cosmopolitanism of globally recognizable writers, of scholarly interest in itself, is not sufficiently reckoning with the far-reaching scope of "English in the world," which circulates in media and markets and is available to many outside of privileges of class, education, and urbanism.

Certainly, the privilege and limits of one language, English, cannot establish the privilege and limits of fields like postcolonial studies and global Anglophone literary studies. But equally importantly, our conception of the English language itself can no longer be limited and a privilege. Global English is not simply the language of technology and software. It is also a language that a man like Moin Khan memorizes and practices to bridge cavernous class disparities. It is also the experience of a language of power as graspable and maneuverable. The sounds of this global English do not just make audible the hegemony of the outsourcing industry but also a man's modest hope-filled attempt to navigate social hierarchies.

Today, the English language continues to animate debates about its legitimacy in the wide fields of African, South Asian, and Eastern European literatures.[67] Indeed, more than three decades after the debate between Achebe and Ngũgĩ, Chimamanda Ngozi Adichie has added a different perspective to the debate by claiming "simply that English is mine."[68] Adichie continues, "Sometimes we talk about English in Africa as if Africans have no agency, as if there is not a distinct form of English spoken in Anglophone African countries. I was educated in it; I spoke it at the same time as I spoke Igbo. My English-speaking is rooted in a Nigerian experience and not in a British or American or Australian one. I have taken ownership of English."[69] Adichie's statement signposts a shifting landscape of English that scholarship must reckon with. It invites us as scholars to read global Anglophone literatures as not simply subverting the hegemony of English but as written in a *native* language. This tension between English as a global and a native language is the tension that vernacular allows us to name.

Chapter Descriptions, or Anglophone in Five Speech Acts

The debates over the global dominance of English have largely been shaped by the realities English obfuscates and the people it does not represent. By contrast, this book reconsiders *how* to read English to capture all that becomes visible and audible in English when it reaches its willing or unwilling users. On the usefulness of the term "Anglophone," Daniel Elam writes that English literature has always been a project of interpellation—one in which English literary studies was used to make colonial subjects. Elam adds that salvaging the Anglophone is akin to salvaging figures like Macaulay. Quite the contrary, right now what should worry us is that we are not able to see beyond the divisive and oppressive colonial education policy.[70] We are not able to pay attention to the different political and symbolic affordances of the English language, beyond its colonial life.

Vernacular English is an attempt to find critical purchase on the allure of English, the affective negotiations, and the political impasses of the English language in India. The following chapters pursue English as a vernacular language of people's democracy through its hope and frustrations. Read through the translational vernacular, the Anglophone illuminates the shared but uneven experience of English. *Vernacular English* convenes wider publics and histories of English in the Anglophone world. It calls attention to the many mediations, translations, and embodiments of a language before or after it is codified textually. English as a vernacular heightens the shared life of a language, whether in the colonialist attempts to introduce English education, or in postindependence attempts to legislate the language, or in global capitalism and media diffusion.

I answer my opening question "what becomes intelligible as English, and how" by examining English through the different modalities of linguistic experience and imagining different strategies of reading. The five chapters consider English as a law, a touch, a sight, and a sound. English is tied to people and their claims to power. In each case, English assumes meaning between its material formations and the body that writes, reads, speaks, and hears. Language, as we know it, appears at its visceral, material, affective limits. Every now and then, I have also drawn on personal experiences of growing up in India with the English language. My experience of English is marked by my gender, class, and caste: it does not represent the experience of everyone in India or in the Anglophone world. Indeed, I invoke these experiences to pose questions and articulate problematics.

The first chapter examines the English language in India as an object of democratic promise shaped by the bilingual English-Hindi Indian Constitution and as part of the bureaucratic scriptural economy. With its opening proclamation of "We, the people of India," the Constitution offers an exemplary case of a people speaking English. Of all the ironies that characterize postcolonial India, perhaps the biggest irony is that the language of the erstwhile colonizer came to be indispensably tied to postcolonial assertion. The Constitution carries a voice that belongs both to the sovereign people and the colonial and postcolonial state. The relation of English with Hindi and other Indian languages, I argue, is a key way in which these competing voices are maintained. This chapter examines the life of English as just such a democratic object—goal, instrument— through *India Demands English Language* (1960), a little-known collection of pro-English essays by influential Indian political leaders, and contrasts the statist vision of English found there with the bureaucratic technics on the ground in Srilal Sukla's satirical Hindi novel *Raag Darbari* (1968) and Upamanyu Chatterjee's English novels, *English, August* (1988) and *Mammaries of the Welfare State* (2004).

Chapter 2 shows that English, unlike any other Indian language, promises a shared space where caste-based injunctions against touch are flouted. It explores English as an experience of touch, shaped in the bodily injunctions of caste and the promise of democracy. Since the nineteenth century, Dalit leaders and writers have cautiously used English to claim the promise of equality associated with the language. Chapter 2 brings together a corpus of Dalit Anglophone literature and Hindi Dalit literature. It shows that key Dalit leaders such as Ambedkar, Jotiba Phule, and Kancha Ilaiah have used English as a principled rejection of the Sanskritized modern registers of many Indian languages, associating Sanskrit with upper-caste dominance. A new generation of Dalit writers insists on English as their own language to reveal the truth of urban caste experience and to further an oppositional politics that seeks a shared discourse in English.

Chapter 3 reads Indian Anglophone novels about caste in the shadow of the caste politics of English noted in chapter 2. Over three hundred years of Indian English literature, there have been only a few low-caste or Dalit protagonists even as almost all of the novels are written by upper-caste and upper-class writers. The narrative logic of these novels rests on the characters' inability to speak English. But despite the literal and literary impossibility of English of those characters, they are also shown desiring English and performing Englishness to manipulate the performativity of caste. This chapter identifies two well-known caste-marked character types in Indian Anglophone literature, Bakha in Mulk Raj Anand's *Untouchable* (1935) and Balram Halwai in Aravind Adiga's *The White Tiger* (2008). It shines a light on an enduring hermeneutic knot in Indian Anglophone literature and imagines a mode of reading beyond suspicion that rehabilitates, rather than dismisses, these characters.

Chapter 4 turns to the English language as a sound object. It considers English as part of global protest vocabulary where it is used to speak back to the Indian state. In a 2004 landmark protest against years of army presence in the state of Manipur in Northeast India, twelve women stood naked in front of the army base to protest the rape and murder of a young woman named Manorama by members of the armed forces. Raising the English-language slogan of "Indian Army Rape Us / We Are All Manorama's Mothers," they used the language of the democratic state to challenge its authority. Northeast India as a geopolitical category and Northeast Indian literature as a body of work both become legible in the postcolonial state's use of English. The chapter argues that the women's political and phonological—figurative and literal—voice offers a decolonial lineage of a mother tongue in English. With a discussion of contemporary literature by northeastern writers like Temsula Ao and Yumlembam Ibomcha, the chapter also reveals the emergence of the English language as specifically aural—an instance of speaking English, of Anglophony—as it represents the nonvocal (guns, bombs) and vocal (human cries, protests) soundscapes of military violence and human suffering.

In the context of traumatic silence that bears witness in English, chapter 5 examines the visual life of English in India. Two recent films—Danny Boyle's Oscar-winning *Slumdog Millionaire* (2008) and Zoya Akhtar's commercially successful *Gully Boy* (2019)—stage English as a thing to be seen rather than read. English appears in Mumbai slums—on public signages and in social media—as the films cinematically produce its pervasiveness. The logic of cinematic signification helps imagine a mode of *not* reading English as it circulates among those who do not know it. The figural character of English—such that its script becomes an image—fractures the authority of the ubiquitous global English.

A coda highlights in the term "Anglophone" a productive emphasis on the *speakers* and *speaking* of English. "Speaker"—as technology, people—reminds us that the speakers of English across the world may have varying levels of competence. It also draws attention to the fundamental role of *tekhne* in the inflection of the phonic (what is spoken) and the sonic (what is heard). The coda proposes that we draw on these mediated and embodied phonic meanings of the word "Anglophone" to consolidate a reading practice that is attuned to the mundane world and that hears marginalized voices in Anglophone studies and India alike.

Together, the texts considered in this book make visible a long history of the English language in India that is not only imbricated in global or colonial logics. This other history of the English language in the colonies by no means disavows the hegemony and violence of English in colonial and neoliberal global processes. Instead, the paradox of the vernacular locates English and its speakers in the world, looking squarely at their democratic aspirations. It offers an opportunity to trace their relations with precisely the multilingual literary and media cultures that the hegemony of metropolitan literary English threatens to subsume. Summoning the many lives and registers of English that make the Anglophone cracks open what has ossified in the name of a colonial or global or literary English.

This book urges greater attention to English, not with or against Indian languages but through them. Vernacular shines new light on both India and English, two topics that have commanded a formidable library of scholarship. While I argue that Hindi is the one language that most centrally shaped the meanings of English in postcolonial India, numerous other languages in the world shape the meanings of English. India was the laboratory for the development of English literary studies as a discipline and has been the paradigmatic site in postcolonial studies. Indeed, it seems to me that there is some wisdom in turning to the new readers and writers of English in erstwhile colonies to imagine disciplinary futures.[71] As we imagine progressively more diffuse teleologies of English—against a monolithic global future for "English studies"—vernacular, a practice of reading modeled in the book, can reposition English via some of these languages.

CHAPTER 1

Law

DEMOCRATIC OBJECTS IN POSTCOLONIAL
INDIA, OR INDIA DEMANDS ENGLISH

A Language of Paper

My father's job with the Department of Education of the Government of India filled our house with a unique kind of papery paraphernalia. There were always books, reports, pamphlets, magazines, and paperwork of the unclassified kind that he brought home. Most of these documents were official publications and communiqués of the Department of Education and the larger ministerial office that housed it. Some were plainly cyclostyled, some attractively bound. Meant for wide circulation within the Indian bureaucracy, their function was pedagogical and documentary. Were these publications to find readers, those readers would probably learn about the then Indian government's educational initiatives for adults or its plans for promoting Hindi in the border states of Northeast India or its self-laudatory prose about India's diverse culture. Most of these documents were written in an overstuffed bureaucratic English, and many had en face translations in Hindi. None, as I recall, featured other Indian languages.

Not even in high school at the time, I wasn't their intended reader, of course. But I would often find myself looking through these documents. I specifically remember three red rexine-bound tomes crammed in the diminishing shelf space of our New Delhi apartment. Published by the Commission for Scientific and Technical Terminology, these were English-Hindi dictionaries of technical terms from botany, zoology, chemistry, and physics. Upon flipping through their pages one evening, I found the

[29]

Hindi definitions were as unpronounceable and unidiomatic as the original English technical terms. There was a pattern: the definitions were either phonetic transliterations of the English word into the *devanagari* script of Hindi or literal explanations of the processes and objects in Hindi. As I slammed the last of the dictionaries shut, I felt disappointed and confused. After hours of poring over them, I really hadn't learned any new meanings!

Referencing a dictionary, writes Walter Hakala, is at once an intimate and a collective experience.[1] The act of looking up a word—perhaps because you don't know it or because you want to confirm its meaning—can be embarrassing or exhilarating. But this deeply personal experience is shaped by a far more abstract and social project. More than any other object, a dictionary is also the modern material artifact of a community that shares a common language or wants to share a language. It constructs historical equivalences between languages, staging them as commensurate entities. A dictionary both presumes that one language has equivalences in another and suggests that they are mutually translatable. Thus, it always provides meanings beyond the literal meaning. Indeed, the English-Hindi dictionaries of scientific terms not only offered purchase on the technical terms but also held their meaning between the two languages, as something that belonged to both.

As I learned later, the Commission for Scientific and Technical Terminology was established in October 1961 to develop technical terminology in all Indian languages and "propagate its use and distribute it widely."[2] The primary function of these dictionaries was not really to define a word but rather to mirror English and construct scientific vocabulary in Hindi. Thus, science itself was imbued with a desirable unfamiliarity that was worth knowing and which Hindi, with its grace, was primed to render. As the genre of the dictionary authorized their commensurability, Hindi and English languages were bridged through mutual translatability. If some Indian nationalists were eager to claim Hindi as a representative national language, the technical dictionaries closed the gap between that "national" Hindi and the English of the colonial state. By ensuring that Hindi could also be scientific like English, the dictionaries brought into being the postcolonial state of India in a way that was both a continuation and a break from colonial rule.

Essentially, then, these dictionaries were an example of the bureaucratese that permeates every aspect of Indian civil society. Their bureaucratic status enhanced their truth value as dictionaries, making them a key part of the self-authorizing scriptural economy of bureaucracy in India and the world. For every dust-laden dictionary, one could (and still, can) find all over India all kinds of bilingual or trilingual Hindi-English public signages, public health messaging, governmental forms, and applications. This scriptural economy of bureaucratic documents, as Akhil Gupta writes, not only commemorates the state but also constitutes it.[3] Documents exist to document, Lisa Gitelman pithily puts it. As an epistemic practice, the "knowing" from the documents is "all wrapped up with showing, and the showing wrapped with knowing."[4] Often, documents are documents, which is to say they make meaning, merely by dint of their potential to show. This know-show function of documents is tied to the work of no-show, of not, in fact, showing anything that is not obvious. Documents of the bureaucratic kind are "paper truths," which derive their truth value from their symbolic value as official papers.[5] As bureaucratic documents, the technical dictionaries instrumentalized English to claim Hindi as scientific. For someone consulting these, English would perhaps be the unfamiliar language, in need of translation. But it would also be a language that is commensurable with Hindi. The deferral of meanings—from Hindi to English, from English to Hindi—where neither was explained, made English meaningful as a language of science, development, and as related to Hindi which was also all of those things now.

The English language is a vital part of the documentary nature of the postcolonial Indian state as also of several other former British colonies in South Asia, Africa, and the Caribbean that have retained English as their official languages. How does the wide spread of the postcolonial state's bureaucratese shape English and how does English shape the state? How does this bureaucratese inflect the relation of English with other Indian languages, and how does it offer a practice of reading English in Indian Anglophone literature? This chapter builds upon Rashmi Sadana's observation in *English Heart, Hindi Heartland* (2012) that English has become deeply entrenched in postcolonial government bureaucracy and is the official language of higher education. Indeed, English circulates in the bureaucratic scriptural economy as a vernacular. Outside of literary circulation, English becomes a vernacular as an administrative language that promises wider reach and control of the populations. It is a reminder of the state's colonial formation, as well as an index of its democratic and developmentalist aspirations. And yet, many people who are confronted with English as the language of the state do not know how to read it. As they comprehend it and contest the power of the state within the context of localized linguistic and political environments, their encounters with the language of governmentality, in turn, makes English a language of the people.

Administrative Anxieties of the Postcolonial State

The use of English in bureaucratic documents in India has a simple explanation: it was the continuation of colonial administrative practices. Aijaz Ahmad identified a "genetic cultural link" between the status of English as "the chief cultural and communicational instrument in the centralization of the bourgeois state in the colonial period," and its continued use after independence.[6] But this critical fact is not the whole story. Globally, the postwar ferment of the 1920s had made communication an important political concern both on the Left and the Right. Governance, democracy, and national cohesion all demanded communication, which in John Durham Peters's words, had the power to "bind a far-flung populace together for good or ill, it had the stuff to make or break political order."[7] This interest in communication demanded a language to communicate in, a language that could reach others and that could be shared and made common.

India's multilingualism didn't fit the monolingual pressures of communication. No one language could serve as the communicational bedrock of the modern democratic nation-state. No one language could bear the administrative task of governing this diversity or the representative weight of a complex linguistic landscape. India is home to four language families—the Indo-Aryan, the Dravidian, the Austro-Asiatic, and the Tibeto-Burman, with hundreds and thousands of different languages and dialects. India's independence movement came with a push to adapt this multilingualism to a monolingual national identity. English offered a solution to the language problem and also secured continuity from colonial administration to the postcolonial state. While scholars tend to examine English in opposition to Indian languages, the life of English is tied to languages like Hindi and Urdu. To understand how and why English emerged as critical to the postcolonial Indian state, we need to cover some well-trodden ground in South Asian studies.

Historically, precolonial and colonial states had preferred the North Indian vernacular for administrative purposes. In continuation of these practices, nationalist leaders like Gandhi touted Hindustani and later Hindi as possible national languages of India after it became independent. For instance, in the twentieth century, Gandhi invoked Hindustani to refer to the North Indian vernacular written either in the *devanagari* script of Sanskrit or the *nastaliq* script of Persian calligraphy. Hindustani, thus, came to be understood as a mix of Hindi and Urdu. With two scripts and widespread use, it promised inclusion, syncretism, and historical continuity. As a more unifying language, Hindustani would potentially be more suitable as a national language. But there was another reason for Gandhi's and others' affinity to Hindustani. Hindustani was a strategy to erase Urdu, which was typecast as a Muslim language potentially appeasing to Indian Muslims.[8] As Aamir Mufti details in *Enlightenment in the Colony* (2007), no language by the name of Hindustani had really existed in India before it was thus politically appropriated. As part of the colonial history of vernacularization, both Hindi and Urdu were effectively invented—standardized as languages—at Fort William College under British colonialism in the early nineteenth century. The British colonialists standardized these languages from the North Indian vernacular to manage the native population and bring the written and spoken languages into alignment. In the nineteenth century, Hindustani referred to the vernacular written in Persian script. Hindi came to be the vernacular written in *devanagari* script. Urdu referred to Persian, which was the state language/language of the court.

By May 1947, as the independence of India and the creation of Pakistan as a separate Muslim state seemed imminent, the language question became ever more charged. In addition to the question of independent India's national identity, the task of governance was also looming. Communication and communicability seemed critical for successful state administration. In the eyes of the nationalist elite, linguistic heterogeneity and plurality posed an insurmountable problem to the idea of a single people and to governing them. While Hindi was still the language of choice for many Indian political leaders, the language did not seem adequate to the task ahead of it.

Amid the Swadeshi movement from 1905–1911, as Indians boycotted and burned British-made goods, Gandhi argued that Indians needed to develop "respect" for their languages in the way that the Boers and the Jews had for their languages, to cultivate the spirit of *swadeshi* (literally meaning "of one's own country").[9] On January 30, 1909, Gandhi wrote to the poet Rabindranath Tagore with a political dilemma: "Is Hindi not the only possible national language?"[10] Gandhi found it hard to reconcile the continued use of English and the struggle for independence from the British. He conceded that English was essential; Indians could learn it as the language of the British government. "One must learn to use it well, when it has to be used. One must learn to read and write in it with facility."[11] But that was as far as Gandhi was willing to go.

Citing the importance of communicability, he added: "There is no point in writing to another in English when that other person knows as little English as one does. It would only lead to a total misunderstanding, apart from encouraging a bad habit. The right approach would be to use English [only] when the other person does not know our mother tongue. English may be learnt but our mother tongue must not be ignored."[12] Gandhi imagined learning a language to be a zero-sum proposition where learning one language would mean forgetting another. He believed that the unintelligibility of English to most Indians would add to linguistic confusion and political chaos. Gandhi considered English to be foreign and Hindi to be native to India. Indians could not win and maintain independence from the British by embracing English and losing Hindi!

Of course, precisely because of India's linguistic diversity, were English to be recruited only when Indians did not share a mother tongue, that would still be very often. No one Indian language, certainly not Hindi, could anchor the idea of India as a democratic nation-state. Spoken predominantly in the northern part of the country, Hindi was as (if not more) artificial, divisive, and exclusionary as English. Severed from Urdu in its Sanskritized form, Hindi also upheld religious, class, and caste distinctions. It did not justify the straight line between nation and language that Gandhi was seeking. The romantic expectations of a national language ran up against the practical necessities of reading, writing, and communicating.

Nonetheless, Gandhi's reasoning that English was unfamiliar to most Indians could not diminish its role in global communication. He acknowledged English as a "world language" to be learned whether one wished to do so or not.[13] English, Gandhi claimed, was central to "the acquisition of modern knowledge, for the study of modern literature, for knowledge of the world, [and] for intercourse with the present rulers."[14] In this role, English was needed to amplify the message and power of an independent India, even if the language was not, in Gandhi's estimation, itself Indian. The knowledge of the world—received via English—would strengthen the image of India's nationalist assertion. Gandhi mobilized English as a prosthesis that could be attached or detached from its colonial provenance and used it to connect an independent and growing India to the rest of the world. Positioned outwards, English would help Indian leaders to communicate with and hear the leaders of the world. It would provide a stage from where India would become influential. Gandhi's reluctant acknowledgment of the usefulness of English was both astute and judicious. English was not a part of India's national identity but the need to assert national identity still determined its role. English could have a role to play in India's future, but only if it did not define India's past.

In Gandhi's vision, English was rendered critical to India's nationalist and democratic aspirations as well as subversively contained. The communicational potential of English resulted in an unexpected role as the language of democracy and its continuation as an administrative language. As Tagore had written in response to Gandhi's question about the inevitability of Hindi, "Political thoughts have naturally taken form in our minds in English."[15] For the time being, Tagore implied, Hindi could not be the language of independent India. English was the language in which most political leaders encountered formative ideas of Western modernity. English may not have been an ontological mother tongue—naturalizing a sentiment of belonging. But, it emerged necessary for the consolidation of India as an idea and a political unit.

The very idea of the nation-state required a different kind of thinking about language and a different kind of language altogether. The rational bourgeois sensibility that necessitated one administrative language also determined that that language be English, and resulted in its conception as instrumentalizable. Thus, the story of English in India is shaped as much by practical and administrative decisions around postcolonial nation-building as it is by the deeper histories of colonialism. The eventual adoption of English as India's associate official language, I show below, was a strategic decision that both drew on colonial governmentality and subversively contained the force of the colonial language. As evident in the dictionaries I began with, English was instrumentalized—in both literal and metaphorical terms—in the service of the postcolonial state's monolingual dreams. This instrumentalization of English was double-edged. On the one hand, it transformed the state's use of English and also became a symbol of its democratic character. On the other hand, this instrumentalization imbibed and furthered the state's violence in a country where only a minority knew the language.

In *Enlightenment in the Colony*, Aamir Mufti makes the critical point that many of the language debates around Hindi, Urdu, and English were led and championed not by writers but by administrators and propagandists.[16] This is true. But while Mufti focuses on the literary use of language, he overlooks the more pernicious and permissive circulation of English as the administrative vernacular. The postcolonial state's democratic aspirations shape English's postcolonial afterlife in India. To understand it better, we need to unpack its relations with other languages as well as its no- and know-showing power in legal and bureaucratic documents.

The Alliance between Hindi and English

The Constitution of India is an exceptional instance of the Anglophone world, of the Indian people speaking in English. It identifies India as a democratic sovereign republic. While the document exists in English and Hindi today, it was first written in English and then translated into Hindi. Beginning with the phrase "We, the People of India," the Constitution both claims the sovereign power of the people and renders it in English. Ambedkar, the father of the Dalit Buddhist movement, led the drafting committee of the Constitution. Thus, the collectivity imagined in the speaking voice of "we" has resonated with historically marginalized peoples as well. But the Constitution is an assertion of the sovereign power of the people as well as an instrument of governmentality and an administrative document.

The voice of the people in the Constitution, thus, writes Sandipto Dasgupta, is accompanied and inflected by that of the administrator as a constituent subject.[17] This double voice explains the model of representative democracy in India, where listening takes precedence over speaking. Usually, a participatory democracy rests notionally on the idea that everyone has a voice, has a vote. In India, however, democracy referred to the state's ability to speak in a language that everyone understood. In the Constituent Assembly debates that led to the adoption of English and Hindi, the concern was not whether everyone could *speak* a shared language. On the contrary, a "national" language was a language that everyone in the country could *hear*. Even Gandhi, you will recall, was worried that one's interlocutor would not understand English. For any language to be considered official and national, it must be understood by a majority of the people, if not literally, then symbolically as the language of the state's power. This emphasis on understanding what was spoken reflected the state's investment in governance and administration. It gave democracy the form of address.

In 1949, when India adopted its new Constitution, it recruited English as an associate official language to offset the factional nature of Hindi, now christened the state's *official* language. The original plan was to end the use of English fifteen years from the commencement of the Constitution in 1950. Part XVII of the Constitution, in its very first clause, recognizes Hindi in *devanagari* script as the official language of the Government of India. However, it follows this statement with the caveat that despite everything in the preceding clause, for the next fifteen years, English would be used for all the official purposes of the Union for which it was being used immediately before such commencement.[18] This meant that all government communication would be in English—all bills, acts, and laws—as it had been during colonial rule.

At the same time as this announcement affirmed the indispensability of English, it also cast Hindi as a language in need of development to actually govern. Articles 343 and 351 of the Indian Constitution, titled "Directive for Development of the Hindi Language," identify Hindi as unprepared for the purposes of governance. As a solution, these articles propose translation to develop and transform Hindi in relation to other languages such as Sanskrit and English. The dictionaries I began with exemplify precisely this simultaneous process of Anglicization and Sanskritization. These latter languages would become the medium as well as the message. Sanskritization would convey the indigeneity and historicity of Hindi whereas Anglicization would convey its modernity.

However, the proposal to end the use of English after fifteen years met with violent protests from the southern states of Tamil Nadu, Karnataka, and Andhra Pradesh as well as the eastern state of West Bengal. These states spoke languages other than Hindi, and the push for Hindi was a threat of its hegemonic consolidation over them. Thus, the Official Language Act of 1963 instead suggested an "intensive and comprehensive program" whereby English would be enlisted to enhance the effectiveness of Hindi for state communication and English-Hindi dictionaries would be developed to expand the vocabulary of Hindi. By 1968, the National Policy Resolution had also adopted a "Three-Language Formula" which suggested that schools in Hindi-speaking states teach two languages—Hindi and English—and that schools in non-Hindi-speaking areas of India additionally teach a modern Indian language, presumably the one spoken in the region. These arrangements located English within an interlocking trellis of Hindi and other regional languages. The role for these languages was not of national identity but of administrative governance. If the adoption of Hindi was a result of an investment in a monolingual nationalist imagination, then the inclusion of English was a concession to the practical work of governance. This negotiation of the practical and the romantic ideals resulted in a critical relationship between Hindi and English.

In their relationship as India's official and associate official languages, Hindi and English came to translate each other into what Lydia Liu, in *The Clash of Empires: The Invention of China in Modern World Making* (2004), has called a super-sign. Liu introduces a "super-sign" as an act of mistranslation that manipulates meaning by locating it outside a language and by concealing that movement. In other words, it is a crosslinguistic act of misinterpretation. Two words that do not necessarily correspond are yoked together into creating the semblance of correspondence. Liu's example of *yi/barbarian* is a series of verbal signs connected by slashes. British/Chinese treaty-making in the early to mid-nineteenth century altered the meaning of the Chinese word *yi* by translating it as *barbarian*. The super-sign *yi/barbarian* "[compelled] the destination of the word *yi* to be 'barbarian' and appointed the latter to inhabit the super-sign and become its proper signified."[19] In doing so, "it require[d] that the word 'barbarian' be sufficiently shielded from *yi* to enjoy a different destiny and a different mode of survival." This act of translation is not necessarily based on a reciprocity or commensurability. Instead, it makes "a verbal sign from one language the destiny and destination of a verbal sign from another language."[20]

While separated by colonial and nationalist injunctions, Hindi and English also announced a self-sufficient and a compound vernacular of languages, ostensibly understood by and an expression of the composite culture of all Indian people. The placement of English proximate to Hindi obscured the foreignness and the history of colonialism embedded in the decision. It also accorded Hindi parity with English for its modern, scientific, and global associations. English and Hindi each became the medium through which the other was transmitted as democratic, and together assumed the role of the "medium of expression." In state discourses and bureaucratic documents, as English fell on the ears of the nation, it secured the postcolonial democratic state just as Nehru's speech had done on the eve of India's independence.

The postcolonial legislation of English and Hindi similarly established commensurability between the two languages and shunted their meanings outside, toward other Indian languages that they were supposed to stand for and stand as. The alliance between the two languages functioned much like the super-sign. Hindi and English assumed the look of something familiar but each deferred its meanings to the other.[21] English supplemented the discourse around Hindi by deflecting meaning both toward and away from itself in a relation of translation. English remains adjacent to India—with no acknowledgement of its colonial history. But it galvanized Hindi by its modern attributes. The interdicted remembering and forgetting of English imbued Hindi with the qualities that were desirable in English: its modernity, rationality, and even, ability to nationalize. At the same time, this relation of proximity and of supplementation drew the English language closer to the ideal (within the discourse of democracy as address) of being a "language of the ordinary people," imbuing it with an enduring political legitimacy without acknowledging it as legitimate.

As English participated in the super-sign and assumed the inequalities Hindi embodied and perpetuated, it also functioned at what may be understood as a national level. Claiming to speak for the people protected not only Sanskritized Hindi (a language that was largely invented) but also English (a language that had, historically, been dominant and exclusive). The deflection of meaning of English to Hindi and of Hindi to English manipulated the foreignness of the two languages, and sustained the illusion of representational democracy.

The relationship of heterolinguistic catachresis and translation between Hindi and English also maintained a familiar foreignness, not intrinsic either to Hindi or to English, but always exterior and proximate to both, creating the conditions necessary to name a democratic language and a language of the democratic state. It was the foreignness of English that enhanced the reach of Hindi. Ironically, the "alien" and the "alienating" capacity of English facilitated a transmission of messages across linguistic and social borders and accorded it a new immediacy. But with its foreignness managed in the address of democracy, English did not so much represent the Indian public as attached to Hindi; it imbued Hindi with the legitimacy to do so. Put differently, today, English represents not as a metaphor but through metonymy. In its legislation as the associate official language, English stands for the many other Indian linguistic and ethnic groups denied exceptional status in favor of Hindi. However, at the same time, it also brings these groups into association and contiguity with Hindi, conferring on it the credence with which to speak for them.

Hindi and English together achieved a representative status as the Indian political elite sought to notionally preserve its linguistic and ethnic diversity. English tempered the regional and communal hegemony of Hindi. In alliance with Hindi, English was no longer nonnative but nationalized. The foreignness of English was key to its potential as a language of communicability and democracy. The cultural distance of English from India was both a historical fact and a justification of the rationality of English. It could, ironically, counter the growing political foreignization of Urdu. For instance, Mufti writes that Madan Mohan Malviya, an Indian educational reformer and an active figure in the independence movement, argued for Hindi in *devanagari* on the basis of the fact that Urdu was foreign to India.[22] English was also not native to India as it came through British colonialism. For that reason, it was not considered partisan and could defuse the regional and linguistic tension in India. Under British rule, the same foreignness of English was oppressive but now it held the promise of democracy.

India Demands English (Anxiously)

The language question—with its entanglement with communalism and caste—has remained one of the most divisive issues in the country. In *Thoughts on Linguistic States* (1955), Bhim Rao Ambedkar—the chairman of the Draft Committee of the Constitution—provided a glimpse of debates surrounding it. "There was no article which proved more controversial than Article 115 which deals with the language question. No article produced more opposition. No article, more heat."[23] Writing during the probationary period after the legislation of English as associate official language, Ambedkar added that no regional language could ever be the official language of the Indian state without risking ethnic rivalry and imperiling the nation. According to him, English needed to continue as India's associate official language so as to preserve the democratic state.[24]

Thus, the adoption of English as an administrative language was enabled by a deferral and displacement of its meanings so that it could effectively confront the "unknowability and potential dangers" of the Indian population and make common a linguistic diversity.[25] Both these facts make English a dispositionally anxious language. A sense of "elsewhereness" accompanies English in India, a sense that the language does not belong in the nation, but just beyond it, outside it. Gandhi's fear that misguided Indians were letting English transgress its place is one example. At the same time, English was always justified by the future in India. This orientation associated English with expectant emotions of anxiety, hope, even shame, which are unmistakable in the 1950 and 1963 legislation that obsessively emphasized the development of Hindi through English.

We see some of the layered anxiety around English in *India Demands English* (1960), a petition published by Isaac Mathai, a publisher from Bombay (now Mumbai). In the midst of a heated political debate over the official language of India, this petition was to be a "forerunner of a thousand pages volume entitled Documentary evidence India demands English language [*sic*]."[26] It was meant to be submitted to Jawaharlal Nehru as a request that English be retained as India's associate official language alongside Hindi. In the face of an impending judgement on the future of English in India, the titular insistence of the anthology is backed by arguments from several Indian political leaders, journalists, and diplomats belonging to a range of religious and ideological persuasions. Most of these writers belonged to the upper class, and several of them were also upper-caste Hindus, thus occupying dominant social positions. Many of the contributors had also drafted longer book-length arguments. For instance, S. N. Moos had already penned a separate volume titled *The Place of English in India* in 1958.

By making the demand for English in English and as a petition, the contributors claim the language as their own and appeal to the state's authority to give it to them. The petition is a typical bureaucratic genre, which works within the system. Anthropologist Akhil Gupta observes that supplicants write petitions to obtain them as favors. Petitions, he explains, "are pleas to the powerful to grant something that is in their capacity to authorize: a favor, an exception, a special dispensation."[27] To make a demand for something is different from desiring it, as desire comes with doubt. As we repeatedly see in our study of English in India, a desire does not come with the guarantee that it would be fulfilled. The "demand" makes the petition a peremptory request and English a right. Whether it is met or not, the right already establishes a claim to English.

The petitioners' demands appear as a means to ensure their elitism as an English-knowing caste and class minority. Some of the arguments were specifically caste-marked and elitist. For instance, writing under the pseudonym of Adib (meaning refined and cultivated), one contributor claimed Hindi to be unsuitable for personal and professional matters. Hindi sounded awkward and gauche, so, according to this writer, one could not use it to place orders at a restaurant. At the same time, Hindi was not precise enough to render a court judgment.[28] These statements are baseless, of course. Still, they illuminate how English came to be entrenched as the language of the Indian elite and the Indian state. The petitioners' appropriation of English in the service of social hierarchies is not unique in itself. Shefali Chandra's *The Sexual Life of English* (2012) shows that upper-caste men taught English to their wives to secure caste hierarchies.[29] Homi Bhabha's "Signs Taken for Wonders" (1985) also showed a group of upper-caste pandits (belonging to the priestly Brahmin caste) using the Bible as a printed text to buttress their own authority. Similarly, Gauri Viswanathan's *Masks of Conquest* (1989) showed a group of upper-caste Bengali men demanding to be taught English. Although the benefactor it is petitioning is the postcolonial state, *India Demands English* similarly consolidates class (and caste) power.

At the same time, the petitioners' claim to English on behalf of India was dubious. If English was "our" language, the claimants did not clarify who the possessive case invoked. The use of the word "our" conflated the speakers with the India on whose behalf they were speaking. It was misleading and majoritarian. The writers also did not dwell on the circumstances in which English became "ours." For instance, K. M. Munshi was an Indian freedom activist and the founder of the educational trust, Bhartiya Vidya Bhavan, whose institutions sought to provide an antidote to modern life. Gandhian in his views, Munshi wrote, "Today English is ours; with its aid we can make ourselves felt throughout the world. It would, therefore, be criminal to ignore or neglect English in this country."[30] Such statements implied that the Indian state needed English to communicate its power globally, so the people of India must also embrace English as their own.

Most of the arguments in the anthology converged on the presumed alliance of English with science and modernity, which it had by virtue of its "Western" and nonnative provenance. Hindi was ideal but it was English that was abreast of the times. It was practical and useful in the daily workings of a nation in a way that Hindi could only hope to be at this point. Given the motivation for the publication of *India Demands English*, many of the anthologized writers specifically compared the merits of English with those of the Sanskritized state-Hindi instead of Hindustani, Urdu, and other languages of India. This is evident in essay titles like "India Is Greater than Hindi," "Against Hindi as the National Language," and "Can Hindi Replace English?." Sanskritized Hindi, these titles suggest, was not and could not be congruent with India. English, *not* Hindi, emerged as central to the sustenance of nationalism and the functioning of the democratic nation-state. Yet, by setting up such a binary, the appeals both obfuscated and abetted the combined violence of English and Hindi, one that we continue to see in Modi's speech discussed in the preface.

Many of the advocates extrapolated on the usefulness of English, comparing it specifically to objects that would exempt the language from further scrutiny. For instance, C. Rajagopalachari observed that English had an "overwhelming utility" for training technicians to carry out national plans. He deemed English "essential" for its role in preserving a "uniformity of laws and administration as also for unity of thought and exchange of ideas until such time as Hindi is organically able to take its place." In the essay included in *India Demands English*, he suggested, "the sooner we give up the attitude towards English as an *instrument* of former alien rule, the better it [would] be for our future progress. We must adopt it as a *lever* for our multisided national advancement."[31] In its objectified role, the alienness of English was not an impediment in the way it was for Gandhi, but was useful in making the laws and administration of India uniform. In *India Demands English*, the English language emerges as necessary to the idea of the Hindi/Hindu nation, to national advancement, to feelings of nationalism, and certainly, to the functioning of the nation-state. It takes on a material form as a tool in Rajagopalachari's "lever" of national advancement. As an object, English could equally be owned by and profit all Indians. "The knowledge and use of English" is a "national asset."³² But, for this to happen, it was important to repress its colonial history by a collective national action of forgetting or, at the very least, of willful negligence.

Fascinatingly, the writers eschewed emotional and affective language to make their case for English. Twentieth-century India witnessed several passionate movements for linguistic determination and separatism. Far from the intense emotionalism of these demands, the petitioners of *India Demands English* struck a rational tone that seemed determined to fight off emotions. Almost all petitioners placed English within a developmental framework that yoked English to democracy, modernity, development, and science. They brought a utilitarian approach to language, seeing it as integral to nation-building and democratic communication. As a language that was not weighed down by regional partisan pressures, English could bring together diverse people. This idea of English as an instrument toward building the nation also cast it as part of the invisible national infrastructure. The writers measured the value of English in terms of its usefulness. They discussed English as if it were itself a technology, an instrument, and the national infrastructure.

Imagining what would happen if Indians were to abandon English, Adib wrote, "We certainly do not want our dams to run dry, our bridges to collapse, our stainless steel to get rusted. For the sake of our future—our second and third and fourth [Five-Year, or national economic] Plans—we have got to stick to English. Why, we cannot even mend a small machine with the aid of Hindi. Even when the light fails in our flat we have recourse to English. Do we have a word for 'Fuse'? It is no use our working ourselves into a temper. A language is not a donkey. No amount of kicking will make it go. And no amount of cajolery either."³³ English was the language of modern-day circuitry and machinery. If a fuse failed in your house, you needed to know English to fix it. The person writing as Adib literally imagined English as an agent in this sentence. English catalyzed technological advancements and performed acts. Abandoning English would have material consequences. Words like cajolery and kicking suggested that those opposing the use of English were being irrational. This rationalism and unemotionalism of English heightened its practicality and scientific associations.

The petitioners also seemed concerned that the argument for Hindi was sentimental. S. N. Moos, the director of public instruction under the British government, pronounced the idea of mother tongue as unnecessarily maudlin. Other petitioners called out Hindi as an artificial and fictitious language that was even less natural than English in India. Echoing Tagore's statement that political thoughts arose naturally in English, they argued that two hundred years of British rule had rendered English more natural than Hindi. In contrast to Gandhi's suspicions about English in the nation, the writers held, not adopting English could be fatal. Attachment to Hindi as a mother tongue could be dangerous to national unity and progress since Hindi was still a language in development. Another contributor, Mirza Ismail, was a storied city planner credited with a civic revolution in the cities of Jaipur, Bengaluru, and Mysore. He wrote, "If India now unlearns English she can never relearn it. Seldom has thoughtless sentiment had a chance of doing so much harm to a nation."[34] His warning made impossible an emotional relationship to language that the nation must use. Language was no longer a personal issue but always determined in terms of public good and national usefulness. It was an opportunity.

Despite this rationalist approach, even the most vigorous advocates of English could not shake off feelings of anxiety and shame. Pothan Joseph, a journalist who launched major Indian newspapers, including the *Hindustan Times*, the *Indian Express*, and the *Deccan Herald*, wrote that "an impatient champion of Hindi once described Indian lovers of English as 'Macaulay's bastards.'" But, according to him, "as Adam and Eve have not been formally wedded in church according to priestly rites, no one need feel particularly hurt at the gibe if applied to mankind."[35] Lovers of English in India found company with all Abrahamic religions' first man and woman. By expanding the meanings of English, Joseph mitigated the shame of using a colonial language in a postcolonial context. English was not only the language of the British but that of a much broader religious sphere. There was no reason to feel offended as Macaulay's illegitimate children when the fates of nations, men, and gods were tied to the English language.

Shame recurs across the different instances discussed in *Vernacular English*—the shame of not speaking English correctly, shame of using the language of the oppressor, humiliation at the imperative. But here, Pothan Joseph's petition deployed humor to urge the reader not to feel any shame. At several points, when they refused to feel maudlin, the petitioners were essentially refusing shame. Shame, writes Elspeth Probyn, is an ethical affect that is tied with communication, felt in its interruption, in the inability to communicate one's self.[36] In the case of these writers, shame arises from the recognition that not all people in India are literate in English and that the promise of communicability in English is distant.

Despite these passionately dispassionate arguments in *India Demands English*, the demand was at no point for English in opposition to Hindi, but for English along with Hindi, for English to buttress Hindi. Even for the most radical advocates of English in this volume, the goal was not to unseat Hindi but to supplement it. The place where English should always stay, according to Gandhi, was still one of proximity to Hindi. If the title of the anthology left some things vague, the essays clarified them. India demands English, but not *instead* of Hindi. It demands English *along with* and *alongside* Hindi. Association with English would make Hindi a language of national and international communication. It would also modernize Hindi through lexicographical and translational efforts. English was considered the conduit to ideas of political modernity, democracy, and science and technology. But in its supplemental role, English was deemed the most democratic, the most secular, and itself a technology. Hindi was already claiming the space of the vernacular. Its association with English endorsed the same status for the latter as well. Even in contemporary times as in the debates around the National Educational Policy 2020, arguments against Hindi as claiming national status rarely throw the usefulness of English in doubt.[37]

Satire, or The View from Below

Thus, the meanings of English as a language of governmentality in postcolonial India are deflected onto Hindi and projected onto the future. As English remains confusing to most people, it creates anxieties and shame about the impossibility of relating and communicating with other citizens in the country—about unifying and governing a nation. The discrepancy between an elite language and the masses who do not know it heightens the structural violence of the state and exacerbates the already mysterious nature of bureaucracy in India.

In both Hindi and English, most of the literary works that have examined the postcolonial Indian state and discussed the cultural and political life of the English language have been satires. Some of the most memorable texts in this category include Srilal Sukla's *Raag Darbari* (1968), and Upamanyu Chatterjee's English novels, *English, August* (1988) and *Mammaries of the Welfare State* (2004). Works by Bengali writer Mahasweta Devi, especially *Hazaar Chaurasir Ma* (1998) and *Draupadi* (1978), have also dramatized bureaucracy's alienation and structural violence. Incongruity, absurd scenarios, and irrational exaggeration are all staples of satire. All of these strategies have the potential to make the anxious temporality and spatiality of English vivid. Satire captures the alienation and abstraction of English as the language of reform, progress, and discipline, as it speaks truth to power in the name of those whom English alienates. It also captures how English is funny in India, precisely because it seems so out of place.

Raag Darbari (written in Hindi), and *English, August*, and its sequel *Mammaries of the Welfare State* (written in English) specifically focus on the relationship between Hindi and English. Both Srilal Sukla and Upamanyu Chatterjee were civil servants with the Indian government. Their novels show the village as a place that, in the government's view, must be developed. But, the potential for development promised by English in *India Demands English* is not just frustrated in the novels but shown to be laughable. In all three novels, the main protagonist and the English language come to the village from the outside. English belongs either to the state capital or to a more undefined locus of modern statecraft. While there are different registers of English, it remains an imposition and circulates widely as an instrument of state power.

The power of English as a state language draws from its abstraction into a dry-as-bone bureaucratic, no-showing, and know-showing discourse. English has no roots or connections with the rural population it governs, which makes its experience both violent and disadvantageous for the people. The novels compare English to a machine and it is indeed a part of the state machine. In *English, August*, the narrator explicitly compares English to infrastructure as he refers to the English language as the "complex and unwieldy bequest of the Raj" like the district administration and the railways.[38] But, abstracted as the language of governmentality, English is also pliable. The compulsory experience of reading English by those who are alienated by it also proves contestatory. There is a subversive element to the instrumentalization of the English language in the service of the democratic state. It is here that, ironically, English approximates its democratic mandate.

Unlike the innocent and morally exemplary village scenes of Hindi writers of rural India such as Premchand or Phanishwarnath Renu, the fictional village of Shivpalganj in eastern Uttar Pradesh in *Raag Darbari* is no idyll. Instead, the novel confronts the reader with narratives of corruption, poverty, and a dysfunctional state. Set in the 1950s, *Raag Darbari* expresses the cynicism and disillusionment resulting from the death of Nehru and the imminent failure of India's welfare-state policies in the 1960s. The novel won an award from Sahitya Akademi, the national academy of letters, in 1969. Writer Srilal Sukla also received the Jnanpith Award in 2009 for his contribution to literature. The Jnanpith Award is an Indian literary award established in the 1960s by the Bhartiya Jnanpith Trust. It has never been awarded to an author in the English language—thus clarifying the institutional imaginations of the category "Indian languages." *Raag Darbari* gained even more popularity with its translation into English by Gillian Wright in 1991 and its adaptation into a Hindi play, *Rangnath Ki Wapsi* (Rangnath's Return).

Raag Darbari puts the idealism of *India Demands English* to test precisely through its discussion of language. It contrasts "we, the people"—as proclaimed in the Constitution—with an aphasic figure of democracy. In a dream sequence, the feudal lord and head of Shivpalganj's political mafia, Vaidyaji, finds an anthropomorphized "democracy" illiterate in either of the two official languages of India. Squatting on the ground next to Vaidyaji's bed, "democracy" appears feeble-looking and suppliant. It repeats the words *huzoor* and *sarkar*. Vaidyaji realizes that democracy looks like a plowman and "could not even speak *shuddha* [pure] Hindi, let alone English!" (उसकी शक्ल हलवाहों जैसी है और अँग्रेज़ी तो अँग्रेज़ी, वह शुद्ध हिन्दी भी नहीं बोल पा रहा था।).[39] Used to address authority figures, the Hindustani words *huzoor* and *sarkar* roughly translate to *sir* and *sir/government*, respectively. Spoken by democracy, these words indicate the extent of Vaidyaji's control over the people of Shivpalganj. However, in their constant repetition by such a beseeching figure of democracy, the words also verge on the nonsensical. Democracy grows feebler stripped of its tongues: English and *shuddha* Sanskritized Hindi.

This episode is reminiscent of Maulana Azad's description of Jawaharlal Nehru in *Ghubar-e-Khatir* (1946). Azad was an independence activist, a senior leader of the Indian National Congress, and the first education minister of India. He wrote *Ghubar-e-Khatir*, a collection of letters to his friend, while in prison with Nehru. The two political leaders had different perspectives on the place of Urdu in Indian nationalism. Nehru, spuriously, called Muslims and Urdu a people and language stuck in the past, which he contrasted with a modern and future-oriented English. Azad wrote that Nehru could often be heard at night muttering in English in his sleep one cell over. In his discussion of this excerpt from *Ghubar-e-Khatir*, Aamir Mufti writes that Azad's remarks were probably a tongue-in-cheek dig at Nehru's rationalism.[40] However, in light of this moment in *Raag Darbari*, this anecdote illustrates how deeply and subconsciously political leaders and laypeople alike deferred to English in nation-making.

Indeed, it is the absence of English and Sanskritized Hindi that horrifies Vaidyaji. In this instance, the novel reminds the reader of the distance between the vision of democracy enshrined in Hindi and English and the average peasant (the subaltern) who speaks neither. *Raag Darbari* is full of references to the misdirected government propaganda that addresses farmers in English, the incongruity of English on billboards in rural India, and the bureaucratese of the government officer. Yet, at this moment, it is not the presence but the *absence* of English that is comical and confusing. But while the novel seems to affirm this centrality of the English language in the heterolingual address of the modern Indian nation-state, it also affirms the very multiplicity of the lived meanings of the language and its sheer futility in the management of populations.

In a mirror reflection of *India Demands English* and the Indian Constitution, the state in *Raag Darbari* presents English as a catalyst of self-improvement, moral amelioration, and national development. English is necessary for the postcolonial state to educate ideal citizen subjects. It is liberal and democratic, with the potential to usher Indian citizens into Anglophonic global circuits of intellectual and economic exchange. As the language of the state, English appears gloriously incorrectly on written requests to the government and in the government's rejections of those requests. These errors index its users' unpreparedness for structures of modern governance. It is the language the magistrate yells in to resume order in the court. English is also the medium of choice for tokenistic speeches on modernization, secularism, and unity in diversity. To the extent that English is a part of the state infrastructure, the only thing that reaches the residents of Shivpalganj from the government in New Delhi is its English bureaucratese. The state machine is defunct. Local politics has little positive effect on the lives of the people, who are shown to be not politically active or aware. The villagers do not vote or care about elections. They think that the nation's Planning Commission is an outfit that simply invents mysterious English names for the nation's problems.

The world of English, imagined as stately and refined, does not always overlap with the world of Shivpalganj. When it does—as it must—the situation leaves everyone confused. The third-person narrator's use of English words and British or American cultural references usually heightens the absurdity of life in Shivpalganj and the ignorance of its residents. The narrator's comparison of the goings-on of village life to what happens in the parliament in New Delhi or more progressive cities in the "West," for instance, performs two functions. These variations in scale make the villagers look ignorant, laughable, and unimportant against the backdrop of the world. At the same time, these variations also serve to cut the bombast of the state and the world down to size by showing us the real people in whose name the state governs.

In one such instance of disorienting overlap, the principal of the local high school refers to Picasso while criticizing a calendar reprint of

Gandhi's photograph in a betel leaf (*paan*) shop. The principal remarks that the cheap print befits the *paan* shop, while a Picasso would be out of place. Before Rangnath disputes the principal's assessment, he bursts out laughing at the mere mention of high art in Shivpalganj. But the familiar joke about the out-of-placeness of Anglophone high culture in rural India veers towards a critique of the revisionist post-independence history systematically delegitimizing lived language experience. English appears as means to legitimize structural disempowerment and to cohere precarious nationalist sentiment. The principal explains that he ended up in Shivpalganj because he once dared to contradict his college professor on the linguistic roots of a word found in the Buddhist edicts on an ancient Indian monument. The professor made sure that the principal never got a good job. The principal knew the meaning of the word that day because of his caste experience of language. However, his professor forced him to accept the definition that was provided by English-language Indological research that strengthened India's historical association with Buddhism. Hinting at the precarity of national sentiment, the principal perceptively points out that his encounter with the professor took place before the recent war with China. Since then, the principal tells Rangnath, he has learned to agree with those in power.

Not many in Shivpalganj know the English language. Much of the novel features dialects of Hindi, most prominently Awadhi, which is spoken in eastern region of the state of Uttar Pradesh. While many scholars consider Awadhi a precursor to Hindustani, the Indian state considers Awadhi a dialect of Hindi. Besides the fact that north Indians speak many different languages (not just Hindi), the Hindi that is spoken is also not the Hindi enshrined in the Constitution. There are several different linguistic cultures such as Awadhi, Braj, and Khadi Boli in North India. When Hindi advocates and the Indian state push for Hindi, they speciously advance the latter to the status of a language while relegating the others to its variants and dialects.

The very few characters like Rangnath who do show a familiarity with the English language are marked as outsiders or, like the principal, have willfully decided to stop using it. Rangnath's degree in Indology, a decidedly colonial invention, further reinforces the status of English as a colonial legacy that isn't quite at home in the village. The teachers who are burdened with the task of transferring the knowledge of English to their students themselves do not fathom its logic or motivation. They are increasingly frustrated as their lectures are met with crushing disinterest. Students do not know either English or the Sanskritized Hindi, as neither of these languages has a place in their linguistic milieu. But their lack of what they never had—of languages engineered in plush Delhi offices—make them look ignorant, uncouth, and incompetent. The training of students at the local high school throws light, microcosmically, on the nationwide attempts at disseminating Hindi and English that followed independence. Calling out the folly of national language policies, a student promptly calls out his instructor for teaching English, not science, when he explains अपेक्षिक घनत्व as "relative density."[41] The explanation of the scientific concept cannot simply be its English-language equivalent when the audience does not understand English at all.

Instead of explaining the terms, the use of English reinforces the alliance between English and scientific knowledge, and renders the latter mysterious. This tautological explanation of a scientific concept refers to the fanatical invention of a technical vocabulary in Sanskritized Hindi as India sought to establish its expertise in the fields of scientific research and development. The Hindi-speaking state of Uttar Pradesh, in which fictional Shivpalganj is set, played an important role in the engineering of the Hindi language because of the "aggressive anti-Urdu attitude of the Hindi group's leaders."[42] Pro-Hindi leaders overwhelmingly dominated the government of Uttar Pradesh, and were well known for their concern for the Sanskritic lineage of Hindi.[43] Radio broadcasting, educational efforts, and teacher training were some of the important ways in which the propaganda of Hindi was disseminated. But in the classroom and in the government's translation efforts, scientific knowledge is removed from the experience and grasp of the non-English-speaking Indian and established as arcane knowledge only to be unlocked by class and caste privileges.

The developmentalist myth embodied in the English language and education has always been frustrating to most who placed their faith in it. The reason for this "failure of English" in India (under the British), Gauri Viswanathan wrote, was a result of the "growing disjunction between the seemingly unlimited possibilities for self-elevation promised by literary training and the restrictive conditions of British rule under which moral and intellectual growth was actually promoted."[44] In the novel, participation in and access to modernity remains contingent on the citizen subject's class and caste position. English education reproduces the same relations of production and division of labor that it ostensibly contests in casteist Hindi. English punctures its potential to speak for and speak to the nation. It fails to be a guarantor of opportunity and advancement. In the heterolingual address of democracy where the state speaks English and Hindi, English exposes as many tensions as it is enlisted to suppress.

If state-sponsored Hindi in *Raag Darbari* is consistently marked as ludicrous, English seems to be taking roots in unexpected places. Advertising and pornography make English more familiar to the residents of Shivpalganj than any state document in Hindi. For instance, Rangnath wonders at the hybrid terminology of the card players. Borrowed from English, card games such as Flash and Bluff have come to produce their own vernacularized equivalents. As Rangnath attempts to make sense of "flash"/*falaas*, "trail"/*tirrail*, a "pair"/*jod*, and "flush"/*langdi*, he realizes that this modified English had become a language in itself.[45] This rough-and-ready functional adaptation is both Hindi and English. As it undoes the binary between Hindi and English, the refashioned idiom of the villagers seemed to Rangnath to be the more appropriate solution to the obsessive linguistic engineering by the state. In an interior monologue that is characteristic of him, Rangnath reminds the reader of the vast "network of professional lexicographers and their committees, who are coining Hindi and regional equivalents for English words." This work, he muses,

> is quite interesting because, on the one hand, a new language is being generated inside a room, and on the other hand, it is taking long enough that the creators are able to clock in enough work hours to qualify for a life-long pension. This work is interesting also because, manufactured in this way, the language is devoid of meaning. It only has a symbolic meaning that conveys: here, the awe-inspiring quality that was in English is now also in your language. Whether the other person cares for it or not is no one's concern.

> देश के पेशेवर कोशकारों और उनकी समितियों का जाल बिछा है जो अँग्रेज़ी शब्दों के लिए हिन्दी और दूसरी क्षेत्रीय भाषाओं में शब्द रच रहे हैं। यह काम काफ़ी दिलचस्प है क्यूंकी एक ओर कमरे के भीतर एक नयी भाषा का निर्माण हो रहा है, दूसरी ओर इतना वक़्त भी लग रहा है कि निर्माण करता पेन्शन पाने भर की नौकरी भी पूरी कर लें। यह इसलिए भी दिलचस्प है कि इस तरह बनायी गयी भाषा का कोई अर्थ नहीं है, सिवाय इसके कि यह कहा जा सकता है कि लो भाई, जो शै हमारी अँग्रेज़ी में थी, वह तुम्हारी भाषा में आ गयी है।[46]

In Rangnath's assessment of India's language policies, the English language does not have any literal meaning. Its gains are symbolic, as he characterizes the association of Hindi with English as largely metonymic. The state developed literal Sanskritized Hindi translation of English words to model Hindi as modern. The colonial legacy of English as an administrative language would strengthen Hindi as the technology of governance. The modernity associated with English, it was hoped, would modernize Hindi and other Indian languages. The potential of Hindi and English to effect change and catalyze social transformation meant that the government used these languages to address even illiterate villagers. But as with the card games, the villagers often transformed the language itself in their reception and reading. Ironically, people's nonstandard reception and use of English is quite different from the Indian state's use of it as an administrative vernacular.

For instance, in the state's wisdom, it wrote all appeals to exterminate mosquitoes and eradicate malaria in Shivpalganj in English.[47] The villagers could not follow the language of this community messaging. Instead, the fact that they saw English as foreign presented malaria as a foreign disease with a foreign-sounding name that was a sure sign of apocalyptic times.[48] From the villagers' perspective, "two men went to every single house and wrote on the front of each house, in ochre paint, prayers to Queen Malaria in English letters. It was because of the majesty of those English letters that all mosquitoes disappeared" (दो आदमी बराबर हर घर के आगे जा-जाकर गेरू से मलेरिया महारानी की इस्तुति अँग्रेज़ी में लिख गये। उन अक्षरों का प्रताप, बाबू, कि सारे मच्छर भाग गये।).[49] To the villagers, the state's English was a paean to please Queen Malaria. They read the scientific nature of English—sought by the state to convey its modernity—in feudal terms. The villagers grasped the authority of the state and the symbolic stateliness of English even as they did not understand the literal meaning of what was written on their doors. The English language, legible only as the Roman script, literally took the form of a benediction and a talisman. The political vernacular of the postcolonial Indian state was further vernacularized, ironically, by situating it in a distant memory of the British queen.

Similarly, the state also marshaled English to encourage the now-healthy villagers to be more productive farmers and to contribute to the growth of the nation. A poster urging its readers to "grow more grain" in English showed a healthy farmer, well dressed and happy, cutting a tall crop of wheat.[50] The omniscient narrator rationalized the language choice of the poster as follows:

> It was assumed that the farmers (clad in a quilted jacket and earrings) who were also scholars of English, would be convinced by the English slogans, and those who were scholars of Hindi, would be won over by the Hindi version. And, those who did not know how to read either language would at least recognize the figures of the man and the woman. The government hoped that as soon as they saw the man and the laughing woman, farmers would turn away from the poster and start growing more grain like a people possessed.[51]

मिर्जई और बालीवाले काश्तकारों में जो अंग्रेजी के विद्वान थे उन्हें अंग्रेजी इबारत से और जो हिंदी के विद्वान थे उन्हें हिंदी से परास्त करने की बात सोची गयी थी; और जो दो में से एक भी भाषा नहीं जानते थे वे भी कम-से-कम आदमी

और औरत को तो पहचानते ही थे। उनसे आशा की जाती थी कि आदमी के पीछे हँसती हुई औरत की तस्वीर देखते ही वे उसकी ओर पीठ फेरकर दीवानों की तरह अधिक अन्न उपजाना शुरू कर देंगे।

The use of the word "scholars" ironized someone who was just literate enough to recognize the words of an informational poster. It drew attention to the enormity of the effort required by the farmers to comprehend the government's address to them. The villagers did not read the poster but saw the figures, making the script of the poster legible as an image. As an address that remains unintelligible, the poster made evident the failure of both Hindi and English. The farmers felt alienated by the two languages that they could not read, as well as by their representation as rich, well dressed, and happy. Ultimately, they did not acknowledge and respond to the ideological message of the poster; in fact, the farmers also did not recognize themselves as the state's subjects.

English, along with Hindi, is the language of address as the state exhorted the villagers to be free of diseases and to grow more grains. However, the responsibility for this productive and healthy life—like the responsibility to read the message—lay with the villagers who must internalize the transformative potential associated with Hindi and English. The double-edged satire of the novel lampooned the political liberalism inherent in the advocacy and exploitation of the English language. In its dissemination to farmers and villagers, and in bureaucratese, English caricatured the developmentalist logic of reform, progress, and discipline that was an important aspect of British imperialism, and remained attractive in the ideology of modern nation formation. The joke was on the government for its ill-thought-out publicity strategies.

The address in English to Indian publics here both capitulates to and exceeds the dynamics of interpellation. The posters are unintelligible to the intended audience and do not, in fact, augment the authority of the state. The nature of translation structuring this address is that of heterolingual catachresis of the super-sign, which also makes it possible to reject, to question, and to not even register the interpellative force of the state. The authority of English, and of Hindi as it draws power from English, defuses the state's democratic impulses.

The English language of the state seems incongruous in relation to people's experiences on the ground. This discrepancy amplifies the heterolingual address of democracy and serves as metonymy for the failing nation-state. Indeed, despite its legislative adoption as India's associate official language, English remains largely unintelligible to the majority of India's population. The unintelligibility of the state's language colors the people's experience of the state. The novel shows that the instrumentalization of English to create an administrative vernacular in India was unsuccessful. However, this bureaucratic circulation of English led to another mode of its vernacularization, as citizen subjects had to muster all discursive and linguistic resources to make sense of the state's address. As English circulated in nonstandard forms and reception by those who did not know the language, it gained a different kind of association, vernacularity, and relevance to their lives.

As a point of contrast to *Raag Darbari*'s focus on the people's confusion, let me briefly discuss Upamanyu Chatterjee's *English, August* and *Mammaries of the Welfare State*, which give us a view of English on the ground through the perspective of the state. Structurally, *English, August* and *Mammaries of the Welfare State* follow *Raag Darbari*. The two novels by Chatterjee have the same protagonist—Agastya Sen—a city-bred high-caste English-speaking Indian Administrative Service officer who travels to a small village called Madna. In these novels, the English language and the government officer are the same. Agastya's friends, who find it hard to pronounce his name, refer to him as August. He is also sometimes called just "English" or "the last Englishman" because of a self-confessed fascination with Anglo-Indians at his boarding school. August, as his subordinate officer Kumar refers to him, is an English type, who "speaks English more fluently than he speaks any Indian language." His names, August and English, make him an embodiment of the language itself. The state and the language come together in his character, making him and his class the rightful owners of English. In the novels, English is august, and August is English.

English, August follows August on his first appointment as an early-career bureaucrat in the village of Madna, and *Mammaries* sees him transferred from Bombay (now Mumbai) and then back to Madna. Both novels show August seeking housing, a process made impossible to navigate by bureaucracy. The story of August's travels thus also becomes the allegory of the out-of-placeness of English in India. Even though he is expected to govern and participate in developing the region, August is fundamentally not at ease in the village. He never learns the language of the village where he is supposed to facilitate developmental work, and by virtue of his city-based upbringing, has no "sense of land, agriculture land."[52] He spends his days smoking weed and fantasizing about sleeping with the village women. As an emissary of the state, he does not inspire confidence, and personifies the life of English in India.

Although August embraces English unquestioningly in urban centers of New Delhi or Calcutta, he is exasperated and baffled by the presence of English in Madna. As in Shivpalganj, English is found in unexpected places—on instruction pamphlets for midwives and as a Shakespeare quote about "innocent sleep" on sleeping pills. *English, August* and *Mammaries* feature numerous genres of bureaucratic documents like circulars, notifications, photocopies, memos, posters, funny acronyms and officialese (BOOBZ), and slogans of the welfare state that neither the state functionaries nor the beneficiaries—citizens—can decipher. As in *Raag Darbari*, changing the names of the places and translating from one language to another was an industry in itself. In the operation of the bureaucracy, writing and documents have great power. And, this power is imbued, in no small measure, by the language in which the documents are written.

Reading *Raag Darbari*, *English, August*, and *Mammaries* together highlights the difference between thinking about English in English and thinking about it through another language. Sukla's Hindi novel focuses on the villagers' reception and confusion, whereas Chatterjee's novels focus on the upper-class and upper-caste male protagonist's confusion and irresponsibility. In both novels, the jokes about English are tendentious jokes, where the male narrator-protagonist has a better understanding of the situation than the villagers who encounter English. August's senior officer, Srivastav, who studied at a Hindi-medium school, offers a contrast to the ease of English for August and his friends, who are urban, upper caste, and upper class. In Srivastav's words, he taught himself "very difficult people" like Wordsworth and Shakespeare to sit for the Administrative Services exam, a legacy of the British Empire that still tests one's knowledge of British literature.[53] He speaks English because it "gives one confidence."[54] He considers English literature a useless subject to study because it does not help one master speaking the language. Srivastav rebuffs the cultural values of English in favor of a manipulable abstraction.

In one particular moment, August's cynicism cracks and he earnestly claims, "We won't make it, you know, as a nation until—to take only one instance—the people who put up our road signs and the people who need to use them, to decipher them from their cars, are the same."[55] Despite this moment of clarity, the novel preoccupies itself with August and his alienation, his inability to feel at home in the India that he is supposed to serve as part of his job. Both *English, August* and *Mammaries* are the stories of the state machinery. The focus is on August, his flawed sense of superiority, and his feeling out of place. Even though August is a representative of the state as far as the villagers are concerned, he does not understand the land or the people. Chatterjee's novels feature an escalating sense of confusion, anxiety, and ironic distance from the people. *Raag Darbari*, by contrast, focuses on the villagers' confusion and puzzlement, where the villagers' "readings" of bureaucratic writing undercut the authority of the state.

Language Ex Machina: English as an Instrument

Raag Darbari, English, August, and *Mammaries of the Welfare State* manifest Gandhi's worst fears. And, it is fair to say that, for the most part, the promise of English hailed by the writers of *India Demands English* and the Indian Constitution fails here. The villagers in *Raag Darbari* do not understand English or Hindi. As a result, their experience of English as the technology of governance is largely one of alienation and confusion. The villagers are forced to make sense of English even when they cannot read it or do not care for it. Such a nonreading of English is an important part of the life of vernacular English in India, as forthcoming chapters will show. As the villagers *do not read* English—sometimes earnestly, sometimes flippantly, English becomes a fetishized object whose power does not always conjure the authority of the state and, in fact, actively rejects it.

The postcolonial life of English is animated by an anomalous maneuvering of the foreignness of English. For advocates of English, the nonnative character of English was desirable but also dangerous to the coherence of the democratic nation-state. One of the ways in which the meanings were contained was by portraying and promoting it as a machinic object. The figuration of language as a machinic object promised two things. It offered a way of controlling and shaping the meanings of English. As an instrumentalized object, the language was not just an object but a modern device that could be joined with animate and inanimate bodies and maneuvered to the desired effect. While the transformative power of English arose from its association with the British Empire, that fact was not the determining point of reference. English was valued for the objects it was associated with, the effects it could produce in specific conditions, the affective relations that those effects enabled, and the meanings it made possible. When the English language is a machine, the relationship between India and English is shaped by creativity and contingency rather than by the ideological workings of the empire. The satiric novels utilize this creativity to resist the power of the state. In fact, the language as a machinic object gives form to the relations between an ex-colony and an erstwhile empire.

For instance, Jawaharlal Nehru called English the "glue" that would seal "the fissiparous tendencies" of India into "national unity."[56] He laid English as the foundation of postcolonial nation-building and third-world solidarity by likening it to India's "national cement."[57] In a 1961 speech in New Delhi, he baldly referred to English as "the key that would unlock the vast treasures of all scientific and humanistic knowledge."[58] Nehru called the English language "the link" between the people of India and the rest of the world.[59] On each of these occasions, speaking and writing in the wake of two hundred years of British rule, Nehru rarely referred to the colonial provenance of the language. Instead, he maintained an interest in it only as an object of global affiliation that could be exerted upon to produce whatever effects one desired.

Comparisons of language to keys, links, or cement can seem throwaway, clichéd, and unsophisticated. Never mind how seductive these figurations be, they invite little critical attention. Nonetheless, for containing the meanings of English, Nehru's metaphors were quite ingenious and deliberate. By comparing English to a key or a link or cement, Nehru manufactured the illusion that English could be desired and controlled with no attachment to its colonial past. Figured so, the cultural value of the English language was perhaps still determined by its colonial provenance. However, the language had a specific delimited role in a newly independent India. It was something extrinsic, serviceable, and familiar. It could be wielded by any human hand—unmarked by caste, class, gender, religion—to produce the same desired results on another object. As a key, cement, or a link, the English language remained firmly in the control of one using it. Its users and speakers were builders of a new nation, a role much different than that of good colonial subjects. Nehru's metaphors reimagined intersubjective relations forged under colonial rule and disambiguated the meanings of English in India.

From a scholarly standpoint, seeing English as an object, a machine, or a machinic object does make English visible as a part of an assemblage where language and animate and inanimate bodies act on each other. Efforts to forge relations based in English or the English language as if they were "free" of the burden of colonial history illuminate another history of the colonial language. They instantiate the vulnerability of what Gilles Deleuze and Felix Guattari called "a major language" as it is continuously reconfigured and made minor. The veracity of the comparison—of language to a machine—is less important. What is important is that this desire to appropriate a language without any claims of subjectification, in fact, highlights a desire to operate in language beyond identity. Beyond even the subject-object dichotomy, we have experiences of language that demand a reconsideration of the dominant narratives of "negative" colonialist oppression and "positive" native rejection that have characterized discussions of colonial language and power in India.

Recently, Rey Chow has theorized this foreignness of colonial language from the perspective of the foreign-sounding colonized subject, the xenophone. Chow notes that the encounter of the colonized with the colonizer's language has typically been characterized in negative terms, as the disruption of "an original connection (the mother tongue) and as the deprivation of linguistic autonomy, spontaneity, and integrity."[60] By contrast, she suggests that we cast colonial language practices and politics as a prosthetic rather than as "essentially originary." As prosthesis, coloniality will overturn the violent burden of a colonial language, "what feels like an inalienable interiority, such as the way one speaks, is—dare I say it?—impermanent, detachable, and (ex)changeable."[61] Conceptualized as a prosthetic, coloniality is exteriorized, it is made into an object, and it is productive. Chow emphasizes the *alienable* exteriority of coloniality, without dwelling much on the idea of exteriority itself. Her reading is powerful in its conception of coloniality as a foreign object.

Still, in the texts above—*Raag Darbari*, *India Demands English*, and Nehru's remarks—language is productive as a machinic object not because it "repairs a loss" instanced by coloniality—as a prosthetic would—but because it visualizes the assemblage of enunciation and machine, enables agency, and plugs these figures into networks of power hitherto unavailable to "native" subjects. In fact, none of the machinic objects we encounter aim to repair a bodily loss of a limb—or a sense of injury to the self—but shed light on the conditionality of meaning and the fundamental otherness of all language. All assemblages are political, and the ones that are thrown into relief by specific articulations of language-as-object show continued negotiations of the colonial and postcolonial meanings of English.

In her argument, Chow draws on Jacques Derrida, who in *Monolingualism of the Other, or the Prosthesis of Origin* (1998) famously claimed that the only language he speaks *"is not mine,"* but it is not "foreign to me."[62] Yet, before we arrive at loss as the paradigmatic characteristic of postcolonial experience, we must confront the Derridean *not mine* that occasions that loss. For Derrida, there can be no mastery of language.

Monolingualism is not an experience of "belonging, property, power of mastery, pure "ipseity." If language cannot be "had" or "possessed," what does it mean to *dispute its loss* in the case of postcolonial languaging? It seems important to acknowledge that the language embodies an inevitable foreignness that extends beyond a simple externally imposed nonindigeneity in a colonial context.

CHAPTER 2

Touch

DALIT ANGLOPHONE WRITERS
AND A LANGUAGE SHARED

The Dalit Writer and the English Language

On July 17, 2018, Sahitya Akademi—India's national academy of letters—hosted five poets for a symposium and reading in New Delhi. Aparna Lanjewar Bose, Aruna Gogulamanda, Chandramohan Sathyanathan, Yogesh Maitreya Wanjari, and Cynthia Stephen were all published authors but were relatively unknown. A few of them had published in online magazines, others were published by small presses. But as literary activists of a new age, all of them had skillfully leveraged social media to share their writing as widely as algorithms would permit. The event itself was made possible by their resourcefulness. Sathyanathan had reached out to the Sahitya Akademi to remind the institution that there were many poets like them across the country, enough in fact, that this key literary institution of postcolonial India should give them a stage. Dalit writers have not always been included in mainstream national and international literary events, so Sathyanathan's ask was important.[1]

Like literary academies worldwide, Sahitya Akademi was established in 1954 to develop and promote India's composite national culture. Given India's multilingualism, however, this decree meant that the Akademi would support literatures from over a dozen Indian languages—including English—and publish translations across them. In this spirit of linguistic pluralism, the five poets gathered that day hailed from different parts of India. They had grown up speaking different languages in the states of Kerala, Maharashtra, and Andhra Pradesh, and had been part of different literary circles. Celebrated as "a rising wave of Dalit English writers" in news reports the following day, what they shared were two key things: their identity as Dalit and their identity as English-language poets.[2] But as the event unfolded, it became clear that the meeting of these identities was far from straightforward.[3]

"I say I am a poet writing in English. But people say I am a Dalit poet." Maitreya, younger and more outspoken of the cohort, would note the distance between the English language and Dalit identity most evocatively that evening. His statement echoed the argument made by Dalit writers and politicians that Hindus within the caste system (known as *savarna* Hindus) have systemically denied them the English language. English, Maitreya argued, was supposed to distinguish literature which is "intelligent, well-written or aesthetic," whereas most literary critics and readers saw Dalit writing as anything but that.[4] In fact, a question from the audience similarly stereotyped Dalit literature by asking why it always tended toward the "political," "negative," and "angry." The factual tone of the question insisted that Dalit literature was all of those things. It also implied that its negative affect compromised the tradition. Of course, the tacit suggestion that Dalit literature instead be "apolitical," "positive," or "pleasing" was both preposterous and insidious.

Still, these assumptions would betray an impoverished understanding of literature as well as obfuscate the dynamics of linguistic and caste experience. For the poets gathered at Sahitya Akademi, the use of English is as much a historical compulsion as it is a political strategy. Comfortably multilingual, they choose to write in English while regularly working with other languages as translators. Their seemingly conflicting identities as Dalit and English poets make them a product of their times in more ways than one. If, as *Raag Darbari, English, August,* and *Mammaries of the Welfare State* illuminated, the sights and sounds of English are everywhere in India today, so is caste. The experience of English is always shaped by caste in India. In the social, cultural, and political world of these poets, the everydayness of caste is illuminated in the modernity of English.

Two radical economic and political breaks around the 1990s made the inequality of English in India more acute. The first event was the liberalization of economic policies that brought English-language media and technology into India, while also making it possible for many Indians to participate in an English-fueled global economy. A major turning point in India's postindependence history as a protected welfare state, it was almost as if "India's twenty-first century began in the 1990s."[5] The second event was the Mandal Commission Report. Headed by Bindeshwari

Prasad Mandal, the Second Backward Class Commission from 1979 came to be known as the Mandal Commission. This commission was appointed to "identify the socially or educationally backward classes" of India and to consider the means of redressal. On August 7, 1990, the government accepted the recommendations of the Mandal Commission Report that 27 percent opportunities be reserved for such backward classes at all levels of the government services. While it was a flicker of hope for these sections of society, the announcement met with vicious resistance from upper-caste Indians that continues to mar its potential.

The heightened pervasiveness of English as a result of economic liberalization was accompanied by a greater awareness of its unavailability to many after the Mandal Commission Report. Having come of age in the shadow of the Mandal Commission Report, the poets' very access to English education speaks to the fraught nexus of caste, class, and language. Their experience of English is different from that of economically disadvantaged Dalits, who, writes Manoranjan Byapari, a Dalit Bengali novelist, must first find a way out of crushing poverty and starvation before they can learn English.[6] But, whatever their path to English—and the paths are different—the poets' decision to write in it is both spectacularly radical and unspectacularly banal.

English may or may not be a language of everyday experience for everyone in India. But, as a linguistic symbol of the democratic public sphere, there is a caste-marked everyday experience of English that encompasses hope and alienation, shame and anxiety. The relationship of English to the idea of Indian democracy in the Indian Constitution—to nationhood, secularism, and social justice—makes it a linguistic space where equality can be imagined in the shadows of other unfreedoms. At the same time, this promised casteless modernity of English remains contested and riven by caste politics. In *The Caste Question* (2009), Anupama Rao has argued that the history of India's political modernity is a history of the term "Dalit" and the "reorganization of caste under political modernity" illuminates a "constitutive relationship between Dalit emancipation and Indian democracy."[7] Thus, not only is there a constitutive relationship between language and democracy, as we saw in the previous chapter, it also exists between democracy and caste. To be clear, the majority of low-caste or Dalit communities do not have formal access to English education. But, for its promise of castelessness—indeed, an annihilation of caste (to invoke the title of Ambedkar's treatise)—English is both an object of desire as well as a negative force that humiliates while also auguring the redressal of that humiliation. Between the imperative, allure, and impossibility to be in English, the language comes to embody the most hopeful promise of social justice and the humiliating caste experience of alienation from it.

Despite the necessary imbrication of caste and English, the vast corpus of Indian Anglophone literature has told us notoriously little about caste experience. Indian Anglophone literature has centered themes of empire and nationhood, of colonialism and Partition, that have not had the same resonance in Dalit writing in any language. Dalit writing has focused on individual and collective oppression within the caste system. We can attribute the silence on the caste question to the Indian Anglophone writers' own caste privilege. In the introduction to a special issue on caste of the journal *Biography*, Charu Gupta and Subramanian Shankar make the astute observation that "caste is not the lived reality of Dalits and Dalitbahujans alone and, accordingly, . . . the critical study of caste cannot be their burden alone." Gupta and Shankar write that while "not all 'upper caste' life narratives acknowledge caste as directly as Dalit life narratives do, they nevertheless remain marked, even in their silence, by caste. Indeed, it has been argued that such silence is itself a mark of caste privilege—after all, is not the ability to ignore caste in itself a mark of privilege?"[8] Discussions of Indian Anglophone writing have also incisively probed only the categories of Indian and English. This line of interrogation draws from the colonial or metropolitan lineage of English. It reads English from a national and monolingual position. Dalit writers and thinkers have not always shared upper-caste nationalist activists' loyalties to the nation. As Ambedkar famously and poignantly said to Gandhi in a conversation in 1931, "Gandhiji, I have no homeland. . . . How can I call this land my own homeland and this religion my own, wherein we are treated worse than cats and dogs, wherein we cannot get water to drink?"[9] Ambedkar, Luis Cabrera writes, staked out a distinctively universalistic approach to democratic citizenship by rejecting uncritical loyalty to one's country of origin. So it would be particularly limited to read Dalit Anglophone writing through a politics of English based in nationalist concerns.

By contrast, the emerging body of Dalit Anglophone writing is not troubled over the colonial provenance of the English language in India. By charging most powerfully the very possibility of writing, this body of literature, in fact, demands more from the English language in the nation. In political terms, English is first and foremost an instrument of Brahminical hegemony—the worthy but incomplete project of the British, the promise of Western European Enlightenment and global capitalism. As perhaps the only language in India without originary caste-based injunctions against who could or could not use it, English is full of promise.[10]

It promises dignity, modernity, and anonymity through an experience of language and subjectivity outside caste.

Between the hope and alienation, between resistance to and in English, Dalit Anglophone writers furnish a vernacular English that seizes the idealism of English and imbues it with the energy to resist Brahminical dominance. By writing in it, they produce a different kind of linguistic meaning from the body than the one imputed by caste. Caste injunctions against scripture, education, and literacy make the very act of writing by a Dalit subject in India radical. Centuries of the caste system have entrenched hierarchies with rules about touchability/untouchability around learning, bodily conduct, food, and clothes. Historically, the knowledge of writing has been in the hands of the Brahmins, and what is valued as literary is itself determined by caste. In this context, the act of writing by a Dalit is always activism, an act of undoing caste as written on the body.

As a haptic act, writing has the psychological and physical potential to touch, sense, feel, and move. It challenges the injunctions against touch by writing Dalits into and within a dominant discourse that is solidified by their exclusion. Hands that write not only define the individual, they also reach out to intentionally touch the other. Against the bodily regulation in the caste system, the physicality of writing in a shared language produces new modalities of seeing and touching the figure of the Dalit as the literary subject. The haptic act of writing transforms English from the administrative vernacular of abstract democracy to a language of transgressive and solidaristic touch.

In the English poem "The Remains of the Name" bilingual English and Gujarati poet Neerav Patel reflects on the impossibility of overwriting or erasing the experience of caste as written on the body. Patel was one of the early Dalit poets to write in English and often wrote about the experience of caste as specifically one that is written on the body. His collections of English poetry, *Burning from Both the Ends* (1980) and *What Did I Do to Be So Black and Blue?* (1987), were published by the Dalit Panthers of the state of Gujarat. In the poem, "The Remains of the Name," Patel writes, "Who is that Satan sculptor who has / inscribed my name on my forehead? / Why like writing letters on the skin of a tree trunk / You are writing my name / Dipping the knife in my veins?"[11] The name here is not an individualist fantasy but caught up in social, spatial, historical, and embodied differences. Given to the poet, the name ties him to his low caste by birth. Thus, caste is ineffably written on the body and it is impossible for the poet to ever free himself from it. But, the poet wants to be rid of his identity-giving name, and it is to forget his name that he seeks the anonymity of the city. Still, caste does not leave him alone even in the cosmopolitan culture promised by English: "I have dissolved every atom of my structure / of name / in the solution of cosmopolitan culture." He worries that his caste will not leave him even in his death: "Oh I am afraid / Will my name not die even with my funeral pyre?" Nothing remains after the name is removed. The poet's act of writing—poetry, English—is steeped in an impossible desire to operate beyond identity.

In an essay titled "Gujarati Is My Mother Tongue, English Is My Foster Mother Tongue" ("Gujarati *Maari Matrubhasha*, English *Maari* Foster Mother"), Patel has called English his "foster mother," marking English as not his own but still maternal. Addressing those who are anxious about the erasure of Gujarati, Patel writes that this position reeks of a plot against the Dalits that *savarna* children are sent to English-medium schools and encouraged to partake of the gifts of globalization while Dalit children are educated in the "mother tongue." By contrast, Patel finds English empowering against Gujarati, his relation to which is determined by his caste. Patel concludes this essay with an embrace of English, "I would like every dalit child to study in an English medium school and love his foster-mother English more than his mother-tongue. In fact I would like English to be their mother-tongue. Dear mother-tongue, I bid you goodbye..."[12] Writing in English, thus, provides the poet the chance to rail against his destiny. It also dares to challenge that destiny by wanting to rub off the name on the forehead, etched with vein-dipped knives. In India, the written language is always an embodied discourse because it is always in relation and response to the embodied discourse of caste. As Patel disowns his mother tongue, the affect of English is noticeably different here. It represents not the anxiety of the democratic state but rather the comfort, intimacy, and empowerment of the foster-mother tongue.

What is it like to obsessively want to write over—to want to erase— caste that is inscribed on the body? Compared to the experience of alienation in English, we know relatively little about this yearning in language. But, attending to it and describing it—not as false consciousness or naïve optimism but as a recognition of agency—can illuminate an experience of English that is rather different from the postcolonial state's: oppositional, nondominant, emotional, and embodied. This chapter threads three disparate bodies of Dalit writing in English—poetry, essays, and short stories—to assemble an archive of Dalit writing in English and to highlight the haptic experience of writing English in postcolonial India. It shows that in Dalit writing, English approximates a shared language where injunctions against touch are flouted both literally and metaphorically.

Spanning political commentaries, polemical pieces, autobiographies, biographies, poetry, and fiction, there exists a distinct tradition of Dalit Anglophone writing. Historically, there have been more Dalit biographies, rather than autobiographies, in the English language because access to English has been limited. For instance, *Viramma: Life of an Untouchable* (1998) was "told to" ethnographers Josiane Racine and Jean-Luc Racine. The biography was later translated into English by Will Hobson. Foundational Dalit thinkers Jotiba Phule and B. R. Ambedkar wrote in English. The manifesto of the Dalit Panthers was written in English. More recently, however, a growing body of autobiographical and testimonial writing, primarily in English, has emerged. These include works by Narendra Jadhav, Yashica Dutta, Suraj Yengde, and Sujatha Gidla, many of whom are based outside India. Meena Kandasamy and Monidipa "Mimi" Mondal write fiction. Mondal is a speculative fiction writer, having authored a novel, *His Footsteps, through Darkness and Light* (2019), and a nonfiction collection titled *Luminescent Threads: Connections to Octavia Butler* (2017).

Alongside this body of writing, there exists a formidable corpus of English translations of Dalit writing, including a few collaborative translations like that of Namdeo Dhasal's Marathi poems into English by Dilip Chitre. English translations of Dalit autobiographies like Sharankumar Limbale's *Akkarmashi* (translated by Sanjay Bhoomkar, 1984), Bama's *Karukku* (translated by Lakshmi Holmstrom, 1992), Omprakash Valmiki's *Joothan* (translated by Arun Prabha Mukherjee, 1997), Daya Pawar's *Baluta* (translated by Jerry Pinto, 2015), and Vasant Moon's *Growing Up Untouchable in India: A Dalit Autobiography* (translated by Gail Omvedt, 2001) have provided Dalit literature greater visibility on a national and a global scale in markets and academies, as well as paths to regional recognition among other Indian languages.

The English-language scholarship of critics such as D. R. Nagaraj, Anand Teltumbde, and Gopal Guru has illuminated the social and political conditions of Dalit experience. Translation anthologies like *Poisoned Bread* (1992), *No Alphabet in Sight* (2011), *Steel Nibs Are Sprouting* (2013), *The Oxford India Anthology of Telugu Dalit Writing* (edited by K. Purushotham, Gita Ramaswamy, and Gogu Shyamala), *The Oxford India Anthology of Tamil Dalit Writing* (edited by Ravikumar and R. Azhagarasan), and *The Oxford India Anthology of Malayalam Dalit Writing* (edited by M. Dasan, V. Pratibha, Pradeepan Pampirikunnu, and C. S. Chandrika) have helped consolidate a tradition of writing in specific languages like Marathi, Telugu, Tamil, and Kannada. The Anglophone publishing ecosystem that includes publishing houses like Navayana and Oxford

University Press India is an important context within which Dalit texts circulate. Laura Brueck and Christi Merrill, who have translated Dalit literature from Hindi, write that by "forming an alliance with English-language readers, Dalit writers are able to call into question some of the dubious moral stances guarded by the indigenous elite in the name of preserving tradition."[13] In light of this fact, Yogesh Maitreya decided to take control of the translation by setting up a publishing house, Panther's Paw, which produces English translations of Dalit writing from languages such as Marathi and Punjabi.

Meena Kandasamy's poetry notes the hopefulness of an English that rises to meet the Dalit poet's language. In her poetry and prose fiction, Kandasamy often writes about her experiences as a Dalit woman in modern India. Many of her poems engage with the promise of the English language to achieve parity with her caste-inflected and vernacular Tamil. She hopes that English will "accept [her] ... to appreciate [her] sensibilities, admire [her] culture and, above all, be accommodating."[14] In vocabulary that resonates with Nehru's midnight tryst with the radio, she has called English a "borrowed language" that has "taken her voice to a larger level and helped in her search for solidarity."[15] In her poem "Mulligatawny Dreams" collected in the anthology *Touch* (2006), Kandasamy petitions—recalling Isaac Mathai's gesture in chapter 1—for her own English: "I dream of an English / full of the words of my language / an English in small letters / an English that shall tire a white man's tongue / an English where small children practice with smooth round / pebbles in their mouth to spell the right *zha*."[16] The dreamscape of English, rather unlike Vaidyaji's dream in *Raag Darbari*, conjures again the ability of English to translate and convey other languages. Sounded by the sounds of another language, this is a lowercase English. *Zha* is the retroflexed sound of *ra* found in Dravidian languages like Tamil and Malayalam that can be hard to pronounce for those who are not used to it. Its tactile production in the mouths of young children gives body and sound to the English language. In poems by Patel and Kandasamy, English is a different physical experience that invites a reassessment of how we understand Anglophone writing from India. The corpus of Dalit Anglophone writers does not match the prodigious and globally recognizable body of Indian Anglophone writing. But, it produces English as a politically and affectively charged vernacular language.

In the shadow of English caricatured as global, then, is an experience of English that is embodied, affective, and oppositional. Unlike the many interrogations of the use of English by Indian Anglophone writers (and their ensuing justifications for its use), the Dalit writers show little nostalgia, guilt, denial, or qualification of their language choice. Their English is not an English of resistance or writing back to the empire but an English of hope and the refusal of shame. It is tentative, idealistic, eager, and limited. Dalit leaders and ideologues—from nineteenth-century reformers like Jotiba and Savitribai Phule to B. R. Ambedkar to contemporary figures like Chandrabhan Prasad and Kancha Ilaiah Shepherd—have all written in the English language and advocated for it. As they insist on English against other Indian languages, regardless of how unequal its experience, these writers not only provide a tradition for contemporary Dalit writers but also conceptualize English as the language of touch. One of the reasons the poets at Sahitya Akademi felt assured in their choice of English is because they saw it as the language of Ambedkar and Phule, and saw themselves as part of a long tradition of linguistic activism. Their writing and publishing in English is very much their response to Ambedkar's call to action to "Agitate, Educate, Organize," and a way to translate embodied experiences into literature.

Across India today, there is a generational shift from the novel form to poetry. Indian Anglophone poetry is a long-established tradition from Michael Madhusudan Dutt, Toru Dutt, and Manmohan Ghose to the *satthohari* poets. Now, many first-time young poets (especially those writing from minority language or subject positions) actively share their works on social media and in poetry readings. The fast-paced, democratizing, hyperconnected culture of the Internet shapes their poetry in very media-specific ways. As we know from the work of globally renowned figures like Rupi Kaur and Cleo Wade, simple and direct poetry is eminently shareable on social media. Platforms like Facebook, Twitter, and Instagram encourage writing styles that can circulate without much contextual information.

In addition to the polyspatiality and polytemporality that Jahan Ramazani discusses in *Poetry in a Global Age* (2020), there's also something unique about the postlingual texture of contemporary poetry that orients it as worldly and global. Global poetics takes shape through the personal lens/memoir that implodes language as we know it to register geographical movements and historical entanglements. Poetry allows a play with visual placement, sounds, and textuality to stage language in translation. This transmedial interplay of the textual, aural, and figural counters the "voluntary deafness" of English. The Sahitya Akademi poets are an interesting product and part of this phenomenon. The reason they have turned to social media is the same reason so many historically marginalized writers have turned to social media. The media platform places these poems in a space where the sincerity of personal narratives meets artifice-free protest poetry. Usually, the poets first share the poems on their social media before publishing them in book form. The Sahitya Akademi poets anchor English in specific locations where it demands to be read through its linguistic and embodied mediations.

All of these Sahitya Akademi poets belong to the post-Mandal generation of writers and started writing around the institutional murder of Rohith Vemula. In this context, they are already sensitive to the promise and failures of English and English education. Their works bring us squarely to a world where the experience of the English language is unquestionably caste marked. At the same time, these Dalit writers are able to tell us something about the experience of writing English in a way that non-Dalit writers are not. Dalit Anglophone poets furnish what Laura Brueck has called "alienistic literary performances," that "confront and affront the non-Dalit world and force Dalits themselves to recognize their own alienation."17 Building upon Brueck's argument, we see that these literary performances do not just challenge caste-marked sense of the literary and the aesthetic but also of language itself.

This chapter heeds Brueck's call to "flip the analytical gaze" and to read historically Brahminical and upper-caste literary tradition through the writings of Dalit writers. Although thinking through the multisensorial nature of the Anglophone world, I wish to build on the gaze with what John Mowitt has called the audit to track the hearing/listening relation (as opposed to vision/gaze) as well other dialogic sensorial relations like that of touch. This chapter begins with writings by Phule and Ambedkar and other Dalit political activists, then turns to Dalit Anglophone poets, and finally brings that knowledge of English to read Hindi Dalit writer Ajay Navaria's use of English in his short story collection, *Yes, Sir* (2012).

Ambedkar, Phule, and the Goddess English of the Bloodless Revolution

The growing success and popularity of Dalit Anglophone writers and their use of social media may suggest that the revolutionary allure of English is recent. This is not true. The Internet has brought English closer home to readers and writers, forcing them to navigate it, but the anticaste pull of English dates back. As Merrill and Brueck write in their introduction to a special issue of *Words without Borders* on Hindi Dalit literature, the English language has always been imagined as an ally of the Dalit struggle. Writing in the early nineteenth century, Jotiba Phule sought in English a language of shared solidarities that could critique Brahminical supremacy and organize resistance to it. Phule and his wife Savitribai Phule were both anticaste social reformers who, like many other reformers of the time, turned to Enlightenment ideas and industrial technology to reform Hindu society. Phule studied in the Scottish Mission's High School in Pune and worked under the British government. The British takeover of the city of Pune in 1818 took power from the hands of the Brahmins. The end of the Maratha rule opened the possibility of challenging their domination in a new political configuration, as evidenced in Phule's challenge to caste from below. The publication of his Marathi-language polemic *Gulamgiri* (1873) (trans. Slavery) was followed by the establishment of the Satyashodhak Samaj (Society of the seekers of truth), which, he hoped, would end the slavery baked into the caste system.

The English-language "Preface" of *Gulamgiri* expands the audience of the book-length critique of the caste system. It is written not only for the Marathi-knowing audience but also to get the attention of the British. This bilingualism is evident in other writers in this chapter and is a common strategy used by Dalit writers who often write to bear witness to their oppression, forge solidarities with others similarly oppressed, and call attention to violence by speaking to many different audiences outside their caste and region at once. As a genre of writing, a preface retroactively gives coherence to the body of the text. As in the case of the Indian Constitution, the power of English manifests in its role as a supplement and in its ability to provide foundational logic to the forthcoming text. Ironically, Phule decries Brahmins as Aryan invaders while not raising any objections to the fact that the British are also, in a manner of speaking, invaders. While he mentions the impositions made by the British, he is more concerned with the fact that they are only educating the upper caste. Brahmins, in fact, are the ones holding India's progress hostage, according to Phule. *Gulamgiri* was dedicated to the people of the United States in acknowledgement of the abolishment of the practice of slavery in 1865. Phule writes:

> Dedicated
> to
> the good people of the United States
> as a token of admiration for their
> sublime disinterested and
> self-sacrificing devotion
> in the cause of Negro Slavery; and with
> an earnest desire, that my countrymen

> may take their noble example as their guide
> in the emancipation of their Sudra Brethren
> from the trammels of Brahmin thraldom [*sic*].[18]

Phule is writing a decade after the First War of Indian Independence in 1857 and a decade before the formation of the Indian National Congress. Yet, the thralldom that he notes is not that of British imperialism but of Brahminical supremacy. Phule's reference to his own "countrymen" suggests an understanding of a political collectivity beyond caste-based distinctions. He expresses admiration for the people of the United States for waging the unselfish struggle against slavery. As he draws on the legacy of the abolitionists to support anticaste efforts, Phule does not acknowledge the continued oppression of African Americans. However, rather than characterizing Phule and other Dalit intellectuals who seek solidarities outside as "naïve interpreters of American history," Tanya Agathocleous has argued that "we might see them as canny authors of a kind of counterfactual history."[19] Phule indeed participates in a counterfactual history as he draws attention to the plight of the lower castes in India by comparing it to that of the African Americans. It is hard to imagine that he was not aware of their depressed status, since historian Nico Slate in *Colored Cosmopolitanism* (2017) argues that Phule's encounters with African American missionaries in India "laid a foundation of mutual awareness," which would serve as the basis of anti-imperial alliances in the future.[20] Novels like Harriet Beecher Stowe's *Uncle Tom's Cabin* also shaped his comparative understanding of caste and race. The praise for the good people of the United States does not diminish the continued oppression of African American brethren in the United States but compares Dalits in India to them to specify the nature of caste oppression by characterizing it as slavery.

Next, Phule recruits three more interlocutors by way of his epigraphs. He first cites an English translation of Homer to register the impact of slavery on the enslaved: "The day that reduces a man to slavery takes from him the half of his virtue." William Godwin's *History of the Commonwealth* (1824–28) also cites this same quotation, using it to establish England's right to protect its freedoms.[21] Phule then invokes Colonel G. J. Hally, who acknowledged that the British education system in India would only "overeducate the few and leave the masses illiterate as ever."[22] As such, it will be "an extension of the demoralizing Brahmin-ridden policy, which, perhaps, has more retarded the progress of civilization and improvement in India generally than anything else." It is a common reading among Dalit readers that Macaulay's "Minute on Indian Education" was not an effective text because it did not extend opportunities to all sections of society. This reading offers a vital corrective to the figuration of Macaulay as an Anglicist British colonialist who offered an unfavorable assessment of Indian literary cultures and imposed English education at the cost of native knowledge.

Finally, Phule quotes from Henry Mead's *Sepoy Revolt: Its Causes and Its Consequences* (1857) to further corroborate the idea that the Brahmins—while custodians of power—have done nothing to uplift others. Rather, they have only "perpetuated the most revolting system known to the world" and "it is only from a diminution of their abused power that we can hope to accomplish the great work of national regeneration."[23] Phule compares the Brahmins to Othello, who finds that "to some extent, his occupation is gone." With the arrival of the British government, according to Phule, the Brahmins find their social position weakened. However, this is not enough. The Brahmin is not going to descend to the same level as the lower castes of his own volition and so a struggle is in order to alter the condition of the *shudra*s. Phule's use of English equips him with a communicative advantage to marshal evidence and allies from outside the caste-marked intellectual discourse. The foreignness of English—with suggestions of neutrality and modernity—also gives his remarks authority and expands his audience. Like Sanskrit and other Sanskritized languages, the English language is dominated by upper castes and is equally exclusive. However, in an important contrast, English is not as severely policed with ritualistic injunctions against speaking and learning it. As a language, English fulfils the promise of universal communicability but in a very different way from its role as a colonial and postcolonial administrative vernacular.

These attributes compel Savitribai Phule, Phule's wife, to specifically refer to English as a mother figure in her poems. Among Phule's many Marathi-language poems that praise the virtues of the English language is one titled "Mother English" (1854). Here, Phule imagines that the English language destroys the caste system. She writes, "Rule of Peshwa is gone / Mother English has come. / In such a dismal time of ours / Come Mother English, this is your hour. / It is all for the good of the poor / Manu's dead at English Mother's door. / Knowledge is poor man's refuge and shade / It's akin to comfort mother-made."[24] Knowledge, which is parsed as the knowledge of English, is the only asylum for the poor Dalits because English protects like a mother.

The wide availability and reach of English shaped Ambedkar's conscious decision to write in English.[25] His linguistic preference contrasted

Gandhi's insistence on Indian languages, especially Hindustani. Because of his class and caste position, Gandhi enjoyed an ease of communication and did not have to struggle to be heard. The drafting of the Indian Constitution in both Hindi and English lends the document the linguistic authority of secularism, equality, and modernity. Symbolically and literally, the Constitution "opens a range of possibilities hitherto unknown in Indian society."[26] It stipulates rights but also tempers the centrality of English. Merrill and Brueck note that, in the decades leading up to independence in 1947, "Ambedkar wrote appeals aimed specifically to foreign readers, in such a way that called into question the elitism of the Congress Party, especially its claim to speak for all Indian subjects in demanding independence from British rule."[27] Besides documents of political thought discussed in the previous chapter, Ambedkar also wrote key autobiographical pieces in the English language. *Waiting for a Visa* (1935–36) is a collection of loosely tied first-person narratives about growing up Dalit in India. The act of writing autobiographically in a language like English is powerful because it imagines the Dalit subject outside of a caste-marked terrain. The linguistic medium of English makes writing an act of bearing witness to suffering and of reclaiming agency and equality.

In contemporary times, activists Kancha Ilaiah Shepherd and Chandrabhan Prasad have advocated for teaching English to Dalits and invoked Ambedkar and Phule as early proponents of the English language for the Dalits. For them, as for many other Dalit writers, English literature refers also to a body of work by these foundational Dalit leaders, as well as the Indian Constitution, which guarantees a measure of equality. Itself unmarked by caste-based injunctions, the English language brings with it the promise of transgressing caste-based rules of decorum and forging transnational solidaristic alliances of resistance.

Shepherd was born into a *shudra* family in the southern state of Telangana. Growing up, he found that his alienation from Telugu textbooks "was more or less the same as it was from the English textbook in terms of language and content."[28] He felt he had been sitting in "hostile anglicized and brahminical [*sic*] classrooms that had been built only by extracting the surplus generated by our own parents."[29] Shepherd and his brother were the first in the family to gain literacy and a formal education, and to move away from their traditional occupation of shepherding. Belonging to the Dalit community, the family was very skeptical of the *savarna* educational institutions. As evidenced in this statement made by Shepherd's aunt, which Shepherd quotes in his memoir, *From a Shepherd Boy to an Intellectual—My Memoirs* (2019): "Saraswati teaches the children of Bapanollu (Brahmins) and Komatollu (trader caste), but she becomes a devil when it comes to our children. She will not allow our children to read and write. She will kill them. That is how my elder son died."[30] Despite the similarity of hostile exploitation between Telugu and English, he chose to write in English because doing so distanced him from the caste violence baked into Telugu history and culture. Over his public career, Shepherd has changed his name and added the English word "Shepherd" because he belonged to the caste of shepherds and felt that the English word brought welcome respect and distance from the caste system that forced their family into this occupational role.[31] His decisions to add to his name or write in English highlight the relational ways in which English gains meaning as a relatively less oppressive language.

Shepherd's essays and two English biographies situate in English the promise of equality, a literal level playing field, and less alienation. His works offer a different view of the postcolonial classroom where English is associated with educating democratic state subjects. In the space of the classroom where citizen subjects are produced, "the real fear is equality in medium of instruction, syllabus content and serious educational environment. They [those in power] are afraid that the poor will challenge the rich, the lower castes will challenge the higher castes once educational equality is established."[32] Shepherd finds the greatest potential of English to be the reckoning of Dalits' economic and political rights. Access to English can mobilize a struggle for equality that could not be achieved in the peasant struggles rooted in land—"from Telangana Armed Struggle to Naxalbari to Srikakulam."[33] According to Shepherd, English can bring about a bloodless revolution that neither the communists nor the liberal thinkers of India can imagine. English can provide access to infrastructure through education, technology, and the Internet. It is itself the infrastructure of such a revolution. Shepherd writes, "The communists... believe in the principle of 'the workers of the world unite.' How do they unite without having a common global language as an instrument of communication among the workers?" A shared language unmarked by caste is not in lieu of a class revolution but is the very condition of its possibility, according to Shepherd. Once again, Shepherd is drawing on English as the language of universal communicability and imagining English as a tool, as a means to an end. In his essay, "Dalit and English," published in the 2020 *Anveshi Broadsheet*, Shepherd echoes Neerav Patel and writes that the "upper castes have handled the contradiction between English and their native culture quite carefully. But when it comes to teaching English to the lower castes they have been proposing a theory that English will destroy the 'culture of the soil.'"[34] He argues for the state to take responsibility for teaching English in schools so that even the poor people, often those belonging to low castes, can learn the language and not simply those who can afford private schools.

Chandrabhan Prasad is another important—indeed the most provocative—advocate of English for Dalits in India today and has called the language a goddess. "If your child learns English it is as if he or she has inherited a hundred acres of land"[35] is one such glorious claim Prasad has made on behalf of English by linking the acquisition of language to the acquisition of land. He is now an affiliated scholar with the libertarian and free-market-oriented think tank, Mercatus Institute, at George Mason University. He is also the cofounder of Dalit Capitalism, a venture capital fund that supports Dalit entrepreneurs.[36] In his journalistic writings he argues that learning the English language wedges small but structural possibilities in the lives of the Dalits. Indeed, learning English is like inheriting a hundred acres of land, with the attendant privileges of wealth, mobility, and dignity.

To drive home his point, in 2010 Prasad even built a temple for the Dalit Goddess of English. The idol of this deity, which stands in the Lakhimpur-Kheri village of the Hindi-speaking state of Uttar Pradesh, is modeled after the Statue of Liberty. Mounted on a computer-shaped pedestal, the idol holds the Indian Constitution in one hand and a pen in the other. Its iconography aligns the English language with a promise of literacy and technology, and it symbolizes freedom and democratic inclusion in much the way the Statue of Liberty is supposed to. The Statue of Liberty, which invokes the United States as an attractive ally in Dalit capitalist endeavors, is also located mischievously in London and the British colonial legacy that topos invokes. In its goddess avatar, English is celebrated as deliverance for those marginalized by centuries of caste oppression. Ironically, the language of British imperialism is invoked to challenge Sanskritized Hindi, one of India's official languages favored by Hindu nationalists to shore up upper-caste Hindu dominance. With a distinct antinostalgic stance, the Goddess English points Dalits in India onwards and outwards.

The idol of Goddess English was unveiled on Thomas Babington Macaulay's birthday, which Prasad also regularly celebrates as "English Day." Macaulay was a British politician, who, in 1835, successfully convinced the British Parliament to spend money on public education in

FIGURE 3. A woman praying to the statue of the Dalit Goddess English in Lakhimpur-Kheri Village, Uttar Pradesh. (Courtesy of Chandrabhan Prasad.)

English in colonial India. Prasad sees Macaulay's primary objective to have not been to enslave Indians with English education but to create a system by which the English-educated Indians could further educate those below them. The full quotation that Prasad refers to from Macaulay's "Minute on Education" is as follows: "*I feel with [Orientalists] that it is impossible for us, with our limited means, to attempt to educate the body of the people.* We must at present do our best to form a class who may be interpreters between us and the millions whom we govern,—a class of persons Indian in blood and colour, but English in tastes, in opinions, in morals and in intellect. *To that class we may leave it to refine the vernacular dialects of the country, to enrich those dialects with terms of science borrowed from the Western nomenclature, and to render them by degrees fit vehicles for conveying knowledge to the great mass of the population.*"[37] Macaulay is a positive figure for Prasad because he exposed the backwardness of casteist indigenous knowledge systems, for which the upper-caste intellectuals disavowed their responsibility. According to Prasad, the scientific rationality of English education makes it impossible to discriminate on the basis

FIGURE 4. Statue of the Dalit Goddess English. (Courtesy of Chandrabhan Prasad.)

of caste. Thus, English education is the only means to right the wrongs of *savarna* history and to enter the exalted space of Western modernity. The English language is not just deified but also cast as the protective and nurturing figure of a mother, a kind of mother tongue. Worshipping this goddess, being raised in the shadow of this mother, launches the devotee and the child into circuits of global modernity, while also drawing English into the most tender sphere of experience.

FIGURE 5. The concept image for the Dalit Goddess English, which Prasad created along with the sculptor Shanti Swarup Baudh. (Courtesy of Chandrabhan Prasad.)

Prasad wanted the unveiling ceremony of the goddess to provide Dalits with their own Dalit Bhagvati Jagran, referring to the congregational devotional Hindu practice of staying up all night to sing prayers to a goddess. The ceremony, thus, featured a song for the Goddess English as well as a few introductory speeches—in Hindi—that emphasized the need for English among Dalits. The devotional song mimicked the convention of popular Hindu devotional songs: "She hails from London, this Mother English / She reigns over computers, she's everybody's mother" (लंदन से चल

कर आयी यह अंग्रेजी देवी मैय्या / कंप्यूटर-वाली मैय्या है अंग्रेजी देवी मैय्या / हम सबकी देवी मैय्या जन-जन की देवी मैय्या).[38] The word मैय्या (*maiyya*)—used for the Goddess English—is regularly used for Hindu goddesses as the mothers of worshippers. This religious and political event recomposes popular devotional songs for Hindu goddesses in praise of the virtues of the Dalit Goddess English. It presents English as much as a *rival* as an *alternative* to the feminine triumvirate of the Hindu goddesses of learning, prosperity, and strength, and to the feminized figure of India as the motherland. C. Rajagopalachari, a figure we encountered in the previous chapter, had also conceived of English as the gift of goddess Saraswati, who is considered the goddess of learning in the Hindu pantheon. In fashioning her so, Prasad continues the caste-based struggle, as identified by Sumathi Ramaswamy, on "an essentially feminized terrain around contending female bodies" and contributes to the "taming" of the goddess.[39] Dialect Hindi and religious rituals translate the deity of English into the quotidian realm of its devotees.

The effectiveness of the Goddess English lies in its potential to enter into the most banal and the most personal experiences. As the goddess-mother, English is located squarely in the everyday smaller moments, where it promises to usher change. Its effectiveness does not come from it magically bestowing the knowledge of English on its worshippers. (It does not, of course!) Its affective power draws from its place in religious and ritualistic practice where it convinces people (mostly women as mothers, according to Prasad) that English will empower them through their children.[40] Prasad's Goddess English, a feminized figure, is expressly an "affect-inflected" appeal to Dalit women as mothers to teach their children the English language. Prasad dreams of the goddess as *maiyya* that will "animate" and "inspire" Dalits to learn English.[41] Indeed, elsewhere in his writing, Prasad has urged Dalit mothers to make sure that the first sounds a Dalit baby hears are those of the English alphabet. English is a mothering tongue. It functions, protects, and nourishes like a mother even if it does not ostensibly activate the "naturalness" of a maternal relationship. The figuration of English as a mother authorizes and legitimizes the claim of the Dalit devotee to the English language.

The Goddess English is not an Indian woman like Mother India, nor is she making a nativist claim to indigeneity like the Hindi lobbyists who present Hindi itself as a mother of Hindustani. Instead, it promises to create a new community and new allies in the aspirational encounter of Dalits with forces of global capital, or what Prasad has called "Dalit capitalism." With a desire to narrativize a life unmarked by caste, the Dalit capitalists imagine power as unlinked from caste. In the concept image created by Shanti Swarup Baudh in concert with Prasad, which was the basis for the statue, the Dalit Goddess stands against a map of India which opens onto the world at large without clear borders. Besides the pith helmet of the British and the global power of the United States, the idol also has several "tropical entanglements" by referring to Frédéric-Auguste Bartholdi's sculpture *Liberty Enlightening the World*, as well as the female peasant woman Bartholdi likely witnessed in Egypt, and her appearance in Cuba, Vietnam, and China.[42] As such, Goddess English not only looks to (neo)imperial powers of England and the United States, but also seeks allies in the working class of the global south.

Prasad's gesture can seem theatrical, misleading, and dangerous for its ready embrace of global capitalism and its language. In my personal communication with him, Prasad has often signed his texts or emails "with the blessings of the Dalit Goddess English," a gesture that seemed playful and self-ironizing. While there are aspects of his political stance that give one pause, he is certainly not the only one to put his faith in English. Prasad points out that caste is maintained by compulsory occupation. English permits mobility by opening new job opportunities for people and making it easier to leave caste-based occupations. He asks, "Will English-speaking Dalits, for instance, be asked to skin dead cows? Will English-speaking Dalits be expected to clean gutters and roads? Will English-speaking Dalits be content to work as menials at landlords' farms? The Goddess English can empower Dalits, giving them a chance to break free from centuries of oppression."[43] Like the writers of *India Demands English*, Prasad imagines that the use of English can effect material transformations. But the answer is not as straightforward as Prasad would like us to think. There are several accounts in literature and film and indeed real life where the promise of English is neither fulfilled nor really fulfillable without structural change. The arguments of activists like Prasad and Shepherd can risk being read as respectability politics, but they are subversive. These writers and activists are aware of the caste bias at the crux of English in India. They know only too well how English greases caste and class stratifications. But they want to adopt English performatively to challenge the inequalities baked into English. The knowledge of English enables mobility that undoes injunctions against touch.

Dalit Anglophone Poets

At the risk of channeling that member of the audience who grills English writers from India about their choice of linguistic medium, I often asked the Sahitya Akademi poets about their stance on the English language. It was possibly the first question I had asked them and it is one that I still bring up. They were not the first Dalits to write in English, I was often told. Many Dalits knew the English language, Jotiba Phule and Ambedkar wrote in English, Kancha Ilaiah Shepherd and Chandrabhan Prasad were advocating for English for Dalits even as we spoke. Sometimes the answers were meaningfully matter-of-fact: because they can, because why not, because why should only *savarna* or caste Hindu writers write in English? This insistence on English as a part of one's tradition led to more pointed reflections on writing in it in their poems.

For instance, Chandramohan Sathyanathan seizes English as a shared linguistic space where his shadow can defile notions of caste purity that mark the postcolonial state. In the poem "On the Need of Common Language" (2019), the poet compares the need to share a language to the need to inhabit the same time for "our shadows to intersect on public roads."[44] The caste system is based on injunctions against touch. For a practising *savarna* Hindu, even overlapping shadows with a Dalit was enough to pollute him. In this context, the poet imagines that this haptic transgression will take place on a "public road"—the infrastructure of modern India much like the English language. In this landscape of total regulation and violence, writing in English becomes an act of self-defense: "Why do you write poetry? / I write poetry—people have the right to bear arms."[45] The syntax of Sathyanathan's sentence—with an em dash instead of a conjunction—renders dubious the fact that the poet's act of writing is *enabled* by the constitutional provisions. The lyric address of the poem overturns the democratic address, and reclaims the act of Dalit writing as independent of any state intervention to authorize it.

The idea of writing as self-defense also appears in the poetry of Yogesh Maitreya, one of the other poets at the Sahitya Akademi symposium. Many of Maitreya's poems establish an imperative to write in English. As a language that the poet shares with *savarna* Hindus, English has the potential of a deeper affront to that audience. Maitreya's poem "Learning to Speak in English" (2017) elaborates on the draw of English. The title turns our attention to a learning situation different from Kancha Ilaiah's hostile classroom. In Maitreya's poem, the act of learning is a reference to the moment of unknowing and wanting prior to writing in English. Learning English in India is learning an affective habitus of shame and hope. The poem itself is five terse lines that neither name the English language nor give us a brass-tacks description of what it was like to learn it. What we get, instead, is a proclamation of rights: "Everybody has the right / To defend himself / And if necessary, attack. / Hence, I write / But not in my mother tongue."[46] The rights-based discourse insists on one's right to English, the *write* to English, against the systemic denials of the English language. This very legal approach also brings to mind the constitutional provision of English, where it guarantees linguistic and political representation to those marginalized by and in modern standard vernaculars. Maitreya considers Varhadi, a dialect of Marathi spoken in the Vidarbha region of Maharashtra, his mother tongue. Eschewing it, his decision to write in English is an act of self-defense, the importance of which is heightened by the following line break. Varhadi, of course, does not have the reach or visibility of English. Writing in English can bring a wider audience and register an unmistakable transgression and scandal. The poem utilizes a common trope of resistance literature—the weaponization of language, though, in this case, it is not so much to attack ("if necessary") but in self-defense.

Yet, the experience of English is embedded deep within a web of shame, risk, greed, and desire. The poem "Dilemma" (2017) specifically names the poet's interest in writing in English as greed: "I grew up much greedy / I wrote in English and kept on writing."[47] Usually, a discussion of greed launches a moral parable. However, here the poet's self-identification as greedy is poignant, conveying an underlying sense of self-reproach, shame, and conflict. The poet imagines himself greedy because the English he pursues threatens his connection with a world without English. Poet Neerav Patel in his essay also feels wistful abdicating his mother tongue of Gujarati but reasons that he needs to do so to resist the hold of caste on his life. Patel writes, "Living as it does in the shadow of oppressors, how would that mother-tongue of mine know that they had cast a web of oppression and hidden it deftly in their language?"[48] For both Patel and Maitreya, to write in English occasionally is a political act but to keep writing in it forges a more intimate, if not all positive, relation with the language. By turning to English, the poet risks being distanced from those before and around him. As the poet later reveals, his covetousness and persistence distance him from the childhood world where his father sang with rage and love, and leave him wondering about the language in which he would sing to his future children. This personal risk is compounded with the economic risks of pursuing an unremunerative life of letters as a first-generation college student. The sense of greed that the poet anticipates, at once critiques linguistic opportunism while also pointing to the reckless experience of an exclusive and exclusionary language in a casteist society.

How does the English language—a bastion of caste, class, and colonial supremacy—come to the defense of the Dalit subject? The language itself does not come to one's defense. It is the physically, and so affectively and politically, charged act of writing in it that arms one. For instance, in writing in English, Maitreya not only takes ownership of a language but also enters a hegemonic discourse that has excluded him. The pages of history have no mention of people like the poet. In his poem "Recollecting an Old Self" (2017), Maitreya writes that the only time someone spoke his grandfather's name was when the man died. "When my grandfather died / People said "Gariba Mahar is dead now." / That was the only time / His name was uttered by their tongues."[49] His poetry is an act of retrieving "history from the rubble" of his grandfather's pyre. His words are gathered so that the poem can literally "give body" to the memory of his grandfather. Many of Maitreya's poems center figures from the Dalit struggle in the state of Maharashtra. In other poems, he stages familial and interpersonal experiences that highlight the way caste contains all life. His poems are shot through with images of the material artifacts of caste discrimination like the Brahmin's sacred white thread, memories of a woman being soaped and washed before being raped, Dalit activists like Pochiram Kamble who died fighting Brahminical hegemony, as well as stories of farmer suicides due to crushing debt and lack of governmental support. At the same time, the gender politics of these poems also demands attention, as it features images of sexual domination over the caste Hindu woman. The hyperlocality and immediacy of Maitreya's poems places them in the tradition of much of Dalit writing that has borne witness to caste injustice through personal testimony. Writing in English gives body to the English language by appropriating it to tell a different history, to name a different people, and to create different traditions of solidarity. In their poetry, both Maitreya and Sathyanathan authoritatively cast the shadow of marginalized Dalit figures onto the casteless modernity of English.

Sathyanathan also brings these figures in contact with oppressed people in other parts of the world. As he writes into existence a history and a present that is consistently forgotten, Sathyanathan forges a point of contact between local and global histories and experiences. To give an example, Sathyanathan's poem "Killing the Shambuka" (2016) was written in response to what he sees as the murder of Rohith Vemula. It compares the institutional murders of Dalit students in institutions of higher education in India to the lynching of African Americans in the United States. The poem is short: "Jim Crow segregated hostel rooms / Ceiling fans bear a strange fruit, / Blood on books and blood on papers, / A black body swinging in mute silence, / Strange fruit hanging from tridents."[50] It models itself after Abel Meeropol's "Strange Fruit" (1937) and references a

Dalit figure from Valmiki's *Ramayana*. Shambuka was a *shudra* who disturbed the order of the Hindu caste system by practicing the presumably pious act of meditation. According to the scriptural accounts, since Shambuka transgressed the caste-based division of labor, the Hindu god Ram was compelled to kill him. By drawing a link with Jim Crow, the poem makes clear that Ram's action was far from inevitable. In fact, it both resulted from and sanctioned the caste-based discrimination (invoked in the Hindu symbol of the trident) that led to Vemula's death. The act of reading and writing in India is a daily confrontation with such bloodstained pages.

Sathyanathan draws upon the African American tradition—a distinctly vernacular literature—to vernacularize and make common the casteist experience of the English language in India. English becomes the grounds for solidarity and a coalitional politics. The African American literary tradition is based in the necessity of having to forge a language within a dominant language. In his study of the relation between Black vernacular tradition and African American literary tradition in *The Signifying Monkey* (1988), Henry Louis Gates Jr. writes that the Black vernacular assumes the corporeality of a Black body and it originates in the orality of the tongue.[51] There is a comparable way in which the turn to English is forged in necessity and bears the corporeal experience of caste. It is by routing his poem through the African American tradition that Sathyanathan is able to touch figures like Rohith Vemula and the Black bodies being lynched. The English literature that writers and activists are engaging with here, as in Phule, is very different from the British canon.

As the inevitable consequence of centuries of oppression, the same English that is the poet's right also assumes criminal transgressive tones. The following lines lend a different hue to Moin Khan's sense of criminality when sitting in an English classroom for the first time. "When hunger / becomes unbearable / one commits crime. / When torture / becomes unbearable / one writes poems / I have / committed crime / to write these poems."[52] Maitreya's poems are criminal in a world riven with casteist injunctions about education and literature. His writing does not just illuminate a "narrative of suffering" but also testifies to the human spirit that strives to witness and to endure. A lot of Maitreya's poems are pithy and direct. Devoid of artifice, they challenge a commonplace sense of the poetic with their desire to bear witness, provoke, outrage, and make sense. The language of the poems has a distrusting rhetoric because it has been appropriated by the *savarna* Hindus to bolster their supremacy: "They talk in smooth language / We don't feel hated."[53] In fact, the rhetoric of the poems is in a sharp contrast to this smoothness. The political force of Maitreya's poems draws from its specifically aesthetic potential, as he writes in a different poem, "The hands confined to pull dead carcasses started to write, and they wrote poems, beautiful stories of our lives."[54] The lyric poems stage feelings that emerge from and address an experience of social injustice. With their unmistakable beauty, they dignify the Dalit experience.

The potential of the poems to aestheticize that which caste dictates should not be so maneuvers the smooth hypocrisy of the English language. On two occasions, Maitreya has published in online magazines personal essays that detail his relation to and experience of the English language. In an essay titled "My English Isn't Broken; Your English is Brahmin," Maitreya names English as not an instrument of British but of Brahminical hegemony. Maitreya describes the event that set him on the path of writing. Maitreya recalls that he read his first English novel in 2010—Charles Dickens's *Great Expectations*. "I read it thrice, back-to-back, for the simple reason that I didn't understand a bit of it in my first reading," he writes.[55] When he shared this experience of reading and *not reading* literature with his English professor, she merely corrected his grammar. "I felt belittled. My understanding had been reduced to errors in grammar. After this incident, I read more and more, voraciously, and I would read anything and everything that was available to me in English. This was also the time when I started to write poems in English."[56] Reading English in the Anglophone world is far from a straightforward process. The meaning of the English novel *Great Expectations* arguably has little to do with its place in the British canon or Dickens's place in Victorian scholarship but more to do with the realities of caste that transform reading into an experience that remakes the body of the novel with the caste-marked body of the reader. Aspects like grammar, enunciation, and accent reproduce the hierarchies of caste in the English language. It is in *writing* in English that Maitreya transforms the experience of shame in speaking English incorrectly. The vernacular is traditionally considered to be oral. Ironically, Maitreya harnesses the resistant potential of the vernacular in writing in English about his shame around reading English literature.

Whether writing in English can ever have the same kind of political radicalism as writing in a lesser-known language, I would leave you to judge. But in this moment, it is so affectively and politically charged that it is hard to miss it. Perhaps, in response to this linguistic policing, Maitreya's poems regularly break down rules in language. For instance, the poem "From Mumbai" articulates a piercing realization that poetry "neither brings money / nor full fills our necessities" but the poet keeps writing. The use of "full fills" instead of "fulfills" strikes at the heart of the idea of fulfilment, even as it creates a sense of plenitude. The splitting of the word into a noun and a verb highlights the insufficiency of the aesthetic potential of poetry. In another poem, "Witnessing," the poet writes, "yet she was the only one who could understood [sic] his desire."[57] These intentional or inadvertent typographical errors result in a material transformation of the English language. In the leveler of the word processor and auto-correct, this syntax is not a "mistake" as much as an indifference to grammatical norms that demands recognition. Instead, rather like transgressing the rules of caste-based decorum, it challenges the performance of purity.

Sathyanathan and Maitreya do not really cite Indian English poets as their influences or interlocutors, but turn to Dalit oral culture in other Indian languages. There have been Indian English poets from different marginal positions—Dom Moraes, Nissim Ezekiel, Eunice De Souza. But Sathyanathan and Maitreya are more identifiably a part of the Dalit poetry tradition than Indian English poetry. With the exception of Arun Kolatkar's bilingual work that figures in one of Sathyanathan's poems, both these poets place themselves in the tradition of Dalit writing by figures such as Tukaram, Savitribai Phule, Namdeo Dhasal, and other Dalit Panther writers. Like other poets, Sathyanathan started writing poetry after the death of Rohit Vemula in the process of creating protest signs.[58] The migration of the word from the streets and the Internet onto the page energizes it as part of an oral protest culture. Maitreya's poetic style draws from Dhasal and the Dalit *shahirs*—actors/singers who use musical performance as a form of caste critique. *Shahiri* is a centuries-old oral tradition that has recently been reimagined to popularize Ambedkar's teachings and philosophy. Both Maitreya and Sathyanathan have a spoken quality to them and part of other modes of resistance heard in the country (chapter 4) and globally.

Dhasal, one of the founders of the Dalit Panther Movement, called himself "a venereal sore in the private part of language."[59] Through his writing, Dhasal created a Dalit idiom in the Brahminical register of the Marathi language.[60] He argued that Dalit literature could only be produced in conditions of radical freedom from caste. Thus, as a body of work, the rise of Dalit literature coincides with increased renunciation of Hinduism and conversion to Buddhism.[61] If Dalit literature can only be an act of an imagination freed from caste, how does a Dalit subject come to be figured as a specifically literary—in this case, lyric and aesthetic—subject? As a political figure, the Dalit subject is defined by caste experience. The agential potential of Dalit writing—what it does—is always understood in political terms. It is understood to perform the work of witnessing. But its aesthetic potential lies in claiming the promise of equality at the heart of postcolonial democracy. Despite their disenchantment with state-based provisions, both poets evince an attachment to the idea of democracy, of a shared space, of the English language full with promise.

It is in writing in English, in centering Dalit figures—themselves and others—that the poets are able to claim equality and be taken seriously as aesthetic subjects. Writing in English enables the possibility of touching the figure of the Dalit anew as well as an act of touching in literature. The lyric address of these poems, often addressing a *savarna* readership—accessible in English—is a response to the democratic address that promises but thwarts equal citizenship. It maps the distance between an Indian English poet and a Dalit Anglophone poet.

Hindi Dalit Writing and the Sensation of Touch

With a majority of Dalit writing in languages besides English, scholars have called for more scholarship in what they call "vernacular" languages to excavate a textured experience of caste. However, given the centrality of English to these stories, we need to complement this work with a more, not less, Anglocentric approach. In their special issue of *Words without Borders* focusing on Hindi Dalit writing, Merrill and Brueck have especially noted Dalit writers' ironic stance toward English that indexes their complicated—at once desirable and conflicted—relationship to modernization. English is at once a language that beguiles and rebuffs. This section turns to the effect of these English words. Specifically, I examine the use of English words in Hindi Dalit literature, with an eye to exploring the interplay of Hindi and English in the stories. While it is not the subject of this chapter, English also forges a relation to this literary Hindi in English-Hindi translations.

If English is the language of touch, how does it inflect the Hindi language narrative? My reading strategy is part of flipping the gaze and the audit, and examining English before it becomes a metaphor. I examine two short stories by Hindi writer Ajay Navaria. Several other Hindi writers used English words, going back to Premchand, for instance, in *Sevasadan* (1919). Brueck and Mitchell, in their introduction to Hindi Dalit writing in *Words without Borders*, show that there are a few Dalit writers who do so as well: Anita Bharti, Kausalya Baisantry, and Mohan Das Namishray. The use of the two languages is also a means of responding to two different readerships—both within and outside the Dalit community. In turn, translators have marked these words as English and often italicized them.

But I am curious about the life of these words before they become English, when they are still a part of the Hindi language as dialogue, in a different linguistic and literary environment.

Navaria's fiction dramatizes the converging banality of caste and English as explored by the Sahitya Akademi poets. Several of his stories show the promise of English to bridge the representational gap in everyday lived experience as well as its failure to do so. By turning to these next, we not only get another look at the way English—as the language of casteless modernity—remains caste marked, we also access the relationship between English and caste via the politics of Hindi. Navaria's stories give us a sensory hold on an English that touches and that permits touch.

In each story, the lower-caste character's use of English has a diminutive effect on the upper-caste figure. Like the works of Maitreya and Sathyanathan, Navaria's characters are a part of a post-Mandal India. Navaria writes about the urban middle-class Dalit male who is educated and politicized, comfortable speaking in English, and enjoys a degree of social mobility. Transgression is an important trope in Dalit narratives, and the unrestricted mobility of Navaria's characters exemplifies a degree of freedom from, and thus an opportunity to transgress, caste-based limitations. English draws its force from its externality—its presumed distance from and neutrality to the experience of caste. The small changes and big reversals that it enables stand out because they would not be possible anywhere else outside the state machinery engineered in English. English, in Navaria's stories, "indicates *both* a heightened political consciousness, Dalit *chetna*, and a deeper alienation from and frustration with a modernity that is marked by native caste politics."[62] English is experienced as a technology, it is active and agential. What makes English manipulable in the hands of Nehru does so also for others. Two stories, "Yes, Sir" and "Cheers," interrogate the limits of such a technologization of English through linguistic and caste transgression.

"Yes, Sir" is told from the perspective of Tiwari, a Brahmin subordinate. It cedes Hindi as a linguistic space but punctuates and punctures it with a few English-language words. The most important of these is the title itself. "Yes, Sir" indicates an attitude of serving and assisting—sincere, submissive, formal, and bureaucratic, all at once. The two words, "yes" and "sir," are easily translatable into Hindi but they are not translated into Hindi in the text. In the kind of caste-neutral relationship they posit between Tiwari and Narottam, his Dalit government officer, they remain untranslatable. The English language, in its bureaucratic use, allows a role reversal which would be impossible in Hindi outside this work arrangement.

Tiwari's tongue *chafes* each time he has to say "Yes, Sir" to Narottam: "Tiwari did end up saying **yes, sir** but it is as if his tongue chafed as he did so" (यस सर कह तो गया तिवारी, पर कहते हुए उसकी जैसे जीभ छिल गयी।).[63] The experience of chafing is hardly comparable to the one Patel describes of caste etched onto one's body. But, it makes vivid the experience, from the perspective of the Brahmin narrator, of being touched in a language imagined as shared by writers like Ilaiah, Kandasamy, and Sathyanathan.

English is not only the language of the democratic state but also of the market. The story deploys a variety of registers of standardized and dialect Hindi, of full English sentences and phrases in an otherwise Hindi sentence to indicate different levels of education and urbanism. Clearly, Tiwari is very bitter at the new order ushered in by reservation, where he has to wait on a generation of uplifted Dalits who would probably be, to use his expression, "sweeping the floor somewhere, if it weren't for the **quota**" (कोटा नहीं होता तो कहीं झाड़ू लगा रहा होता।).[64] The word "quota" appears in *devanagari* script in the text of the story, and is a colloquial term for post-Mandal reservation of employment opportunities for socially and educationally "backward" members of the society. Tiwari's use of the English word draws attention to its intrusive quality—as an arguably foreign and invasive language—that has upset a traditional order that worked to his advantage. Indeed, the English word "quota" has become an easy criticism in popular discourse that delegitimizes a lower-caste candidate with the insinuation that they succeeded only because of the unfair "advantage" of the quota. This is despite the fact that there are new reports every day which show that positions reserved for marginalized castes and tribes/ethnic groups are rarely filled, and that many qualified members still find themselves unemployed due to prejudice. Yet, by virtue of precisely its foreign quality, the word "quota" also stands for a modicum of legal enfranchisement and promise of social mobility. It confirms the symbolic power of English in its promise of breaking with years of upper-caste hegemony.

Besides bureaucratese, the other category of English words used in the stories is brand names. As brand names English words and phrases used by different characters announce increased participation in global markets for the Dalits. One conversation between Tiwari and Narottam dramatizes very clearly the reversal in roles brought about by the Mandal Commission Report. Narottam is very proud of his accomplishments and remains unfazed by the gossip that he rose in ranks only because of employment reservation. He can also be slightly patronizing—especially in an instance where he is discussing hygiene and water purification with Tiwari. As Tiwari pours Narottam water from the latter's water bottle,

Narottam tells Tiwari that he has owned an R. O. System at his house for a long time. He then asks Tiwari if he even knows what an R. O. System is. R. O. System here refers not only to the reverse osmosis system of purifying water but also to a brand of water filters in India, which advertises it as its patented technology. Tiwari feels humiliated by Narottam's tone and snaps back with the word "Aquaguard." This is a brand name for another kind of water purifier in India. Narottam is exasperated with Tiwari's ignorance and responds with a lesson in language, science, and consumerism:

> This is the one problem with you folk, you don't know the difference between horses and donkeys. If you go to buy **toothpaste**, you will just ask for **"Colgate"** and if you are buying **detergent**, you will say you are buying **"Surf."** Idiot! **Aquaguard** is the name of the **company**. This is called a **water purifier**. A **machine** that filters water and an **R. O. System** are two different things.[65]

> बस तुम लोगों में यही कमी है, गधे घोड़े सब बराबर। टूथपेस्ट खरीदने जाओगे तो कहोगे कोलगेट खरीदने जा रहा हूँ और डिटरजेंट ख़रीदो तो कहोगे सर्फ़ खरीद रहा हूँ। अरे बेवक़ूफ़ एक़ागार्ड तो कंपनी का नाम है। इसे वॉटर प्यूरिफाइयर कहते हैं, पानी साफ़ करने वाली मशीन और र.ओ. सिस्टम दो अलग चीज़ें हैं।

Narottam's response shows the reversal of social and political roles between the Brahmin and the Dalit. These altered roles are further secured by the vocabulary of an informed consumer that overhauls what counts as knowledge. After all, the knowledge of brand names in English and consumer goods is very different from the literary and religious knowledge that the Brahmins have monopoly over. Historically, Brahmins have appointed themselves as the custodians of knowledge, prohibiting the Dalits from entering the temple or reading the Hindu scriptures. Narottam's reading of brands brings to mind a capitalist system where, as Chandrabhan Prasad also argues, caste injunctions can be more malleable. It also shines a light on a different way of reading the English language as he encourages Tiwari to not confuse brands. Narottam shows a canny grasp of the connotational and denotational, iconic and indexical ways in which a brand works and separates these registers of meanings of the language from its literal meaning. For many Dalit writers the subversive use of English draws precisely from distinguishing the symbolic and literal registers of the language.

The topic of water purity features in many Dalit narratives as the site of caste violence. Considered "impure" by *savarna* Hindus, Dalits continue to be prohibited from communal and high-caste sources of water and have to rely on the mercy of higher caste members for this basic right. Approached in the vocabulary of a rightfully appointed government officer, in "Yes, Sir," the subject of water purity does not stigmatize the Dalit figure but offers an opportunity to confirm his state-bestowed elevated office. The technology of the English word comes to stand for the capacity of English-language regimes—as in the new "quota" order at the government office—to upend caste hierarchy. The association of English with technology, the sociotechnical effects of the English word itself, holds the power to address and redress caste-based violence. As I showed in chapter 1, the association of English with science and technology has long been the source of its fascination and its validation—from Macaulay to Nehru to Chandrabhan Prasad. The significance of the technology of a water purifier in "Yes, Sir" is thrown further into relief by a comparison with Mulk Raj Anand's *Untouchable* (next chapter): it is the modern technology of the toilet flush that the young Dalit protagonist, Bakha, finds most alluring as it renders his caste-based profession of manual scavenging obsolete. Bakha's faith in technology seems to be manifested and justified, about seventy years later, when Narottam sitting before Tiwari takes pride in his R. O. System water purifier.

The scene at the office where Narottam explains the R. O. System to Tiwari, and the story at large, also sheds light on the government office as a space where the subordinate-who-is-now-the-officer consolidates the hegemony of the English language. Navaria's story offers an important contrast with chapter 6 of Ambedkar's English-language collection of his personal experiences of untouchability, *Waiting for a Visa*, "A Young Clerk Is Abused and Threatened until He Gives Up His Job." Ambedkar describes the experience of a young "Bhangi (Dalit) boy" who upon completing his education and passing the requisite exams, becomes a clerk in a government office in British India. The young man named Parmar Kalidas Shivdas is surprised to encounter caste-based discrimination in a government office. He finds that the caste Hindus in the office refuse to respect him or let him do any work. He is denied water, humiliated, made to sleep on the floor, and his life is even threatened, until he quits his job and returns home.[66] Narottam operates in a different kind of knowledge economy that allows him to assert his authority. The fact that Tiwari even stands there and listens to Narottam is because of the latter's higher status in the office, which has been possible because of the state's liberal dispensation to reserve a certain percentage of employment opportunities for lower castes. But, in this specific instance, the knowledge that cements

Narottam's superiority is specifically a knowledge of English, science, and consumerism.

Even when not spoken by educated and well-placed Dalit characters like Narottam, English words in the story add emphasis to statements (as in Tiwari's about "quota" earlier). For instance, one of the lower caste characters who is also a peon in the office says the following, "Brahmins have a **disease** that makes them want to **show** their **caste**" (बामनों को कास्ट शो करने का डिसीज़ होता है।).[67] This is a reference to the fact that many members of lower castes choose not to use their family name as it reveals their specific occupation and caste in the society, whereas members of the upper caste usually do use their family name as it makes them readily legible within a social hierarchy. In this short story, in fact, "Tiwari" is a family name and Narottam is a first name. The sentence is in dialect Hindi since the word used for Brahmins is *baaman*, and it contains three English words transliterated into *devanagari*: *caste*, *show*, and *disease*. All these words have equivalents in Hindi, with the exception, arguably, of the word "caste" itself.

The untranslatability of the English word "caste" into Hindi marks it as an extraneous practice and thus disenfranchises the concept. In *Castes of Mind: Colonialism and the Making of Modern India* (2001), Nicholas Dirks has shown that the caste system was, to a large extent, shaped by British colonial practices. It was the Portuguese who first suggested caste identities. The British expanded on that idea to create administrative order in Indian society, and the discipline required for census surveys helped establish a clear hierarchy of caste categories. This is not to say that caste practices and discrimination did not exist in India. Shankar in *Flesh and Fish Blood* also uses the phrase "*varna-jati* complex" instead of the word "caste" to denote social and occupational stratifications in India, as he finds "caste" to be an inaccurate and imperfect translation. Thus, the foreignness of English that attaches to "caste" discredits—as a relic of the colonial order—the very system that subordinates Dalits. "Show" and "disease," however, evoke the objective and scientific valences of English, respectively. These words variously summon the foreignness of English to highlight the inadequacy of the language to native categories and its prestige value to bolster the speaker's empirical critique of caste. The use of these words in an otherwise dialect Hindi marshals the "foreign" language within a familiar idiom to critique Brahmin supremacy. The simultaneous untranslatability and translatability of English, its foreignness and objectivity, further buttress this critique. If English were to be entirely absorbed into Hindi by a complete translation, if it were rendered *translatable*, it would lose its power to validate, modernize, and democratize: power on which not only this speaker relies, but also the Indian state at large. The selective use of English in such experiences reveals a relationship with the question of caste in which English makes possible a willful elision and anonymity. To access these, we do not need a less Anglocentric approach to literary studies, but rather an approach that is attuned to these vernacular experiences.

The story "Cheers" also elaborates on the effects of caste-marked writing in English. It uses English words as bureaucratese and advertising, and presents English as a language of change, a language with which to critique caste emphatically. For instance, the English language word and colonial relic of "scheduled caste" makes it possible for the young narrator of this story not to reveal his specific caste to his co-workers who also belong to low castes. He only identifies as the state subject as Scheduled Caste (referring to the list of low-caste groups officially recognized by the Indian state). Having found a temporary refuge in the ambiguity of the English language, the narrator wonders if the Hindi language is so humiliating because it is intimate, "Was this language so humiliating because it was familiar?" (क्या यह भाषा अपनेपन के कारण इतनी अपमानजनक है?).[68] Across Dalit Anglophone writing, the intimate humiliation of Hindi is often contrasted with the amnesia of English, such that it carries no memory of familial and ancestral humiliation. Rita Kothari writes that Neerav Patel's essay "Gujarati *Maari Matrubhasha*, English *Maari* Foster Mother" calls English his foster mother precisely because it does not have the social and cultural memory of caste. Patel writes, "I am grateful to the other tongue which became my foster language; it is this English that provided scientific thought and showed a way out of oppression and torture."[69] English emerges as the site where authority and dignity are reclaimed for and by the Dalit.

Only one of the characters in "Cheers" can speak English fluently. C. Lal is a low-caste man who has shortened his name from "Chunni Lal" to "C. Lal" because the former iteration undermined his "dignity" by sounding too informal. The English word "dignity" appears in *devanagari* script in the story and reveals how foreign the idea of dignity is for lower castes in modern Hindi—so foreign that it has to be found and rendered in English. C. Lal's grasp of structural racism and his knowledge of English and of African American literature make him a force to reckon with at the school. Even though Chandgi Sharma, the school principal, is high caste and of a higher official rank, he does not know the English language and literature as well as Lal, and is shown to be nervous around him.

In a key scene in the story, someone graffities the principal's name plate, which is supposed to read, in the Roman script, "Chandgi Sharma."

However, as someone draws a line on the letter "C," it now reads as Ghandgi, a Hindustani word which means "dirt."

> There in blue letters on a white washed wall, it read "Ghandgi Sharma"... someone had drawn a line across the "C" and had turned it into a "G." Just like the tiny adjustment of the reservation, thanks to this little line, Principal Chandgi Ram Sharma turned into a heap of Ghandgi Ram Sharma.[70]

> वहाँ सामने दीवार पर, सफेद पेंट से पुती, लकड़ी की प्लेट पर, अँग्रेज़ी में, नीले अक्षरों में 'गंदगी शर्मा' लिखा था... किसी ने 'सी' के नीचे डंडा खींचकर उसे 'जी' में बदल दिया था। आरक्षण की छोटी-सी व्यवस्था की तरह, इस छोटे से डंडे की कृपा से, प्रिन्सिपल चंदगीराम शर्मा, गंदगीराम शर्मा के ढेर में बदल गये।

C. Lal goads the principal by saying that had he stuck to *devanagari* script for his name plate, this would have never happened.

> I had told you that you should have your name plate written in *devanagari*, not English. That would have saved you your reputation, met the government's stipulation, and preserved old memories as well. C. Lal purposefully emphasized *devanagari* and old memories. (53)

> मैं तो आपसे पहले ही कहता था कि अँग्रेज़ी की बजाय नेम प्लेट 'देवनागरी' में बनवाई जाए, इससे इज़्ज़त भी बचती, सरकारी नियम भी पूरा होता और 'पुरानी याद' भी बनी रहती। सी लाल ने जान-बूझकर देवनागरी और पुरानी याद पर ज़्यादा ज़ोर दिया।

The phrase "old memories" refers to an unchallenged upper-caste exclusivity in government jobs (and all arenas of social and political existence, by extension) before the induction of lower castes into the government. "Government's stipulation" is a reference to the government's encouragement to use Hindi in *devanagari* script for state administrative tasks in The Official Language Act of 1963. The act also concedes the use of English in the official work of the government. It is this use of English that C. Lal seems to have satirically warned the principal against. By writing his name in the Roman script (conflated with the English language in the story), the principal perhaps hoped to associate himself with a language of power that he does not speak very well. The principal's act mobilizes English as a symbol, as a "brand" one buys, to enhance his status and prestige at the school. Ironically, the same language provides the stage to humiliate him. Thus, the relationship between English and caste marginality, as it emerges in this scene, is not simply one of exclusion. English makes it possible to critique Brahmin supremacy in the high school, which had not been possible in the regime of the *devanagari* script, or before the modern postcolonial state outlawed untouchability and introduced caste-based reservation.

At one level, the principal's new name, "dirt," captures the long-enduring belief that even the shadow—to say nothing of the touch—of a person considered untouchable can pollute the upper-caste person. As he considers the defacement of the name plate, the principal remarks on the changing composition of the student body as well, looking back nostalgically at a time when all students were from "respectable" upper-caste families. Presuming that it was a (lower-caste) student who tampered with the name plate, it is not a surprise that Chandgi Sharma collapsed into a heap of dirt. However, as the graphic inscription defiles, it also defies the caste-based hierarchy that is reproduced at the government school.

This incident draws our attention to the symbolic value of English not only in the word "quota" but also in the legislation of English as India's associate official language, which further animates its vernacular force. English plays an important role in this surreptitious coup that parallels the imagined progressive energy of reservation of employment opportunities after the Mandal Commission. The vernacular and symbolic force of English, however, is allegedly guided and goaded by its global force. The principal suspects—though he would never dare to say as much—that C. Lal incited one of the students to tamper with the name plate. As far as C. Lal is concerned, the English language allows him to access a global lexicon of political radicalism from English and African American literature.

Nevertheless, the promise of English is limited, and by the end of the story, we see its complicity and complexities in lower-caste oppression. The story does reference the fact that access to English is not simple and while C. Lal as an autodidact is able to speak the language and familiarize himself with radical literature available in English, many of his own students are not. As it catalyzes a transitional narrative into global modernity, English also signals an alienation from the specificity of the caste experience and a critique of an abstracted modernity. The story makes it clear through two English phrases that appear in *devanagari*, "cheers for our victory" and "cheers," that respectively open and close the narrative in two scenes where the teachers are celebrating the election results with a drink. The opening "cheers" is celebratory: it announces the arrival of a new order where the various lower-caste teachers will finally have their own representative. The process of deciding who their candidate will be reveals more differences than similarities among the gamut of lower castes present in the school. It is in this process that the narrator is asked what his precise caste affiliation is. While the story begins ambivalently, the elections make clear the internal differences and hierarchies between the various low castes. As they are clinking their glasses at the end, C. Lal says that with these elections, the position of the secretary at least slipped down a little. It is Rampal—belonging to the pastoral community called the Gurjars—who wins the election. Gurjars are not Dalits. They enjoy an elite status in some states of India and are classified as "socially backward" in certain others. C. Lal's acknowledgement and affirmation of a hierarchy in the phrase "at least slipped down a little" reveals that even the English language cannot obliterate caste hierarchies.

Reading English after Touch

In a world marked by injunctions against touch, the power of a shared language can scarcely be overstated. Debates about linguistic representation in India have been marked by the desire for or dread of a language that is shared—between the state and the people as well as among the people themselves. To varying degrees, it is this desire for a shared language that motivates Mathai and the others to *demand* English, it is this desire that leads Ambedkar to *insist* on the retention of English in India, and it is the absence of such a language that throws *Raag Darbari*'s Shivpalganj into confusion. Yet, if English were meant to be the language that leveled the unevenness of the democratic address, it has never done so.

In the early 1990s, two political leaders belonging to the same cow-herding low caste and espousing similar socialist politics championed two diametrically opposite positions regarding English. While one rallied for the banishment of English in India, the other adopted a pro-English policy in his state. Both, ironically, were guided by the anti-elitist agenda of validating a shared language. But, what widened the gap between English and the masses was not a policy but the response to these proposals. The call to replace English with Hindi was a familiar one to scholars because it did not question the hegemony of English. Instead, it set up the erstwhile colonizer as the enemy with the upper castes and classes as its beneficiary. The push to make English a mandatory subject in the state school curriculum was met with "confusion."[71] A news report made sense of the low-caste politician's embrace of the English language as its *hijacking*. "Like gunboat diplomacy, in the hands of a few, English helps maintain a kind of balance that will be destroyed if the instrument passes to those who have been kept beyond its reach so far. By wanting to hand over the instrument to the backward castes or the local people, [he] has in fact committed piracy."[72]

According to the writer, this politician could only want English-language education for the lower-caste people as piracy. Carrying meanings of both rightful and glorious robbery as well as of illegal reproduction, his call for English was deemed criminal.

Why is the response to English in India always supposed to constitute a rejection or subversion of the foreign *colonizer's* language? Why do we need metaphors to understand the low-caste subject's desire for English? How do we recapture and reinterpret the *foreignness* of this English which has donned an all-too-familiar mask of the foreign? The next chapter turns to Indian Anglophone literature to make legible the low-caste and Dalit characters' relationship to English within and outside the text. Reading English as a language of touch—of aspirations of commonality, democracy, and transnational solidarity—can dissolve these metaphors.

CHAPTER 3

Text

A DESIRE CALLED ENGLISH IN INDIAN ANGLOPHONE LITERATURE

Caste and Representation in Indian Anglophone Literature

The problem of reading is always a little circular. How we read delimits what we know but how we read is itself conditioned by the surrounding institutional field, by what we already know. Repeatedly, the physical and political perimeter of the Anglophone world has been inscribed by what, where, and how Anglophone literature is read. But as the preceding chapters show, what is read under the sign of English is shaped far more by linguistic environments and mediations than by the colonial provenance or global literary formation of English. English is coercive and freeing, material and affective, a global language with vernacular ambitions of governance. The previous chapter examined the caste politics of English through the corpus of Dalit writing across two languages. As a linguistic cognate for the promise of equality and democracy, English emerged as a site for social and cultural reimagination, and the Dalit Anglophone writers claimed it as a vernacular language of caste assertion. But, while the knowledge of English may unlock many real and metaphoric doors, the path to English is itself paved with the immeasurable violence of class and caste disparities. How do we read (in the shadow of) English as a vernacular language of caste assertion? How do we meet Anglophone literature in and from vernacular worlds of caste politics?

This chapter considers these questions by redirecting attention to English as a caste-marked desire in Indian Anglophone literature. The banal convergences of caste and English in the last chapter would lead us to think that the two overlap often in Indian Anglophone literature and criticism. This is not always the case. None of the Anglophone novels are examples of Dalit literature or written by Dalit authors; thus, it is incumbent upon us to bring to bear on our readings a caste politics of English. For instance, in the vast body of scholarship on Mulk Raj Anand's 1935 novel *Untouchable*, I have thus far found relatively few discussions of the relationship of English (the novel's linguistic medium, among other things) and caste (one of its themes). A majority of these readings begin with an implicit concession that a caste-marked character is fundamentally out of place in an English novel. This gesture is inadequate, if not ironic, because *Untouchable* was published around the same year that Dalit leader B. R. Ambedkar was writing *Waiting for a Visa*, mentioned in the previous chapter. *Untouchable* is one of a small number of Indian Anglophone novels to thematize untouchability. Bakha—an untouchable, the protagonist of Anand's novel—is still one of only a few Dalit and caste-marked protagonists in all of Indian Anglophone literature.

Bakha wishes to secure respect in society and deliverance from the Hindu caste system by learning English. When he finds that no one will teach him, Bakha transposes his faith from the English language to Englishness as a material discourse of clothes, machines, and sound objects. Bakha's attachment to English and way of being in language before knowing how to read or write or speak is poignant because he is never able to learn it. This fact is especially poignant because in a 1948 pamphlet titled *The King Emperor's English*, Mulk Raj Anand enthusiastically advocated for the English language.[1] Yet, while the narrative in *Untouchable* shows the protagonist desiring the language, it also casts doubt on all means and rationales for achieving it. The novel presents Bakha with three different routes—Christianity, Gandhi, and modern Western science—with a clear argument in favor of a modern Western science organically grafted onto the native landscape. *Untouchable* stages the English language as a panacea, but also undermines its potential. If, as Anand argues in *The King Emperor's English*, "the unashamed study of literary English" is important for India to become a modern nation, then why can Bakha not be imagined as learning it?[2]

The question of who can learn and use English—who gets to have it—is not merely rhetorical but a thorny one in India. In *English Heart, Hindi Heartland*, Rashmi Sadana notes, "In India, as elsewhere in the world, the social distinction of English has alienated non-English speakers to such an extent that people speak not of "knowing" English but of "having" it."[3]

In various instances, ranging from Thomas Babington Macaulay's "Minute on Indian Education" to Isaac Mathai's *India Demands English* to pieces by Dalit writers and activists, the question of who gets to have English marks the limits of liberal imperial and national paternalism. As chapter 1 shows, English is the language upon which hangs the tale of Indian democracy. Thus, the refusal to acknowledge the allure of English is tantamount to denying what many see as a rightful and hopeful *shared* space. In writing and reading literature, giving or not giving a character English is a representational claim on behalf of the language about what it can and cannot accommodate. It should come as no surprise that the question of who can have English—who rightfully speaks it and for whom English can speak— also bears upon literary criticism. Offhand reviews and scholarly works show that reading English literature in India is often a negotiation—over the meanings the reader concedes and doesn't, the experiences they recognize and don't, the spaces they hold apart and don't, the worlds they see and don't. For instance, many popular reviews of Aravind Adiga's Man Booker Prize-winning novel, *The White Tiger* (2008) interrogate Balram's use of English and ask how a cosmopolitan, educated writer like Aravind Adiga could write about a character like Balram.[4] In the methodologically fraught space of the literary text, what is heard and seen as English?

Consider a few seemingly irrelevant English sentences in Arundhati Roy's novel *The God of Small Things* (1997). In the key scene of the Communist protest, random English letters critique the representational affordances of English. Rahel, Estha, their maternal great aunt Baby Kochamma, mother Ammu, and uncle Chacko are all stuck in their sky-blue Plymouth in the midst of a protest. Their immobilization, as members of the upper class, is the goal of the protest, but it is not enough. One of the protestors further suspends the family's privileged immunity by pulling open the car door. As the family sits exposed, the protester first mocks them in Malayalam and then in English. He addresses Baby Kochamma directly: "Hello sister. What is your name please?"[5] When the question is met with discomfited silence, another protester "irrelevantly," the author tells us, recites the first and last few letters of the alphabet: "A, B, C, D, X, Y, Z."[6] Though they sound silly and meaningless, these words—by mocking as irrelevant the English language of the elite—are not, in fact, as irrelevant as the narrator informs us. Before we know it, Baby Kochamma is handed the Marxist flag to hold and wave and asked to shout the Hindustani slogan from the Indian freedom struggle, *Inquilab zindabad* (Long live the revolution). Held hostage in her own car, she speaks and moves as directed by the protesters. The protestors roar with laughter. "'Okay then,' the man says to Baby Kochamma in English, as though they had successfully concluded a business deal. 'Bye-bye!'"⁷

I imagine this as a film scene where the subtitles indicate that dialogue in languages subsequently deemed foreign is unimportant. In an Anglophone novel, such would be the fate of Malayalam or Hindi. But here, it is the protesters' English that risks receding into gibberish if we read it only as the irrelevant language of the rich. It is tempting to hear the working-class protestor speaking English as speaking the language of the rich. But the political force of the speech comes from the fact that *he* speaks it, from *his* ownership of the language, even when that language is a literal throwaway object. While the protesters speak in English to mock and express disdain for the rich, they pose a deeper affront by wanting to be understood as speaking in English. Along with the open car door, their speech act dissolves the cocoon of privilege where English presumably belongs. The protesters' English critiques the other English, the language of the Indian democratic state and global capitalism mouthed by the family. The protesters' English expands the representational possibilities of English in both politics and literature.

The narrative logic of many Indian Anglophone novels about caste rests similarly on English as an index of economic and social disparity. Ironically, novels that render English and caste proximate are read as sites of cleavage between them. The English language spoken by caste-marked characters is never their own but that of the author. The characters' use of English either feels like ventriloquism or highlights the distance between the characters and the medium in which they find themselves. Either way, English remains palpable as an absence. It is a negative force that illuminates the inadequacy of the characters' literary and political representation.

Low-caste or Dalit characters have met with a peculiar fate in Indian Anglophone literature. In the roughly three hundred years of Indian writing in English, there have been only a few novels that feature caste-marked characters. Some of these characters, like Bakha in *Untouchable* or Velutha in *The God of Small Things*, are validated as morally exceptional. Their personal attributes neutralize the caste hierarchies. More often, however, low-caste and Dalit characters are not so distinguished. Low-caste characters are usually secondary characters, like Kalo in Bhabhani Bhattacharya's *He Who Rides the Tiger* (1954), the pariahs and the Dalit women in Raja Rao's *Kanthapura* (1963), Chandri in U. R. Ananthamurthy's *Samskara* (1965), Ishvar and Om Prakash in Rohinton Mistry's *A Fine Balance* (1997), and Kalua in Amitav Ghosh's

The Ibis Trilogy (2008, 2011, 2012). Very often, the low-caste characters are shown to be dissemblers. The moral critique intrinsic to such a characterization weakens the characters' credibility and explains their presence in the Anglophonic literary world of the novel, where they are not supposed to belong. That these characters can speak English means they are lying. Several of the low-caste characters have either been con artists or have been accused of being so. These characters include Balram Halwai in Aravind Adiga's *The White Tiger* (2008) and Ayyan Mani in Manu Joseph's *Serious Men* (2011). In each case, the moral critique inherent to this portrayal is tied to the characters' desire for or access to English. The punctum of the stories is the characters' transgression, the conceit that they have or want to have something not rightfully their own.

On the caste question, Anand's *Untouchable* and Adiga's *The White Tiger* exemplify the two types of caste-marked characters in the existing corpus of Indian Anglophone literature. While *Untouchable* is located in the tension between colonial modernity, Gandhian nationalism, and anticaste radicalism, *The White Tiger* commands attention from within the neoliberal Indian state and its newfound economic prowess.[8] In each case, the caste-marked character desires English for its colonial and global affiliation, in order to contest national imaginations. There are two distinct kinds of English in each text. The first kind is English used as the medium of the novel. Here, English is the class- and caste-marked language of global literary production in which Anglophone novels appear as born translated from other languages more native to the specific geopolitical context. The second kind of English is the language that is attributed to the low-caste or Dalit character. Here, English appears as itself—a language to be read, seen, spoken, and heard—standing for the character's subjective visceral and psychic experience. As the characters claim English to imagine an identity beyond caste, its legibility as a caste-marked desire presses against narrative coherence. English becomes its own other. It turns from the language of political and literary representation to an idiom of their critique.

Following the caste-marked desire in these two well-known novels leads us to the repressed polyphony of the Indian Anglophone novel. The narrative logic of novels from the English-speaking world has often presumed the caste-marked character's inability to speak in English. This phonic lack makes for compelling tales of meteoric success and sensational fraud. However, it also directs English through different sensorial, political, and material mediations. Paying attention to the wide range of linguistic experiences in these two novels can voice the character and illuminate the Anglophonic habitus. This chapter stages the proximity and banality of worlds considered global with those considered vernacular, and urges a reassessment of the relationship of English with experiences of subalternity.

How Does a Dalit Character Sound?
Reading Anand's Untouchable

Priyamvada Gopal writes that *Untouchable* was inspired by "Gandhi's character sketch of the unknown sweeper, Uka, in the pages of *Young India*" and was written at Gandhi's ashram in Sabarmati, Gujarat.[9] When *Untouchable* was still in draft form, Gandhi noted that Bakha sounded like a Bloomsbury intellectual and warned Anand against characterizing him as such. Gandhi claimed that *Harijans* (God's people, Gandhi's name for "untouchables") "[did] not use big words."[10] Anand recalls, "The next day [Gandhi] told me, 'I have looked at your novel. You seem to use big words. Harijans sigh, moan, groan! They do not use such heavy words. Write in a simpler language and transliterate what they say.'"[11] Gandhi's observation of the kinds of words that the *Harijans* used already betrays a curious understanding of language as "things." Gandhi extends the socioeconomic poverty of a *Harijan* life to a poverty of vocabulary and emotions. The revisions Gandhi suggests police the language that Bakha can speak as well as the emotions he can feel, according him a questionable economy of emotions. The act of transliteration that Gandhi recommends is aimed at preserving this presumed economy as well as at managing the potentially distortive effects of the English language. Perhaps because of Gandhi's admonition, most of the novel is recounted as an internal monologue. Bakha does not speak much, in English or out loud. At the heart of the novel simmers a tension between the absent aspirational English of the protagonist Bakha and the awkward frame of Anand's use of the language.

The imposition of linguistic austerity on Bakha's imagination and the translational and literary project advocated by Gandhi results in an impasse for Bakha. Over the course of the day that constitutes the novel, Bakha asks several characters to teach him English, but no one responds favorably to his request. Bakha wants to learn English as a means to the unmarked status (within the Hindu caste system) that the Tommies, or soldiers, in the barracks (outside of the Hindu caste system) have. Several critics have noted a disjunction between Bakha's and Anand's voice that arises from their different social positions, and that becomes evident in the kind of language either the character or the author would use in keeping with their caste and class positions.[12] The implicit suggestion in Gandhi's advice, in Anand's usage of English in the novel, and in many of the critical positions is plainly this: the elite caste-marked and colonial language of English is not the language of Dalits, and it cannot voice a character like Bakha.

However, the liberal axiom of "voice" obfuscates many other experiences of language in the novel. Language—not necessarily just English—regularly exceeds concerns of writing and voicing to manifest other possibilities, such as experiences of listening, hearing, wearing, and weaving.[13] Even though the larger political vision and the plot of the novel thwart the possibility of its actualization, Bakha "voices" his desire—betrays his inclinations—in ways that are neither vocal nor literary. The fact that scholarship has missed these moments is ironic because for critics (beginning with Gandhi) who have discussed language in terms of what Bakha can or cannot have, language does have profoundly objectified meanings. (Bakha cannot be given English, but he can be given other things that might produce similar effects.)

Overall, Bakha's experiences of language incarnate a bodily experience of caste that Toral Gajarawala rightly notices is absent from the topology of class in the Indian English novel and its readings. Gajarawala in *Untouchable Fictions: Literary Realism and the Crisis of Caste* (2012) and Tabish Khair in *Babu Fictions: Alienation in Contemporary Indian English Novels* (2001) both point out that the Indian English novel and its readings have tended to subsume the category of caste within the category of class. Gajarawala argues that a critical aspect of this slippage is the negligence of caste as a bodily experience. The conditions under which Bakha hears or speaks a language, his inability to learn and speak a classical and religious language like Sanskrit, and his desire (and inability) to learn English are all indices of his caste identity. For instance, in the novel, Bakha is often the one observing and listening from afar, a role that reinscribes his position as an outcaste and highlights language as a bodily experience. Sample these reports of narrative action: "Bakha had listened hard to the *babu*," "he heard the yokel say," "the phrase, as it had dropped from the mouth of the volunteer," "Bakha heard a schoolboy whisper," and "he had heard each syllable of the Hindu hymn."[14] Configurations of power include structures of listening as well as structures of speaking and voicing, and the ear can offer paths to making shifts in relations of power. Remember that the *shudra* is expressly prohibited from listening to the vedic scriptures.

By listening in and listening to, Bakha "participates" in conversations between *savarna* men from whom he must remain physically distanced because of his status as an outcaste. As he draws upon his sense of hearing, Bakha becomes an important archetype in the genre of Indian English novels where there have not been many first-person narratives about low-caste figures even as more autobiographies are published.

Unable to learn and speak English, Bakha turns to the next thing that promises to similarly address and redress caste-based violence: Western-style "English clothes." Clothes work almost as efficiently as the knowledge of English, because Bakha's caste position is made legible by the broom and basket that he must carry. Wearing clothes discarded by the Englishman would visibly distinguish him from others of his caste. In the framework of the novel, this distinction not only provides him with a quiet dignity that did "not belong to the ordinary scavenger" and instates him as the hero of the novel, it also challenges his caste-based disadvantage.[15] Bakha's English clothes make visible the language that he does not quite possess, effecting what Deleuze and Guattari call an "incorporeal transformation," which "changes nothing in the bodies upon which they act but everything in the social position and situation of these bodies."[16] The clothes do not actually change anything about Bakha's caste identity. However, by flouting the caste-based sartorial and social mores, the clothes do recalibrate his social positioning and make those mores momentarily inoperative.

Ben Baer has observed in Western-style clothes "a haphazard parallel with the language of the novel itself, English."[17] He describes Bakha's decision to wear Western-style clothes as "anglophile transvestism," arguing that it categorically does not offer a way out of caste oppression even as it operates as a sign of crisis in subalternity.[18] Baer's use of the word "transvestism" implies a falsity in Bakha's sartorial choices, an ineffectiveness, and a departure from a bodily truth that may be embedded in one's anatomy. It does not recognize the productive value of transvestism in *critiquing* binary thinking, as for instance of male and female. Transvestism is valuable for what it makes possible rather than for what it does not correspond to. In *Vested Interests: Cross-Dressing and Cultural Anxiety* (1991), Marjorie Garber maintains that "the compelling force of transvestism in literature and culture comes . . . from its instatement of metaphor itself, not as that for which a literal meaning must be found, but precisely as that without which there would be no such thing as meaning in the first place."[19] Bakha's "transvestism" is not simply an inadequate answer to the caste problem that dates back more than three thousand years. Instead, manifested through an "incorporeal transformation," it is also a performative interrogation of the distinctions between upper castes and the "untouchables," or even between the natives and the Englishmen.

Ironically, this performative interrogation of hierarchical distinctions is made possible by strategically harnessing the colonial power of the white man and his clothes. As the narrator informs us, Bakha "had felt that to put on their clothes made one a *sahib* too."[20] Bakha wants to *be* the *sahib*—the master—only so as to invoke the authority of that position to critique another system of oppression. Apropos, it is also worth noting that the "English" clothes desired and worn by Bakha are meaningfully reminiscent of the "English" three-piece suit worn by Ambedkar.[21] Ambedkar's suit was a sharp contrast to the asceticism and the "*swadeshi* cloth*" (Indian-made cloth) championed by Gandhi. Fully aware of the affront that a well-clad Dalit would be to the upper caste, Ambedkar, in one of his poems, "Yadi acchoot pahanta hai saaf kapdey" (If the Untouchable wears clean clothes), asks: "Why is there atrocity on an untouchable, when he puts on clothes that are clean? How is a Hindu hurt by it?."[22] For Ambedkar, wearing the suit was a means to break the humiliating mandate that the Dalit should not be fully clad, that they should not wear footwear or the color white, or that they should only use ragged, old, and dirty clothes retrieved from corpses. Donning "English" clothes for Ambedkar, as for Bakha, was a strategy of political resistance to the Brahminical system and an assertion of Dalit power.

Ordinary routines and sartorial practices provide the conditions for a mutually transformative assemblage of (in)animate bodies and language practices, an assemblage that renegotiates the relations among natives. Bakha is not the only one to participate in such an assemblage. Colonel Hutchinson is reported to have "stuffed the pockets of his jacket and overcoat with the gospel of St. Luke to thrust in the hands of any passer-by, willing or unwilling."[23] The native clothes donned by the colonel are filled with Christian literature and manifest the translational powers that Bakha expects of *his* sartorial choices. The Indian clothes are meant to convey solidarity and oneness with the locals. The literature carried in the folds of the colonel's clothing draws on that trust to convert native Indians to Christianity and, possibly, to remove them from caste-based structures.[24] Of course, like the petitioners in *India Demands English* in chapter 1, Bakha only desires the English language, not the British Empire or the religion of Christianity. He only wants to shed caste-based marginalization—not, in fact, to imbibe some "Englishness" or to embrace the logic of the British rule. This presentation of Bakha's desire for the English language seems to be a means by which Anand affirms Bakha's exceptionalism as an ideal untouchable subject in the wake of decolonization. While Bakha appears as one who does not support the British Empire and remains vaguely nationalist, his desire for English confirms that the foreignness of English is double-edged. The very quality of foreignness that makes English exclusive in the hands and mouths of the colonial elite is what makes it exclusive—that is, capable of excluding the reigning native order and its hierarchies—for the Dalit who marshals it.

Bakha rejects Colonel Hutchinson's missionary overtures, as he wants the clothes to elevate him among the Hindus but does not want to become a Christian in the process: "To him the *padres* were of interest because of their European clothes."[25] In the same episode, the colonel is described as one "who had originated the idea that the Salvation Army ought to be dressed in the costume of the natives and live among them."[26] Ironically, the fact that the colonel wears Indian clothes and mixes with the natives diminishes in Bakha's eyes some of the "glamor attaching to the superior, remote and reticent Englishman."[27] Bakha wishes to leverage the differences between the native and the colonial, but the colonel's habits muddy them. While Bakha is flattered that an Englishman would come and talk to him, he cannot help but think wistfully that all he really wanted was a "pair of cast off trousers."[28] He does not reject or contest the British rule or religion, since the transformative power of the clothes stems from them. However, as Bakha fetishizes the clothes, he consistently imagines wearing them without embracing them, without being ideologically interpellated by them.

Colonel Hutchinson also finds that he cannot just learn the native language to ingratiate himself among the natives, but that he will always have to contend with his own skin tone and role in imperial expansion. In contrast to the efficiency—the "incorporeal transformation"—attributed to material and sartorial translational strategies, literal and literary translation seems lacking. Colonel Hutchinson's intention to learn Hindustani—though a noble one—is shown to have disastrous consequences. In his conversation with Bakha, he struggles to convey the expression "Come all ye that labor and I will give you rest" and constructs an awkward sentence sans copula, "*Tum udas?*" (You sad?), to reach out to the dispirited boy.[29] *Untouchable* does not include many Hindustani words and expressions, and "*Tum udas?*" is one of a handful of Hindustani phrases spoken mostly by nondescript beggar boys.

According to Ben Baer, the awkward English language syntax is an example of the many techniques used by Anand "to make the reader painfully aware of the lack of fit between the various levels of street Hindi or Punjabi and English."³⁰ For instance, Anand translates literally the Hindustani expletive *saala* (साला) as "brother-in-law" rather than as "sister fucker" and uses "dead over her" for the Hindi/Punjabi *uss par marta tha* (उस पर मरता था) rather than the more idiomatic "be willing to give his life for her." Examples like these confirm, writes Baer, that "*Untouchable* depicts the medium of English as inadequate to the task of reaching the subaltern," making "vivid a problem of disarticulation between two languages and two spaces."³¹ The translatese certainly seems to convey a problem of disarticulation, especially as it is often used to convey the attitudes of the British—for example, in "*kaala aadmi, zameen par hagne wala*"³² (dark man who defecates on the ground).

However, if the inclusion of Hindustani transliteration is meant to indicate incommensurability and incompatibility between English and native discourses, then it is worth noting that none of Bakha's dialogues is in Hindustani or in Hindustani translatese. The absence of transliteration for Bakha's dialogues only validates his approach to English and affirms his rightful ownership of the language for which he yearns. The lack of discrepancy when Bakha talks creates an unexpected immediacy between the untouchable boy and the colonial language in which Anand is writing. Of course, this immediacy is also dissolved by the end of the novel, when the subaltern subject is categorically denied the English language in the plot. In a novel that is concerned with language as something that can be had and with the question of who can have it, the fact that the narrative "gives" Bakha English is remarkable. Such a giving and taking away of language reveal the interrelated ways in which language does not simply lead to a desired result, but is continually transformed through its relationship with other human and nonhuman actants.

The narrator of *Untouchable* suggests that Bakha and his friends are not wholly "unconscious of the falseness of their instinct" in desiring English clothes.³³ The community elders often sarcastically remark, "*Look at this gentreman!*," and the boys, recognizing the scorn in their criticism, repeat the statement to each other. The appearance of the sound *gentreman* in the novel, likely drawing from and even meaning "gentleman," can be read as criticizing Bakha's anglophilic desire. *Gentreman* is a sound object in the sense that it is a construct of what Rey Chow and James A. Steintrager call "iterative perception."³⁴ A sound becomes an object for the listener by virtue of its consistent repetition, usually made possible through technologies of sound isolation and reproduction like the phonograph. The miscomprehension and mishearing of the word that makes *gentreman* into such a sound object constitutes both aspiration and criticism. Anand's use of the phrase *gentreman* is notable because he has chosen to translate into "correct" English the rest of Bakha's dialogues, making him sound like a "Bloomsbury intellectual," to recall Gandhi's criticism. The word invokes an idea/l but also conveys how ridiculous it is for Bakha and his friends to be pursuing it. In mishearing or misspeaking it, the village elders and the boys themselves betray their immeasurable cultural distance from a "gentleman."

Still, it is arguable that *gentreman* is not the same as "gentleman," but a phonetic variation resulting from a deliberate misspeaking or mishearing. As such, the sound is ironic but perhaps also a little liberating. Constituting *gentreman* as a homophone for "gentleman" resituates it from a colonial racialized hierarchical terrain to a native racialized one. While the meaning of the sound *gentreman* is shaped in relation to the word "gentleman," it remains relatively unencumbered by the structures of power anchoring the presumably colonial and comprador idea of a "gentleman." This relation becomes clearer in an exchange between Charat Singh, a Hindu and a havildar in the Indian army, and Bakha. Charat Singh exclaims: "'You are becoming a *gentreman, ohe* Bakhya! Where did you get that uniform?' Bakha was shy, knowing he had no right to indulge in such luxuries as apeing [*sic*] the high-caste people. He humbly mumbles: '*Huzoor* it is all your blessing.'"[35] Clearly, by wearing English-style clothes, Bakha knows that he is *not* challenging the relationship between the English man and the native but is, in fact, upsetting the caste-based hierarchy among the natives themselves. The use of the word *gentreman* becomes an especially critical gesture as it unmoors the English language and English cultural ideals from their colonial hierarchy and draws on the power of the language. While the word *gentreman* domesticates the spelling and the sound of "gentleman," the word still serves as a persistent reminder of a foreignness. In fact, because any power or currency that the word *gentreman* has is because of this foreignness, the word is not really a disarticulation from "gentleman," but is rather a strategic deployment of the sound of the English word. *Gentreman* translates "gentleman" by triangulating with the signifier of "gentleman" and the signified of the British Empire. As such it does not disrupt the empire but profits from its displaced sounds to push back against—however humbly and timidly—the localized caste-based hierarchies.

The experience of the sound of the word "gentleman" as English and the English language itself as an object becomes even clearer as we attend to the precise nature of Bakha's desire: "He had felt a burning desire, while he was in the British barracks, to speak the *tish-mish, tish-mish* which the Tommies spoke."[36] Sonically, the soft sounds of *tish-mish* counter the "undertone [of] untouchable, untouchable" in the other sound that Bakha and his broom regularly make, "*posh* [sound of the broom sweeping the ground], sweeper coming, *posh*, sweeper coming."[37] As someone who is considered impure by virtue of his caste, Bakha has to announce his arrival and warn others. The *tish-mish, tish-mish* also evacuates the English language of any discursive meaning as Bakha wishes to claim it as a vaguely imitative sound, as the form that is the signifier. As in the case of the word *gentreman*, it is the meaninglessness—the placing of the signifier before or as the signified—that is important, precisely because it is gibberish. Bakha is able to achieve this meaninglessness by a deliberate mishearing or misspeaking. Inasmuch as the language of English is also a socially circulating sound, the imprecision of *tish-mish* opens up possibilities for Bakha and his friends. Baer writes that the "novel represents a displacement of the sound of English (the language in which it is written) as meaningless onomatopoeia, and thus as a lingual space as yet inaccessible to the very subaltern whose consciousness is being depicted in that language."[38] But seizing and enjoying the English language only as its nonsensical sound object does not only exhibit an unmistakable indifference to the ideologies of the British Empire; it also manifests a fascinating mimicry of the Orientalist colonial attitudes to native literatures and languages that consigned them to inscrutability, gibberish and (as a result) worthlessness.

What many do not know about this episode in the novel is that it is autobiographical, and a verbatim transposition of Anand's own desire as recalled in *The King Emperor's English*. Anand records his joy in the "new Indo-Anglian style of writing."[39] He writes:

> From my childhood I felt a fascination for the English language through hearing *git-mit, git-mit*, as the sepoys called the speech of English Army officers and "Tommies" in the Indian Cantonments. And it was that early interest, part curiosity and part snobbery, that made me learn quickly. I remember the thrill I had when I could collar some "Tommy" and practice my vocabulary on him. Usually, he could not understand my sing-song, even as I could not catch a word of his jerky staccato, except the familiar, unprintable swear words. But later, at school, I excelled at recitation of both English prose and verse.[40]

The ease of Anand's experience is in sharp contrast to Bakha's frustration. Anand's ability to "collar a Tommy" is an attribute of his caste and class position, neither of which is shared by Bakha. What is also striking in this episode is the portability of the desire for English as a sound object, the way that the desire can be transposed from one situation to another. The desire can have different motivations (Anand's curiosity and snobbery, Bakha's quest for an identity unmarked by caste) and can be met with different fates (Anand is able to learn English, Bakha is not). Yet, the essential shape of the desire—in an evacuated signifier either misheard or mispronounced—remains identifiable. It is worth noting that *King Emperor's English* was published after *Untouchable*. To that extent, this moment not only exemplifies the portability of an anglophilic desire as a sound object but also instantiates the domain of physical objects that inflect language.

Anand imputes his desire for English to Bakha before he is able to write about it himself in a sort of auto-fiction. Perhaps the "untouchable" subject's burning yet unfulfilled desire is simply a stage in Anand's evolving stance on English. Perhaps it marks the limits of Anand's liberal humanism and anticolonial nationalist politics. Either way, Anand's ideological inconsistency only confirms the meaning of English in India as policed by class and caste hierarchies. *King Emperor's English* overlaps so much with *Untouchable* that I feel emboldened to say that the novel is as much about English as it is about caste, just as *King Emperor's English* is as much about caste as English. Of course, the inconsistency between Anand's and Bakha's interests in English also reminds us that postcolonial and South Asian Anglophone literary criticism seldom reconciles with the colonized and caste-marked subject's desire for the colonial language.

As previous chapters have shown, there are a number of arguments like Anand's own in *The King Emperor's English*, and many instances when English appears desired in colonized spaces. Ironically, the narrative of *Untouchable* establishes the allure and importance of English through an anecdote that validates the upper-caste figure of Gandhi himself! This is a critical gesture on the part of the novelist, given Bakha's unfulfilled desire for English in the novel and Gandhi's influential admonition of Anand. Toward the end of the novel, Bakha finds himself amid a crowd waiting for Gandhi to arrive and address them. As he stands there, Bakha recalls all that he had heard of the *Mahatma*:

> People said he was a saint, that he was an *avatar* (incarnation) of the gods Vishnu and Krishna. Only recently he had heard a spider had woven a web in the house of the Lat Sahib (viceroy) at Dilli (Delhi), making a portrait of the sage, and *writing his name under it in English*. That was said to be a warning to the sahibs to depart from Hindustan, since God Almighty Himself had sent a message to a little insect that Gandhi was to be the Maharaja of the whole of Hindustan. That the spider's web appeared in Lat Sahib's *kothi* (viceroy's residence) was

surely significant. And they said no sword could cut his body, no bullet could pierce his skin, no fire could scorch him.[41]

This instance is the only time that the narrative straightforwardly advocates for the English language, and it is used, quite literally, to write back to and warn the viceroy of Gandhi's power. In this instance, Gandhi is cast as the eternal character of the human soul in Hinduism (via translations of the Hindu scripture, the Bhagavad Gita) and validated not only by the "God Almighty Himself" but also by the language of the British Empire. The mythic power of Gandhi is confirmed when the message is delivered to the sahibs in a spider's web that spells out his name in English. It is only through an association of the colonial language with native monarchy and animal superstition that Gandhi registers his warning to the British and accedes to the status of royalty, the Maharaja of Hindustan. Often associated with Western secular modernity, English is used here to reinforce a monarchical vision of independent India. There is no doubt that Gandhi's power in the novel is in English.

At the same time, Gandhi's power is also itself specifically machinic, in the spider's web and emerging as "a faint whisper at first, the Mahatma's voice, as it came through a loud speaker" had "the genius that could, by a single dramatic act, rally multicoloured, multitongued India to himself."[42] Gandhi's voice, amplified by and almost inseparable from the microphone, is able to bring a dispersed India together just as Nehru's post-independence address did. It is precisely the materiality of Gandhi's speech that allows Bakha to see his hypocrisy: "In one breath Gandhi says he wants to abolish untouchability, in another he asserts he is an orthodox Hindu."[43] As ideological political struggles take place on the terrain of language, Bakha encounters language itself piecemeal. Language is broken down word by word, sound by sound, part of and itself a machine.

Such an ungrammatical understanding of English, one that constantly disrupts the signifier and the signified, perhaps best mirrors the protagonist's grasp of it, as we have seen already. The fact that Bakha consistently grasps what he hears word-for-word, as sight and sound and rumor, rather than syntagmatically, disrupts the discursive power of his perception of Gandhi's mythology, even as it does not unequivocally disrupt Bakha's perception of the authority of the British. Ben Baer reads this moment as the subaltern borrowing of the name of Gandhi. He argues that this episode demonstrates the difference between literacy in the modern public sphere and general subaltern history. While this particular moment does manifest a subaltern borrowing of the name of Gandhi, it is clear that that borrowing occurs in English, a patently non-subaltern language by the novel's own logic. If anything, in its use only as a script formed by a spider's web, this episode reveals English as the subaltern language of rumor and myth that authorizes and disseminates Gandhi as a feudal figure.

So, as the novel concludes, the machine (the flush) and the language (English) as part of and as a machine become central. "Yes, yes, all that, but no catch-words and cheap phrases. The change [in a caste-based system] will be organic and not mechanical," a left-leaning poet in the novel named Iqbal Nath Sharsar, an alter ego for Anand himself, reminds his rapt audience.[44] Repeating "cheap phrases" without a deep knowledge of the larger context is, of course, discouraged by the novel. Yet, this claim is not a criticism of the machine in the vein of Gandhi, who was deeply critical of Western modernity and saw no place for machines in postcolonial India. In fact, E. M. Forster in the "Preface" has already established the centrality of the machine to Anand's vision when he writes, "No god is needed to rescue the Untouchables, no vows of self-sacrifice and abnegation on the part of more fortunate Indians, but simply and solely—the flush system. Introduce water-closets and main-drainage throughout India, and all this wicked rubbish about untouchability will disappear."[45]

The poet's "yes, yes, all that" is in response to the invocation of "Marxian materialism" by an English-educated critic of Gandhi. In the world of the novel, authority is located not in the philosophy of the "West"— that is, Marxian materialism—but in its machine. The emptiness of a machine without catch phrases is akin to language without the colonial discourse imagined by someone like Nehru. The poet Sharsar and Anand seem to say that to make change organic, and not mechanical, the language as machine does not have to be rejected, it only has to be grafted organically—broken down and then reassembled. But, as Bakha's experiences with language as machinic objects show, this process is far from straightforward.

Performing English in Adiga's The White Tiger

Although Bakha only speaks in English through Anand, his desire and disappointments make him an important archetype in Indian Anglophone novels. His desire to know how it feels to not be marked by class and by caste marginality resonates across the range of works that imagine caste experience. Balram Halwai, Aravind Adiga's protagonist in *The White Tiger*, shares this impulse with Bakha. For Bakha as for Balram, English becomes the site from which to protest national and nationalist imaginaries. Unlike Bakha, however, Balram is able to pick up enough knowledge of the English language by emulating his English-speaking employer, and thus escape his life of social, political, and economic marginality. Many readers—from scholars to book reviewers—question both Bakha's and Balram's claim to English. Indeed, the transgressive nature of these characters' access to English is cast as a moral and an ethical problem that threatens to delegitimize their textual and political existence.

Framed as an epistle, *The White Tiger* is a long letter from Balram to the Chinese premier, Wen Jiabao, that Balram dictates into a recorder. Balram opens his letter with the irony of Nehru's first address to independent India in English. He speaks into the recorder: "Neither you nor I speak English, but there are some things that can be said only in English."[46] Balram is speaking into the recorder because he is supposed to be unlettered. Yet, the first thing he voices is his lack of English. This imperative and impossibility is the very paradox of global Anglophone literature that, to use Rebecca Walkowitz's formulation, is "born translated." It is written and read not only in English as it mediates non-English speakers and non-English languages through English. At the same time, this paradox also renders English a vernacular when figures who do not know the language must encounter it.

In *The White Tiger*, English is mediated via the upper-caste and upper-class employer who has returned from the United States. As they travel through global hubs of New Delhi and Gurgaon, and spend more and more time in the car together, Balram and Ashok curiously meld into one person. Balram often catches his glance in the rearview mirror while driving his employer. He copies the cultivated mannerisms and tastes of his employer. He begins to see the world through Ashok's eyes, to react to it in a way that Ashok would. If Ashok seeks a Caucasian sex worker who oddly looks like Kim Basinger, then Balram also dredges up the last of his savings to sleep with a golden-haired girl. If his employer sits with a woman in the car, then it is Balram who gets aroused. Balram explains this closeness with the man he murders by saying that one tends to feel surprisingly attached to the person one kills.

Balram's phonic dictated letter is an attempt to generate political power in the face of representational anxieties in a democracy. Jiabao is slated to visit India soon, and Balram wishes to expose the dysfunctionality of the Indian state and the acute class disparity plaguing neoliberal India. Equally importantly, Balram wishes to present Jiabao with the secrets of India's entrepreneurial success and inform the latter of "the real truth" about it before Indian state officials give him their misleading version. While Balram was happy to know that the premier was visiting to "learn how to make a few Chinese entrepreneurs," he was also filled with an "*anxiety*. It hit me that in keeping with international protocol, the prime minister and foreign minister of my country will meet you at the airport with garlands, small take-home sandalwood statues of Gandhi, and a booklet full of information about India's past, present, and future."⁴⁷ This is when Balram decides to write his narrative to counter the prime minister's.

Arguably, the "thing" that can only be said in English refers to the entirety of the letter that forms the novel. But, more contextually, it refers to "what a fucking joke!," an exclamation that Balram has heard his employer Ashok Sharma's wife use.⁴⁸ That Balram singles out "What a fucking joke!" as a statement to be articulated in English immediately draws attention to the use of English in the novel. In this letter to the Chinese premier, Balram uses the exclamation, at different points, to mock the democratic process in India, to show the dark underside of recent entrepreneurial successes in the country, and to draw attention to his own wrongful framing as a murderer by his employers. Balram does not pursue political action for the collective good. Many critics see that fact as the novel's most damning flaw. Nevertheless, his "What a fucking joke!" immediately offers a critique of the state narratives found in police actions, among parliamentarians, and in the "welcome." Balram never voted in elections because rich landlords routinely bought off his votes, nor did he find himself represented by "politicians and parliamentarians" who only exploit the rural poor.⁴⁹ Balram's "What a fucking joke!" and his contestatory letter expand the possibilities of protest in the English language, quite like in the Communist protest scene in *The God of Small Things*, where letters are pelted like stones.

From the beginning of the novel, Balram's doubtful ability to speak English renders his authorship suspect and challenges the idea that voice is an assertion of identity. Balram also positions his letter as a managerial how-to on entrepreneurial strategies. In this endeavor, he is his own case study. The novel-as-letter describes Balram Halwai's rise from the acute poverty of rural Bihar (Darkness) to entrepreneurial success as a cab service owner in Bangalore (the Light). Balram's rags-to-riches story would have been a middle-class fantasy had it been made possible by difficult yet rightful access to education. Instead, he accomplishes these feats by recklessly lying about almost everything: his name, caste, age, level of education, religious beliefs, work experience, and sexual experience. He lies not only to other characters in the text but also to the reader. What is worse is that he murders his employer, Ashok, and steals his money, which serves as seed money for his start-up, White Tiger Drivers. By the end of the novel, he is a small-time gangster, in cahoots with the Bangalore Police, flouting the law, and harboring visions of starting a school for children.

While English is recruited to contest the nation's lies, the language is itself mired in lies and falsehood, as Balram uses it to fake his identity and commit homicide. Almost all aspects of Balram's person were invented by the state. He was given the name Balram because his government schoolteacher was dissatisfied with his generic name that literally meant "boy." Since none of his family members remembered his birth date, that was also invented for him by the schoolteacher. What we know of Balram's height and weight, even the details of the crime, are from a Wanted poster issued by the police in his name. This poster, like the posters found in Shivpalganj in *Raag Darbari* in chapter 1, is not only meaningless but also erroneous in its information about Balram. Yet, by the end of the novel, Balram skillfully manipulates his lack of social coordinates and his ignorance through his knowledge of the English language. *The White Tiger* thus dramatizes the ways in which not knowing the English language, or not revealing how much he knows, allows Balram to sign his name as his master, Ashok Sharma, in the final instance.

Balram scales class differences and caste injunctions by exploiting language as performance. He encounters English like the majority of Indians who must learn it to remain relevant in a changing economic order but who have no means to do so. While Balram is self-taught, his learning style invokes the strategies that Moin Khan—the milkman who, by learning English, became known as "The English Man"—deployed when taking English classes. Both Balram and Khan break the English language into sounds to be memorized and repeated. This language, largely made up of nouns and short sentences, is devoid of any grammatical adherence. English is configured as portable mathematical formulae that can be applied to a range of social situations. This idea of the English language as a set of formulae is literalized in the film *Gully Boy* when the protagonist Murad graffities on the walls of Mumbai (chapter 5). This experience of the English language shows Anglophone India as a space not where everyone speaks in English but where everyone hears and mimics what is understood as English as an acousmatic sound.

A self-confessed "original listener, not original thinker," Balram learns how to pronounce the word "pizza" in the "right way" by repeating it under his breath as he hears Ashok correct his wife. Balram also memorizes the names of expensive whiskey, picks up stray words like "pri-va-see," "income tax."[50] Balram had encountered an injunction against English during his childhood in the form of his low caste and class position, which prevented him from completing his education. As an adult, Balram seizes on every opportunity to learn the language and to capitalize on his knowledge of it—thus making good use of his talent as an "original listener." Balram picks up English words by listening to Ashok from the driver's seat and from the ubiquitous presence of the language in urban Delhi and Gurgaon. Like Bakha, what Balram learns is also not a formal knowledge of the English language but more the symbolic associations of the language, its shapes and sounds.

Balram's attempt to learn a few words of English with the customary pronunciation underscores his transgressive desires to move across classes. Balram describes this imitation of Ashok as his "first taste of a fugitive's life," which conveys a sense of the illicit as he overhears snatches of English phrases and as he mouths them later.[51] Describing his first English lesson at the English-speaking school, Moin Khan had also said that he felt "criminal." Both instances attest to the thrill of forbidden knowledge. This idea of the fugitive implicitly also criminalizes Balram for overhearing and learning English—the master's language that he is not supposed to access, learn, and know—even before he is criminalized as Ashok's murderer. Ashok and his family conduct their unscrupulous business in the car with unabashed candor because they do not think that Balram can understand them. The value and success of Balram as a servant and as a driver depend on his illiteracy. Thus, the fact that he learns the English language in secret signifies that he has outgrown his submissive role as the employee. Balram's knowledge of English is, in fact, a step towards his crime of literally unseating the employer and occupying his position.

Despite the centrality of English as arguably the *only* linguistic medium that affords a critique of the state, the indeterminacy of how much Balram understands when he repeats and uses English words stages a struggle over representation and claims to a language. While Balram Halwai does not rise against the injustices of the rich in an identifiably glorious gesture such as participating in an overthrow or an uprising, what he does is as political as these acts. He falters in his self-appointed position as a guide to Wen Jiabao through the lies and truths about India. However, he falters not because he is not a "proper guide," as some critics have claimed, but because—as Balram shows—this process of guiding itself is murky. Through his self-conscious tropes of narration and blatant lies, Balram magnifies and parodies the representational process of democratic politics itself. Thus, the unreliability of Balram as a narrator does not so much weaken his critique as it strengthens it.

Balram appropriates ideas and words, and the neoliberal rhetoric that he picks up from his driver's seat. Betty Joseph has argued that almost all of Balram's neoliberal rhetoric can be traced back to Ashok. So the views he expresses are not his own, or not only his own or of his class. Joseph writes that it is precisely the "neurotic symptomatology" of neoliberalism that a poor low-caste driver unquestioningly internalizes its ideology. This reading does not account for the ambiguity with which Balram receives that neoliberal rhetoric, and the powerful double-edged-ness with which he deploys it.[52] One of the most compelling images in this respect is that of the Johnnie Walker Black whiskey bottle. Balram knows from other drivers and from his own experience that English liquor is more expensive than country-made liquor. He also knows that an empty Johnnie Walker bottle, carelessly left behind by the employer in the car, is just as expensive because of its resale value. It can be refilled with cheap liquor and sold at a profit. The usefulness of the empty bottle of Johnnie Walker Black usually lies in the possibility of refilling it and selling it on the black market. The way that the other drivers would use such a bottle couples the bottle's use value with its exchange value, by virtue of the English brand name.

By killing his master with that bottle, Balram uses it to exchange his person, name, and financial means with those of Ashok Sharma. Further increasing the exchange value of such a bottle, Balram uses it to establish an equivalence between himself and his master. As he transitions from a marginalized citizen to a citizen as consumer, the knowledge of the English language helps Balram to claim a new political space and identity for himself. "English" here is not simply the literal language of English but encompasses its materiality and its visual life. Balram splits English along its symbolic and literal meanings, transforming it into an object and a commodity that he can wield. In this political economy of the sign, form (signifier) takes priority over content (signified); the English language literally functions like a currency and as an object of use—a murder weapon—as in the example above. After murdering Ashok, Balram not only absconds with his former employer's money but also takes on his name. In the ultimate act of political reinvention, he signs his letter to Wen Jiabao as "Ashok Sharma."

While Ashok was still alive, Balram emulated him by paying attention to his choices as a consumer. Blending the sartorial, the visual, and the linguistic registers into a single semiotic register, Balram describes Ashok's attire thus: "It was like no T-shirt I would ever choose to buy at a store. The larger part of it was empty and white and there was a small design in the centre. I would have bought something very colorful, with lots of words and designs on it. Better value for the money."⁵³ Balram decides to buy a similar shirt the next time he goes shopping for clothes, and picks up a pair of black shoes and toothpaste as well. The value of the T-shirt, in this case, is not simply as a piece of clothing to cover a human body but is indistinguishable from its exchange value as a shirt of a specific English brand that is also worn by Ashok. By virtue of this association with the T-shirt, the English language is really the commodity that Balram wishes to purchase. Balram rejects many T-shirts before he chooses this one with the one English word.

The T-shirt and that one English word furnish him with a new "fugitive" identity. One transgression—or *crime,* as the narrative would have the reader believe—leads to another. That plain white T-shirt with only one English word on it is like an empty canvas, which Balram fashions to his own freedom from the colors and multitude of narratives of his servant's attire. With this tastefully selected attire, Balram is no longer dressed like a servant but as an English-speaking master who belongs in a Honda City car. The clothes and the one English word equip Balram with the anonymity from class and caste branding that Modi, Bakha, and the Dalit characters of Navaria's stories cherish. The *value* of Balram's shirt, then, is not simply its use value but also its exchange value—almost in excess of what can be captured by the brand name—that literally opens the doors that had historically been closed for Balram and others belonging to his caste and class. This quality of the single English word is talismanic, and recalls the fetishistic quality of the commodity in Marxist theory as well as the talismanic quality of the Indian Constitution for historically marginalized people like the Dalits in India. The shirt allows Balram to be read as an upper-class figure and facilitates his admission into that class via the mall. Reading, in this moment, is not just the way Balram reads the English word but also the way that others read English itself as encoding a class and caste position.

Just before he actually murders Ashok, Balram again displays an uncanny comprehension of the "value" of the English language. Like the protestor in *The God of Small Things*, he had planned to draw Ashok out of the car on a deserted road at night, on the pretext of a problem with the tire, and kill him when Ashok was bent over examining it. But as it turns out, Ashok seems reluctant to step out and wants to telephone for help. This leaves Balram with no other option but to blackmail Ashok with the knowledge of his previous sexual liaisons. Referring to the car, he says, "It's been giving me problems ever since that night we went to the hotel . . .

the one with the big T sign on it. You remember it, don't you, sir?"⁵⁴ In the scope of the novel, Balram's use of his knowledge of the "T" sign, one Ashok did not even presume he could read, ironically does not establish him as literate in English because he reads the letter like a sign. However, it transforms the terms of his everyday experience because of its symbolic meaning. After he hints to his knowledge here, Ashok is more willing to listen to him. This tendency to claim signifiers culminates in Balram taking on Ashok's name after murdering him.

Balram's tussle to wrench English from where it is ensconced culminates in a textual genealogy for himself that, ironically, severs him from a modern English textual lineage. Balram often mentions that he finds literature comforting and inspiring and quotes Urdu poets to prove his point—Iqbal, Rumi, Mirza Ghalib. There is "a fourth fellow, also a Muslim, whose name I've forgotten—has written a poem where he says this about slaves: 'They remain slaves because they can't see what is beautiful in this world.'"⁵⁵ Together, these lines become formative in strengthening Balram's resolve to murder Ashok. Balram's inability to remember the name of the fourth poet is intriguing. In quoting these lines without credit, a plagiarism akin to his other practices in the novel, Balram establishes something like a *silsilah* of poets. The word *silsilah* literally means a chain of succession, or transmission, usually established by quotation and invocation between an *ustad* (master-poet) and a *shagird* (student/apprentice). Balram Halwai can be read as participating in a *silsilah* when he quotes Rumi, Ghalib, and Iqbal, indicating that *that* is the tradition he wants to place himself in. His love for Urdu poetry, and not an English novel, is a disavowal of the distinctly modern ideology of the postcolonial Anglophone novel and the English language. Balram inserts himself in the *silsilah* of Urdu poets by reciting lines that invite the listener to escape slavery by noticing what's beautiful in the world.

This act of insertion on the part of Balram also realizes his desire to break out of the rooster coop that maintains the master-and-slave dialectic. Balram uses the "rooster coop" as a metaphor for the lives of the poor in India: "Go to Old Delhi, and look at the way they keep chickens there in the market. Hundreds of pale hens and brightly colored roosters, stuffed tightly into wire-mesh cages. They see the organs of their brothers lying around them. They know they are next, yet they cannot rebel. They do not try to get out of the coop. The very same thing is done with humans in this country."⁵⁶ As he offers his analysis of inequality and injustice in India in his letter to Jiabao, Balram declares that it is the servant himself who is responsible for his own suffering. It is the mentality of the servant class to surrender to "perpetual servitude." This ideology of the "rooster coop" is so strong that "you can put the key of his emancipation in a man's hands and he will throw it back at you with a curse."⁵⁷ The way to break out of it, arguably, is to recognize the servile mentality.

Later, when Ashok is despondent after his wife has left him, Balram again invokes the metaphor of the rooster coop. As he wipes Ashok's vomit and takes care of him, Balram wonders where his genuine concern for his master ends and where his self-interest begins: "Do we loathe our masters behind a facade of love—or do we love them behind a facade of loathing? 'We are made mysteries to ourselves by the Rooster Coop [sic] we are locked in.'"⁵⁸ Balram echoes the lines from Urdu poetry, exhorting the slaves to look for beauty in the world. The alliance with the poets separates Balram from the social tussle that English and Hindi languages represent. Instead, it places him in the space of Urdu literary tradition, which at once presents a theoretical space to upend the Hindi-English social and literary hegemony, as well as the historical space to complicate their binary dynamics. Balram, ironically, rises to the middle class—no longer remaining a slave—by rejecting the Hindu majority culture and the forward-moving conception of modernity enshrined in English. The final word in the novel goes to the minority Muslim culture in India, which is rendered in English that has assumed an anti-institutional and antimodern character.

Fugitive Fictions

Untouchable and *The White Tiger* dramatize the quest for a language that is equal, and stage the promise and anxiety of English as a purported language of equality. In this quest, English appears in the hands (and mouths) of the "masses" and "the common people" who do not have access to it and in whose name the language occupies its state-sponsored position. The protagonists Bakha and Balram interrogate the symbolic affordances of the English language to effect social transformation. But the novels leave them with correctives and criticism. The fact that Balram murders his employer furnishes a moral critique of his character arc. Bakha is reprimanded in the novel by upper-caste men for not observing caste-based decorum, and instead given Gandhi and the machine as solutions. Between competing narratorial and characterological impulses, *Untouchable* and *The White Tiger* present fictions about fugitives of different kinds while also showing the fugitivity of those fictions.

Indeed, the figure of the fugitive/trickster/con/fraud appears with disquieting regularity in Indian Anglophone literature about low-caste characters. Recent novels like Manu Joseph's *Serious Men* and *The White Tiger* draw on a globalizing India to fuel the attempts of the poor to act like the rich. And many of the earlier novels, like R. K. Narayan's *Guide* (1958) and Bhabhani Bhattacharya's *He Who Rides the Tiger*, evince similar social anxieties around the maneuverability of caste. Let me briefly turn to the latter, as much has been written on *The Guide*. Kalo, the protagonist of the latter novel, is a blacksmith in the small town of Jharna. The Bengal famine of 1942–43 pushes him to look for a job in the city. Driven by joblessness and hunger, Kalo arrives in Calcutta to realize that he does not have any of his tools, markers of his caste identity. Without these, he cannot find any work. What seems like an impediment at first turns out to be a great opportunity to fashion his life outside caste determinations. Kalo pretends to be a Brahmin and the custodian of a temple. Despite his eventual success in tricking people, Kalo remains morally troubled by his lie. Bhattacharya's tale of "modern India" explores the promise of modernity but culminates, like *The White Tiger*, as a cautionary tale. As the title has warned the readers, once you tell a lie—that is, mount a tiger—you cannot dismount it without risking death itself.

As seen in *The White Tiger*, the trope of the fugitive both challenges the performativity of caste and class, and blunts that challenge. The idea of dissembling offers its own moral critique, preserves whatever social order the characters are navigating, and regulates the incongruity of the characters and the linguistic medium. But, when these fraught characters are the protagonists or first-person narrators, they pose a challenge to literary representation itself. The acts of speaking in English or wanting to perform Englishness are particularly fraught, as the narrative rests on the fact they cannot speak. In this context, the trope of the con renders certain characters as authentic and inauthentic and reliable and unreliable. The friction between the affective modalities of the hope of transgression and the anxiety of equality is conveyed in the tension between the character and the narrator. This tension between the written English of the author and narrator and the spoken English of these characters destabilizes the *letter* of the novel.

Novels like *Untouchable* and *The White Tiger* give clarity to the term "Anglophone" by showing the social, political, and affective conditions in which English is spoken. In India, speaking English is a modality of linguistic engagement that draws on more than one sense. To put our scholarly finger on the politics of English in readings of Anglophone literature, we would do well to locate other experiences of English beyond speaking or writing. The prosthetic nature of language, as if it were a machinic object and a commodity, offers a transformative perspective on the meanings of English. *Untouchable* and *The White Tiger*, considered alongside the previous chapter's readings of Dalit writing, reveal new relations of power and intersubjectivity. Examining the complexity of Bakha's desire can help us better grasp the importance of English as a symbol or as a language that contemporary Dalit writers have chosen to use in contemporary Dalit writing. As a story about a low-caste subject's desire for English, *Untouchable* emerges as an early sounding out of the resonance of English beyond the education of native elites. It provides a necessary context for recent discussions on caste and the English language by reminding us that characters who may not normally "speak" English may still perhaps hear and see the language.

Vernacular English, as it figures in the texts, is not relegated to the expensively gained formal education of a few but circulates, tantalizingly, within everyday experiences. Especially within global capitalism, the English language is available to variously nonelite characters as a graspable catalyst of social mobility and individual advancement. These informal brushes with, and experiences of, the English language provide complex negotiation of a language of power from positions of marginality. The prospect of success here illuminates English as a caste-marked desire.

CHAPTER 4

Sound

THE MOTHER'S VOICE AND ANGLOPHONIC SOUNDSCAPES IN NORTHEAST INDIA

Orality, or English as a Mother Tongue

One of my earliest lessons in the English language was from my mother, who would carefully read out loud the letters of the English alphabet from a primer. I remember imitating her pronunciations and matching the letters with words. For me and for her, this practice of matching sound to sound—of memorizing and repeating in the name of reading and speaking—was a natural pedagogical strategy. It did not strike me then, as it does now, that my mother is not someone I would call an English speaker. In everyday conversations, she recognizes the sounds of common English expressions. As part of her job in a government office, she can read, spell, and trace many English words of the Indian bureaucratese. Despite this functional linguistic competency, what has always also been clear to me is that my mother is not comfortable in any of it. Outside of our scenes of learning, I have never heard her speak a full sentence in the English language. Yet, it is my mother, who never speaks English, who taught me to speak English.

I am certain that linguists have specific terminology to categorize language users like my mother. Terms like "bilingual," "emergent bilingual," "ESL or English as Second Language," and "English Language Learner" come to mind. However, none of these would be accurate descriptions of a speaking subject like her who could still tutor someone in English without being comfortably bilingual herself. Literacy—as a quantifiable relation to language—remains undertheorized in discussions of language and multilingualism in literary studies.¹ Nonetheless, I am interested in the different conceptions of language and orality that emerge in my childhood scene of learning and in similar scenes, theorized countless times by philosophers like Sigmund Freud, Jacques Lacan, Luce Irigaray, and Julia Kristeva.

Take, for instance, Friedrich Kittler's description of the historically inductive construction of the metaphysics of presence in phonetic script in *Discourse Networks 1800/1900* (1990). In nineteenth-century Germany, writes Kittler, the oralization of the German alphabet and the development of primers directed at the mother created the woman as a source of poetic feeling. The mother, teaching children how to read, would "give voice" to the printed text by sounding out the letters in the primer. She would thus embed a seemingly natural, original voice in the child's head so that "when later in life children picked up a book, they would not see letters but hear, with irrepressible longing, a voice between the lines."² The mouth of the mother, as it sounded the letters, would transform language as divinely ordained—"a creation *ex nihilo*"—to a phenomenon rooted in nature and "maternal gestation."³ It would elide the coerciveness of language learning, producing instead a naturalness and affinity that did not otherwise exist in German. Kittler imagines the mother as a biologically grounded sociological figure—not the biographical mother—whose voice sutures the distance between the signifier and the signified, between writing and speech, thus producing the mode of silent phonetic reading. Mediation by the mother transforms the rote activity of language learning to one that might feel as natural as sitting in her lap.

My experience could not be more different. Very often, my mother's careful enunciation was distracted by the sounds of the Hindi language that she primarily speaks. On such occasions, *I* would "correct" her pronunciation by repeating how I recalled the teacher at school to have pronounced the same word. Our collective uncertainty would soon morph into shared embarrassment and frustration, where we persisted with English lessons only because we felt we had to. These moments of unknowing combined with the fact that, as a family, we never conversed in English with each other only diminished for me any naturalness in the English language. I remember learning the language mostly as navigating an absurd refraction chamber of random English words and their fickle pronunciations. Although we did not realize it then, these English lessons took place in the postcolonial shadow of the pedagogical project of the British Empire which had created colonial subjects as the ideal learners of the English language.

When I now consider Kittler's seductive formulation that the mother's voice authorizes a mother tongue, several questions come to mind. What kinds of affective and political associations accrete when a mother figure voices not the comforting familiarity of an indigenous language but the distressing foreignness of a language of colonial, global, and national power? Does the mother's voice make the language more familiar, or does it render the mother strange? Does it matter in this process *how* the mother figure speaks?

Spurred by these questions, in this chapter I turn to aural and gendered experiences of English in postcolonial India. I am especially interested in situations where English is spoken by gendered figures who neither know English nor want to speak it, or in situations where English approximates the affective and political resonances of an identity-giving mother tongue. My pursuit of English as a kind of mother tongue may seem ironic, if not entirely misguided, since English is often the language against which the idea of a native and intimate mother tongue makes sense in South Asian literary contexts. The Census of India—including the most recent one in 2011—focuses quite solely on "mother tongues" that must be claimed by at least ten thousand citizens. In terms that are both romantic and literal— much like Kittler's—the census defines the mother tongue as "the language spoken in childhood by the person's mother to the person. If the mother died in infancy, the language mainly spoken in the person's home in childhood will be the mother tongue. In case of doubt, the language mainly spoken in the household may be recorded."[4] This strategy of noting only languages with a certain number of speakers quite blatantly disadvantages linguistic minorities.[5] Speaking statistically, as mentioned in the introduction, only 259,678 people reported English as their mother tongue in the 2011 Census of India. Compare this to the whopping numbers that distinguished other Indian languages such as Hindi (528,347,193), Telugu (81,127,740), and Marathi (83,026,680). The Indian subcontinent has seen bloody wars, territorial divisions, and fervid riots defending many such "mother tongues." Beyond the passionate dispassion of the petitioners in *India Demands English*, there have been no wars or riots in India about English.

Yet, as previous chapters have shown, English has also elicited passionate defenses and espousals. For instance, as an object of caste-based desire and as an instrument of caste-policing, the language is a site for a different kind of struggle. It is claimed as a different kind of mother tongue. As noted in chapter 2, Savitribai Phule, a pioneering anticaste social reformer, specifically referred to English as a mother figure in her poems, and Chandrabhan Prasad has led the popularity of English as a Dalit mother goddess. These explicit invocations of English as a mother—and even a goddess!—make the language an affectively charged mother tongue that holds the promise of a social revolution and social mobility.

The fact that an ever-growing number of people speak or want to or are forced to speak English in India today has elicited much consternation among cultural commentators. G. N. Devy has argued that the promise of social mobility in English has diminished interest in and opportunities to speak any other language. As a result, many people who report Hindi or Marathi or Telugu as their mother tongues are not, in fact, regular speakers of these languages. Devy goes on to claim that Anglophony—the speaking of English—is related to, perhaps even responsible for, a growing "phonocide" in India.[6] Still, despite the oversupply of such claims about the phonocidal tendencies of English, very little is actually known about the oral and aural experience of English. What *is* the experience of speaking English in India? What is the experience of hearing it? Orality is often neglected in studies of major languages like English, only to be reauthorized—à la Kittler—in the idea of the mother tongue as a different, *less-global* language. But, beyond its elevation to the terminus a quo in the idea of the mother tongue, orality encompasses a much wider gamut of experiences. This chapter charts the uncertain paths from sound to phoneme that are often mediated through gender.[7] These spoken experiences of English not only defetishize the oral against the written but also take seriously the potential of the different speaking situations and speaker subjects named by the adjective "Anglophone" in descriptions of world, people, and literatures.

In what follows, I turn to two sites from northeastern India, an area seldom heard from in global Anglophone and South Asian literary studies alike, to examine aural and gendered experiences of English as they bear witness to life in a war zone. The first site is a political site of maternal speech—an iconic radical protest in Manipur by women who identified themselves as mothers and raised English language slogans against the undemocratic regime of the Indian army in the region. The women's voices are not directed at the colonial or global metropole. With their English-language slogan, the women speak back to the Anglophone state-military apparatus that has destroyed the land and classified people as traitors, suspects, and targets. Their voices sound the contestatory potential of the English language not because the women, as mothers, appeal to some harmonious maternal principle, but because their embodied protest makes visible the coercive logics of a language that secures a state of siege. As they stand at the seat of state power to mourn the death of their daughter, the women's voices make the English language deeply intimate, and so, deeply political.

The second site is a literary site—short stories by Manipuri writer Yumlembam Ibomcha and Naga writer Temsula Ao that draw on local oral traditions to forge a literary language that bears witness to the physical damage and the psychic desubjectivation of life in the region. The stories are characterized by a distinct interplay of nonvocal and nonverbal sounds of suffering and violence that resonate in the English language. Ibomcha writes in Meitelon and is translated into English, Ao writes in English. Together, these writers offer instances of English-language literature from northeastern India as exemplarily Anglophonic because it begins in the *absence* or the repudiation of language in a state of siege. It is important to note that both Northeast literature and Northeast India are constructs of mainland India that obscure the complexity and diversity of region. Emerging as a geopolitical category, the Northeast offers an example of the Anglophonic state's hegemony. In both the political and the literary example, the oral experience of speaking English or the aural experience of hearing it as sound undermine the dominant ideology of a democratic nation-state associated with the English language. The chapter also engages with works by Mahasweta Devi and Arundhati Roy to show how English emerges as a site of revolutionary counterdiscourse against the Indian state beyond this region.

Almost all of the northeastern states of India, like Kashmir, have been under military occupation by the Indian state for almost as long as India has been independent from the British in 1947. The region comprises eight states—Manipur, Assam, Nagaland, Meghalaya, Tripura, Sikkim, Arunachal Pradesh, and Mizoram. It is sandwiched between mainland India, China, Burma, Bangladesh, and Bhutan. Seven of these states have armed insurgent groups who wish to claim political sovereignty from India—either as autonomous within the nation-state or as independent from it. The Naga National Council declared sovereignty before India even became independent from the British. There are many separatist movements in the region. In the name of managing ethnic insurgency, the Indian army also has unchecked extrajudicial powers to execute counterinsurgency operations. The army flagrantly abuses these powers, resulting in arbitrary arrests, detentions, custodial deaths, disappearances, and acts of sexual violence. Manipur, where the protest took place, has been under the Armed Forces Special Powers Act (AFSPA) since the 1980s. Under the sweeping provisions of AFSPA, the armed forces can kill any suspect or arrest them without a warrant on mere suspicion. The army can also enter and search any premises without warrant to make such arrests. Given the provisions of the AFSPA, the guilty personnel are not prosecuted for their crimes. Unfortunately, it is not an exaggeration at all to say that the rest of India has little knowledge or care for the daily war waged between civilians, insurgents, and the army.

Previous chapters have shown that the English language justifies the democratic character of the Indian state and that conversely, the language has also enabled claims for power by those marginalized by the state. It would be tempting (and not wholly unreasonable) to argue that English amplifies the protesting women's voices or that its use by them renders English an unexpected mother tongue in the Kittlerian vein. These are not the arguments I want to make, however—or, at least, not the *only* arguments I want to make. Instead, I pursue both "voice" and "mother" as sites of difference in order to hear the geopolitical trauma, affective structures, and resistant feminist subjectivities that make the English language audible. By following the sounds of English in postcolonial India, this chapter recovers in English a rival lineage of a revolutionary mother tongue. The political and literary sites identified above offer critical instances of the orality of English in India, also in the spirit of attuning literary criticism to the sonic materiality of Anglophony. In speaking, the materialities of affective and embodied mediation unmake the English that we know all too well into a vernacular English that enables solidarities and speaks truth to (state) power.

Voice has long featured as a metaphor for political participation and as an essential axiom of human rights discourse. It is something to be claimed in defiance of political oppression and unspeakable trauma. Yet, the verifiability of voice—central to these formulations—is heard only in listening and is often belied by conditions of aurality. Voice is always more than, and independent of, language. This excess of voice and its independence from language aligns language to "bones, flesh, and blood."[8] Voice brings to auditory attention an embodied experience of language that makes utterance possible.[9] By uniting the idea of voice as agency and voice as sound, we can foreground English, beyond its literary and visual life, as part of an aural sensorial public sphere in India. By examining the tension *between* these two valences of sound, we encounter language at its representational limits, where speaking subjects claim their humanity and their right to live in the face of the sexual-political violence of the postcolonial state.

If the voice has been prized as the most naturalized form of subjective self-expression, the mother's voice has still greater cultural associations.

The mother's role in patriarchal society shapes the meanings of a language given by the mother (and it is always given by the mother). The valuation of the maternal principle also elevates the mother's voice or her language to the status of the mother tongue, where it connotes origin, nativity, intimacy, immediacy, and naturalness. As a concept cognate to the vernacular, the mother tongue undergirds the subject as well as the imagined collectives of cultures and nations.[10] Psychoanalytic feminist criticism has fixed on the figure of the mother to speak outside patriarchal discourse and associated the mother tongue with the pre-Oedipal order. Yet, as long as matricide is at the origin of the speaking voice, the language learned at the mother's breast *remains* a patriarchal language.

Perhaps the radicalism of the fantasized object of the mother lies neither in biology nor in culture but in this paradox. It lies in the reminder that the subject enabled by the symbolic order of the mother in fact lacks a foundation. The maternal body does not so much name an origin but lay bare the coercive logics that produce the mother. Understood so, the mother's voice or the mother tongue do not stand at the source of discourse—the wellspring of life and language—but are always mediated and embodied experiences that disable the sovereign power of the subject.

This chapter centers the mother's voice—as a concept—to explore both the sounds of English and the sounds mediated in English. In doing so, it centers the bodies of those who speak English, and acknowledges both the affective attachments and the bodily violences of language. At the same time, my mother's literal voice from my childhood scene of learning performs the discordance between what is said and what is heard. While my mother has always been a speaker of English, I have only just heard her as one. In comparable ways, the real and imagined figures we hear raising their voice in the following pages are not normally considered English speakers. They are not who come to mind in discussions of the global Anglophone of literary studies. Yet, they not only speak English but, in doing so, they also inflect it. In the next two chapters, I take seriously my new awareness of my mother's voice to listen again to Anglophone India.

"Indian Army Rape Us":
Political Mothers and the Indian State

On July 15, 2004, twelve Meitei women protestors (locally known as the Meira Paibis or the Torch Bearers, and belonging to an ethnic group native to the region) stood naked in front of Kangla Fort, the army base in Imphal, in the northeastern state of Manipur. Their middle-aged bodies were only

FIGURE 6. Women's protest in Manipur, 2004: "Indian Army Rape Us." (Courtesy of UB Photos.)

partly concealed by a white cloth banner that read "Indian Army Rape Us" in blood-red typography. The immediate context for this protest was the rape, torture, mutilation, and murder of Thangjam Manorama, a thirty-two-year-old woman, by soldiers of the 17th Assam Rifles, a counterinsurgency paramilitary battalion.[11] The larger context was the rampant rapes and extrajudicial killings by the Indian army in the name of maintaining order in "disturbed" areas across most states of northeastern India. One can find several secondhand accounts of the protest and interviews with the women. Despite some minor inconsistencies between these narratives, what remains consistent is the maddening frenzy of all that the women felt leading up to that moment—grief, anger, courage, doubts that tested that courage. When the women faced the historic seat of power that morning, they did so with tears in their eyes but without fear. For a moment, no one spoke. But soon the air was ringing with slogans: "[Indian Army] Rape us, kill us! Rape us, kill us!" Available video recordings of the protest show Ima Lourembam Ngambi, one of the women, defiantly screaming in the direction of the army base, "We are all Manorama's mothers! Come, rape us, you bastards!"

Of these twelve women, Lourembam is the only one who knew English. So, while her coprotestors repeated the slogan of "Rape Us" or raised other slogans in Manipuri, she angrily continued: "Understand?" "Come on, flesh us!" If you listen carefully to the video recordings, the word "flesh" would stand out. Its "f" sounding labial and aspirated and its "sh" intermixed with the "s" of "us." The accented English on the lips of Lourembam and others heightened the abstract nature of the representative democracy that spoke on their behalf. But, beyond the specificity of Lourembam's accent, which an ear may or may not pick up on, the voices of these women gave the spectacular protest an auditory referent. Each time the women spoke, they flung their words and bodies fiercely towards the army base. And, each time they challenged the army so, the Meira Paibis also drew the English language inwards—towards their naked maternal bodies and deep into the vortex of their emotions.

This speech act of these political mothers of Manorama echoes the original scene of learning at the mother's breast. But, rather unlike "the mother [who] has a (sweet) voice, but no speech," the Meira Paibis's voices sound angry, tear-soaked, and tireless.[12] Their tone and timbre produce a very different English from the one that justifies the coercive logics and mechanisms of majoritarian democracy in the Indian Constitution. While the naked bodies of the mothers conjure the primal maternal bond before language, they make visible not a pre-Oedipal mother but years of geopolitical trauma and a people's collective emotional and physical pain. The banner held by the women renders their bodies scriptural, making legible the violence of political and linguistic mediation. Ironically, the protest *does* constitute a pedagogical moment where the Meira Paibis demonstrate what democracy looks like for those who operate in its name but remain far from it in spirit.

As the first chapter shows, democracy in India is imagined as a situation where only the state speaks to its people and never the people to the state. Debates over language politics show that the number of people the Indian state speaks to, the number of constituencies it *wants* to or *can* address in a common language, is a measure of its democracy. With Hindi and English as India's official languages—the primary media of address—this number is already rather small. The literal and figurative address to the people is a performative gesture that "constitutes a 'we' of the community," in this case, the "we" of the Indian Constitution's "we, the people."[13] However, this act of speaking is neither simple nor straightforward as we witnessed in the farcically confused reception of the state's English in *Raag Darbari* in the first chapter. As foregoing chapters showed, there is no guarantee that what is said will, indeed, be heard. For instance, the political history of the northeastern states is a history of unproductive peace talks between the government of India and one of the many ethnonationalist groups, talks that make no positive difference to the people who live there. The Indian state uses these talks as political techniques of conflict management, and ethnic insurgents use them to legitimize their political difference and gain political recognition from the state.[14] Far from uniting a nation under its phonic authority, the state's address reveals more differences in the Indian polity than it conceals.

There is no communication, despite the line of communication that is thrown to people. Due to this communicative asymmetry, the region of Northeast India has been called a politically "illegible space" or a political "nonspace" that thrives as a "durable disorder."[15] The political unevenness between the Indian state and the people of the Northeast, writes Papori Bora, is also a result of colonial cartography that represented inhabitants of the region as immigrants from East and Southeast Asia, and ignored the region's history and its numerous ethnic and indigenous tribes. Colonial-era philological and racial classification has resulted in the political differentiation of the people of the northeastern states and mainland India.[16] While the region is included in the Indian state, its "inclusion in the political community of the Indian nation is always deferred."[17] This deferral—the status of the Northeast as a part of India that is in waiting—positions "India and the Northeast as unequal speaking subjects." It ensures that "[the Northeast] can never speak for India; India speaks for it."[18] The Northeast is always forced to speak the language of nationalism without ever being included in a vision of the nation.

The Meira Paibis's provocative address to the Indian Army, thus, demands an audience where there is none. It defies the deadlock that has shaped politics in and from Northeast India. How do the women do that? How do they make themselves legible from a geopolitical region that is itself unrecognized, and how do they ensure they are heard amid political impasses? The Meira Paibis circumvent the political and philosophical challenges of a representative democracy by acting as mothers and not as political subjects of the state. In interview after interview, the women have explicitly rejected the idea that their protest was premeditated or emboldened by the support of any militant outfit. They maintain that they "had reacted just as any mother would when her daughter was killed or raped" and that their actions should be read as their distinctly maternal response as mothers and as *independent* political actors. "The army didn't just rape Manorama," the women claimed, "they denied the right of the people of the Northeast to live."[19] With these claims, the Meira Paibis emphasize the spontaneity and the immediacy of their actions. At the same time, they claim that they act in the name of a bigger community. An attack on Manorama was an attack on all the vulnerable people of the region. By insisting that they acted as mothers—spontaneously, emotionally, viscerally, and *apolitically*, the Meira Paibis clarify their political position: they spoke on behalf of *everyone* unwittingly caught in the crossfire between insurgents and counterinsurgents. By giving voice to this unheard and unseen majority, the Meira Paibis overturn the state's address, in which it always speaks to the people but the people do not speak to it.

Unclothed, aged, and angry, the women enact the humiliation of speaking in a political situation that is defined by the speakers' "constitutive desubjectivation," that is endured in becoming a subject of enunciation in order to bear witness to the impossibility of speaking.[20] Where the people's voices are stifled, Soibom Momon Leima (one of the protestors) explained, they had to adopt a different strategy: "[The Army] had their weapons, we only had our bodies.... Together the mothers gave a war cry."[21] The war cry draws attention to the vulnerability of the women's bodies amid the extraordinary ordinariness of sexual violence in the region, such that the women may well walk in the streets naked. It also makes those bodies visible in a very disembodied discourse of democratic political participation. In discussions of democracy, "political voices" usually refers to "discursive speech, analytic or reasoned discourse," writes Laura Kunreuther. "Other forms of political utterance, sound, or even noise—voices shouting, collective chanting ... active performance of silence" are sounds that are produced collectively. These do not depend on a single speaker and rarely register as democratic participation.[22] The spectacle of pain and resilience caught national and international attention by giving human face to a region that had thus far been represented as a mix of touristy exoticism and necessary violence. Standing at the army base—which is effectively the seat of governmental power in the region—the women made visible the link between their naked bodies and the violent national body.

The banner that dared the "Indian Army [to] Rape Us" barely concealed the women's bodies. It presents the limit point of the representational language of democracy that the army personnel cannot risk breaching. The English language and the Roman script have a favorable position in Northeast India because of its relation with religion and other tribal languages. Nandana Dutta writes that intense missionary activity, especially in education, resulted in English proficiency.[23] Arkotong Longkumer's research on the American Baptist mission in Nagaland shows how the Baptist mission's philosophy on education led to the rise of a sense of "national community" among the Nagas.[24] In her introduction to the *Oxford Anthology of Writings from Northeast India* (volumes 1 and 2), Tilottama Misra also describes the different political valence of English in the region.

If there is a hegemonic language in the region, it is not English but Assamese. If there is any threat from a "foreign" language, it is not from English but from the neighboring Chinese. To fight "Indianization," insurgent groups order bans on Hindi language films and television channels. Indeed, it is more likely to find Korean films and shows in the region than Bollywood films. However, English is also the substantive language of nationalism and democracy that the Northeast is expected to parrot. Linguistically diverse regions like Manipur are precisely the parts of India in whose name English was legislated as India's associate official language. In the banner, doused in a bloody hue, the English language is turned in on itself as it calls out the impunity of the army. Removing the banner—and exposing the nudity of the women—is far riskier for the army and the state than for the women themselves. It would call attention to the hypocrisy of a democratic state that seeks to represent the people. The ensuing shame would be theirs and not that of the women.

The slogan that the women raise—"Indian Army Rape Us. We are all Manorama's Mothers"—transforms the protest from a dissenting voice *within* democracy to one that invalidates its power. Like voting, a protest is a means of democratic participation. But, as the Meira Paibis sound the literal (English) and figurative (protest) language of democracy, they make audible its violence and insufficiency. The women challenge the army and state personnel to do in broad daylight exactly what they have been doing to the people of the region. Their slogans bring attention to the covert and cowardly operations of the army. Their voices jar the metaphorical and literal language of the democratic state by foregrounding the pained bodies that make it heard. Once the women raise their slogans, they are no longer asking that the state redress their grievances; they are at war with the state itself. When the Meira Paibis shout the English language slogans that simply state back the crimes of the army, their repetition constitutes an effective response to the brutality of the military-state apparatus.

Yet, the women do not exactly respond by literally dissenting. Instead, they state a fact and stage a mock affirmation—yes, rape us. In doing so, the Meira Paibis conjure a kind of "autistic voice that lurks in the shadow of humanistic language and overturns the axioms of humanitarian recognition."[25] In her study of documentary voice, Pooja Rangan has argued that figures like the autistic blogger Amanda Baggs produce a critical counterdiscourse of the voice that stages "compelling critique of humanitarian notions of having and giving a voice.... Rather than capitulating to the humanitarian call to 'speak out' or 'come to voice,' these writers redefine voice as something that is not oriented exclusively toward the human, as it is understood in the logocentric tradition."²⁶ Similarly, by inserting themselves in the language order that has denied people like them subjectivity, by repeating the language without always accepting its violence, the women not only defy the army but also the proper language of dissent that they are expected to use.

The political voice of the "Mothers of Manorama" draws its power from the affective and embodied character of their phonological voice. In the Meira Paibis's telling, the protest was a felt compulsion. "At first," remembers Gyaneshwari, another one of the protestors, "we all just sat and cried."²⁷ The women also recall crying through the night before the protest and not being able to sleep. Their act of baring bodies and shouting slogans turns the women's inner *felt* compulsion outward. Their maternal rage and grief offer a pointed contrast to the toxic masculinity of the army and the paternalism of the postcolonial state. While their nudity heightens the immediacy attributed to the spoken, the banner—barely adequate—demonstrates the trauma of equivalences forged between different linguistic orders. If a mother tongue is supposed to consolidate imagined collectivities, the Meira Paibis's literal sounding of the English language, in fact, shreds the national imaginary. The affirmation of the people's right to live is not a *demand* one can make of the state. It is an especially difficult message to register when the state does not acknowledge your existence. By speaking as mothers, the women are able to assume an unavailable subject position. Their lack of English unmakes the English language of their subjection.

A Language of Protest: Mahasweta Devi and Arundhati Roy

While the Meira Paibis have insisted that the protest was not a planned operation but a spontaneous outpouring of emotion, their own interviews elsewhere belie this idea. In *The Mothers of Manipur: Twelve Women Who Made History* (2017), Teresa Rehman recreates the women's deliberations prior to the protest to suggest that its seed likely lay in a "radical idea" pitched by one of them, who "remember[ed] seeing a photograph of a nude male protester in a magazine once and wonder[ed] if they [could] do something similar."²⁸ This photo is likely from Manipuri theater director and playwright Oja Heisnam Kanhailal's staging of Mahasweta Devi's Bengali short story, "Draupadi" (1981) in Imphal. Like the rest of Kanhailal's oeuvre, this play also sought a language of the body to give form to the political suffering of the Manipuri people. Deepti Misri has read the Meira Paibis's protest as a citation of Kanhailal's play, which she argues "imports the willfully naked figure of the raped Draupadi into the political framework of counterinsurgency state terrorism in Manipur."²⁹ The reason why the women would hesitate to claim the protest as a political strategy is clear. Nevertheless, the spectacular force of the Meira Paibis's actions is only enhanced by its resonance with global protests such as Las Madres de la Plaza de Mayo during Argentina's "Dirty War." Resonating through a global vocabulary of protest, English emerges as a language of revolution. These contestatory meanings of English as a language of international wars are sounded in the precariat's attempts to live in and through it.

Devi's story also offers a powerful literary example of the orality and vernacularity of English. It is set against the Naxalite movement, a peasant insurgent rebellion in the late 1960s in the Naxalbari region of the Indian state of West Bengal. Lower-caste cultivators rebelled against upper-caste feudal landowners to protest their economic and sexual exploitation. The story follows a couple from the Santhal tribe, Dopdi Mejhen and Dhulna Majhi; Dhulna has murdered a wealthy landlord. The Special Forces use Dhulna's corpse as bait to capture Draupadi, who is also known as Dopdi. The ensuing struggle between the state and its others plays out on the terrain of language. Led by Senanayak—a government specialist "in combat and extreme-Left politics"[30]—the men of the forces know neither the people of the area nor their language. They puzzle over the tribal language for efficient ways to apprehend their "target" and are shown consulting the army handbook often. English words appear in italics in the translation to show that they, in fact, also appear transliterated in the original Bengali version. Gayatri Chakravorty Spivak's translation stages these English words by italicizing them, conjuring the theatrical nature of the state-military apparatus. The English-language vocabulary used by the Senanayak—evident in words like "target"—reflects the Special Forces' criminalization and objectification of the tribal people they wish to discipline. In the unequal conversation between the state and its people, Senanayak instructs his men to "make" Dopdi reveal information about the peasants' uprising and modes of organization. The expression "make her" appears a few times in the English language in the story. As part of the militaryspeak for torture, it translates to Dopdi's rape by the Special Forces men.

Still, the story of Dopdi is a story of unexpected defiance in the face of state violence. Refusing to be shamed by her multiple rapes, her bleeding vagina, and bruised breasts, Dopdi throws the last bit of cloth off her body when she is being taken to the leader of the Special Forces. The men who had raped her the night before are scandalized by Dopdi's naked and wounded body. They insist that she wear some clothes to look respectable enough to be presented to their leader. Dopdi responds to their flustered commands by not acknowledging any shame in being naked. Dopdi's protest, like the Meira Paibis's, refuses to accept the meanings of the state's language and of her own naked body. Both Dopdi and the Meira Paibis, thus, invalidate the state's power by neither recognizing it nor seeking accommodation in it.

Shaking with laughter, Dopdi "wipes the blood on her palm and says in a voice that is as terrifying, sky splitting, and sharp as her ululation, What's the use of clothes? You can strip me, but how can you clothe me again? Are you a man? . . . There isn't a man here that I should be ashamed of. I will not let you put my cloth on me. What more can you do? Come on, *counter* me-come on, *counter* me-? Draupadi pushes Senanayak with her two mangled breasts, and for the first time Senanayak is afraid to stand before an unarmed *target*, terribly afraid."[31] Much like the Meira Paibis's use of the English language slogan, Dopdi's use of the English word "counter" and Devi's use of the English word "target" are awe-inspiring. They demand a redefinition of notions of governance, masculinity, and power. These visceral linguistic formations defy the corporal violence of the state's linguistic and political vocabulary as it insists on "making" the people do their bidding. By turning the language of torture back toward the army, Dopdi literally reaches the point of abjection where she has nothing more that can be taken from her.

In the translator's preface, Gayatri Chakravorty Spivak argues that the knowledge of English, often thought of as political privilege, in fact stands in the way of "a deconstructive practice of language—using it 'correctly' through a political displacement, or operating the language of the other side."[32] Had Dopdi been well versed in the language, her words would not have had the same effect. It is her *lack* of English that enables a critique of English as the "language of war—offense and defense . . . that nameless and heterogeneous world language."[33] Dopdi's use of English is a use of English through political displacement, through its appropriation in a different political discourse. Spivak's italicization of English-language words spoken by Dopdi stages them as semantically different from the rest of the English-language translation. To the extent that there is a consensus on what words such as "target" and "counter" mean, Dopdi's use of those words and Senanayak's earlier invocation overlap.

But, there's more—in Senanayak's speech, the words are part of a military-state vocabulary and its attitude towards its subjects. In Dopdi's performance, the words constitute a taunt that takes power away from the state. Dopdi's use of the English words "counter" and "target" are preceded by her unexpected laughter and sky-splitting ululation. It is her lack of shame about her lack of English that is important. English words are made meaningful through Dopdi's bruised and violated body. The vocalities of laughter and ululation fly in the face of the humiliation that is expected of a "rape victim." Effectively, the language that Dopdi and the Meira Paibis use is not the English of the army. These two disparate political acts must be named as separate to nuance what is read under the sign of English in postcolonial India.

As if to distinguish this English language transformed in and as the site of resistance, Arundhati Roy's *The Ministry of Utmost Happiness* (2017) features a separate dictionary for it. The novel focuses on the region of Kashmir, where the language of war, state violence, and governmentality is English, just as in the Northeast. Tilo, one of the characters, compiles within the pages of the novel a Kashmiri-English dictionary that associates all the letters of the English alphabet with terms that are meaningful in the military siege of Kashmir. This improvised lexicon glosses terms from English and the Hindi/Urdu/Kashmiri languages, according to the meanings they have in the lived reality of the people of Kashmir. The former category includes words like "army," "bullet," "curfew," "disappeared," "encounter," "fake encounter," and so on. The latter category includes words like *azadi* (meaning freedom), *jihad* (meaning struggle), and *zulm* (meaning oppression), as Roy acknowledges the values of those fighting for freedom from the imperialist state.

In a region where people, but especially Kashmiri Muslims, are targets before they are citizens, Tilo's dictionary gathers the knowledge they need to live their daily lives. Far from the philologist's ossified dictionary or the Hindi-English dictionaries of the Commission for Scientific and Technical Terminology discussed in chapter 1, Tilo's dictionary is vital like the spoken word, as she records the transformation *of* language and transformation *in* language. In the dictionary, she makes sense of life in Kashmir and also begins to name the trauma. The rest of the novel also features words like "'neutralize' attack" and "seek 'permission'" within air quotes, to highlight that the meanings of language in Kashmir are not the same as its meanings elsewhere. The equivalences forged in the dictionary, still in the Roman script and the English language via transliteration, transform English from a language of control to a language of resistance.

Tilo's personal archive, dotted with doodles, serves as metonymy for *The Ministry of Utmost Happiness*. The novel itself translates and transliterates many Urdu-language words and poetries within its text. Urdu is relegated to a "minority language" in the Indian Constitution, and its speakers are read as Muslims and so necessarily anti-(Hindu) India. The concurrence of English and Urdu languages makes the novel into a politically charged site where Roy establishes a commensurability between them. As English translates Urdu, it not only bears witness to the damage done to its speakers by the state and by state violence; it also stages a dialogue between them. The appearance of English and Urdu together interrupts the heterolinguistic catachresis of Hindi and English in the Indian Constitution, in which the meaning of the English words used is deflected to Hindi, and the meaning of the Hindi words to English. The novel, like the dictionary, forges a language that offers a "way of binding together worlds that have been ripped apart." This quest for language was something that impeded Roy's return to fiction after the larger-than-life success of *The God of Small Things*, where English words are pelted like stones. In the essay "What Is the Morally Appropriate Language in Which to Think and Write?" (2018), Roy writes that she wanted to "find a language to tell the story I want to tell. By language, I don't mean English, Hindi, Urdu, Malayalam, of course. I mean something else. A way of binding together worlds that have been ripped apart."[34] Unlike the playful language of *The God of Small Things*, which was told from the perspective of children, here we have an omniscient and first-person narrator, who tells the story in English and a transliterated idiom with Urdu. This lexicographical gesture in *The Ministry of Utmost Happiness* is as much in the interest of realism (*language as it is*) as in the interest of arriving at language as a locus of witnessing the sundered worlds (*look, what has been done!*) in which Roy's characters now find themselves. The Meira Paibis, Dopdi, and Tilo all activate a comparable mode of English. They acknowledge that the language is weaponized by the state in times of terror, and respond to that language by estranging it further.

Sonic English and the Aesthetics of Witness in Literature from Northeast India

English literature from Northeast India sounds the English language in yet-unheard ways to bear witness to ordinary life in the state of siege in the region. Many of the stories feature characters who are killed, or characters who are or go missing. The literary language does not restore with an overabundance of dialogues the literal or figurative voice robbed by dehumanizing violence. Amit R. Baishya observes a preponderance of figures or materializations of nonhuman entities and of disabled characters in contemporary literature from the Northeast India. He argues that forms of disability offer "ordinary modes of survival, endurance and agency through which figurations of life escape, endure and survive beyond the constrictions imposed by necropower."[35] The aphasia of literary figures creates the effect of hollowing language out to convey with immediacy the sounds of human suffering and military violence. Literary critic Robin Ngangom has called this sonic hyperrealism of literature from Northeast India an aesthetic of witness and an aesthetic of survival.

Across contemporary Manipuri literature in particular and literature from the northeastern states broadly, writers have produced distinctly sound-based literary worlds of violence, humiliation, and trauma to capture the experience of everyday bodily and psychic violence. Much of Northeast literature is characterized by a very discernible interplay of sound and soundlessness, of silence, gunshots, cries, and folk singing, all of which are reported by a nondiegetic or a heterodiegetic narrator who belongs to the community. This limited third-person narration sees and hears everything but is not privy to the inner thoughts of the characters. Many literary works altogether lack verbal dialogues or reported speech, often because the characters they feature no longer exist. Instead, they teem with pre- and postlinguistic vocalities that strain against the verbal limitations of English as the linguistic medium. Ironically, to speak the unspeakable physical and psychic pains of life in a war zone, many literary works eschew verbal orality.

In the absence of an adequate language to represent pain, nonverbal sounds are the locus of ethical witnessing. These nonverbal sounds make English literature from Northeast India uniquely Anglophonic, as these literary texts begin in the *absence* or the repudiation of language. The Northeast Indian English-language literary work is an echolalic or antiphrastic repetition of language—both English and humanitarian—that challenges the authority of any narrator or literary work to actually represent the trauma. Its repetition of sounds offers a political commentary precisely by *not* commenting and by simply relaying the horror and the absurdity of the situation. The abundance of sensory details in the literature produces linguistic meaning through affect and embodiment. The cacophony of sound and silence—while influenced by oral cultures—is not orature, but forges a comparable register of estrangement and intimacy. In a deviation from the contemporary Anglophone novel as born translated, these literary works neither describe nor narrate other languages. Anglophone literature here is surprisingly *localized*. While it certainly begins elsewhere, that elsewhere is not linguistic in the traditional sense.

For instance, Yumlembam Ibomcha's short story "Nightmare" (1990) uses an overpowering crescendo of muteness to articulate the dehumanization of life in Manipur.[36] The story opens with a young girl watching army personnel harass her father by asking him to make animal sounds.

The humiliation of the father as he is asked to sound his nonhumanity takes an even more gruesome turn when the army men cut off his tongue. The daughter watches in helplessness and anguish. Before she can report or decry the harassment, the army men gag her mouth as well. The father and daughter are both unvoiced, completing, one would assume, their abject desubjectivization. But the horror does not end here. Ibomcha's story builds the progressive annihilation of the subject. The army men bury the father alive, forcing the daughter to wordlessly witness the traumatic sight. The daughter's inability to breathe or say something or to even cry is the horrific (and literal) nightmare for which even the title has not sufficiently prepared us. The release only comes when the daughter wakes up and sobs loudly with her mother to mourn the absence of the father. In their waking life, neither of them knows what happened to him. The story names both the pain of physical torture as well as the psychic trauma resulting from not knowing and from not being able to bear witness to that torture.

Starting with the father's glossectomy, the literal absence of voice is not compensated by verbal language. In fact, with its nonverbal and prelinguistic testimony, the powerful act of crying challenges the humanistic valuation of having language. Still, it is actually through the act of describing that crying, through linguistically mediated sounds, that the girl can respond in some way to the trauma of watching her father be buried alive. The moral and ethical imperative to make visible the daily tragedies in the postcolonial state empties the English language to resound the daughter's cry. The site of resistance, of reclamation of any modicum of agency, is not a romanticized dubious mother tongue—or, indeed English as the language of humanitarian recognition—but a deeply phonic experience of English available in translation from Meitelon.

Like Ibomcha's story, Temsula Ao's stories also create ambient soundscapes as it searches for a literary language to capture the pain that belongs to others. Along with Easterine Kire and Monalisa Changkija, Ao is one of the most well-known contemporary English writers from Northeast India. Her writing is influenced by her ethnographic work of recording the oral traditions of her community, the people of the Ao Naga tribe. Ao's short-story collection, *These Hills Called Home: Stories from a War Zone* (2005), is a part of a culture of "postmemory." Marianne Hirsch defined "postmemory" as "the relationship that the 'generation after' bears to the personal, collective, and cultural trauma of those who came before," to experiences that "were transmitted to them so deeply and affectively as to seem to constitute memories in their own right."[37] *These Hills Called*

Home includes a number of stories that remember the violence in the 1950s during Nagaland's demand for independence from the Indian state and to reclaim the land before it was ravaged by state violence. Ao opens the collection with the preface "Lest We Forget," which situates the stories as an attempt to "re-visit the lives of those people whose pain has so far gone unmentioned and unacknowledged."[38]

I examine two of Ao's stories—"Soaba" and "The Last Song." In both stories, the narrative highlights nonverbal vocalities when faced with protagonists who either cannot speak or refuse to do so. While this focus on the nonverbal can seem like a phonocentric overvaluation of the oral, it serves to push the linguistic medium at hand to acknowledge, accommodate, and express the trauma of "those scarred in mind and soul."[39] Nonverbal sounds of confusion, horror, or resilience voice contestation in the absence of a "linguistic vocabulary" of protest, and affirm the subjecthood of those whose very identity is under attack.

The story "Soaba" explicitly sets up a contrast between the "lack" of language of the eponymous town orphan and the linguistic surplus of the war zone. The narrator describes Soaba as "slow in the head" and his speech style as "incoherent."[40] As someone who is likely on the autism spectrum, Soaba mainly expresses his feelings through grunts and screams. His vocabulary consists of simple sentences like "I am hungry," "Give me more" and at times loud screams of "No, don't do that."[41] His language seems deficient, as ordinary words like "situation" (for the political situation), "errant" (for an incompatible political position), and "fight" (for independence from the Indian state) acquire new meanings in the conflict between the Indian state and underground armies in Nagaland. In a divisive political situation, one's loyalties and language are both life-and-death decisions, resulting in new terms to distinguish the self from the other and to label political affiliations. For instance, the atmosphere of distrust necessitates "Home Guards," referring to a group of entrepreneurial locals without affiliation with the separatists, who spy on the state for money.[42] As in "Draupadi," the Indian state, which knows neither the land nor the people it seeks to control, invents new words like "curfew" and "traitor" to objectify the former and criminalize the latter. In fact, as I write, "sedition" and "antinational" are two other words in the contemporary mainstream Indian political context that criminalize dissent.

Soaba reacts strongly and visibly to this transformation of language around him. Many of the sounds he hears—gunshots, people yelling, motor vehicles zipping around—are acousmatic sounds, in the sense that they are heard by Soaba without his knowing or fathoming the source.

Michel Chion has argued that an acousmatic voice "evokes archaic and dramatic psychic vulnerabilities for the spectating subject, including those associated with the mother's unseen voice."[43] Indeed, the first time Soaba hears a squad vehicle scream past him, he becomes obsessed with it. He spends more and more time outside the squad leader's house, where he first hears the sound. As the squad leader tortures and interrogates a "traitor," Soaba, who is standing outside, mishears the phrase "stupid bastard" as "supiba." Obsessed with the sound, Soaba insists that people call him that. In mishearing, the words "stupid, bastard"—like the sounds of squad vehicles zipping by—migrate from an economy of torture to one of desire. Soaba's attempt to vocalize the English language—through hearing and mishearing—is similar to the primary scene of learning where the mother gives the child language. It establishes, perhaps more effectively, the coercive logic of language learning. In Soaba's case, there is no such mother, and the language that he hears is the violent language of torture as the state clamps down on its subjects. The heartless yelling of the squad leader, in place of the dulcet sounds of a mother, is ironic, because in Kittler's assessment, it is the mother's voice that drowns out the ideological workings of the state (here represented by the squad leader).

Soaba's fascination with words that are yelled by the squad leader draws him to his unfortunate death. Following the sounds he hears and desires, Soaba finds himself between the squad leader and the "traitor" he wants to shoot. Thus, Soaba literally intercepts the meaning of the language employed by the squad leader. Arguably, Soaba's vulnerability in the story arises from *his* personal language, which situates him at odds with language in a normative and verbal sense. In a world being claimed by warring factions, words themselves are divided, and language does not quite mean what it is supposed to mean. Soaba typifies a yearning for relations that are not linguistically mediated. His prelinguistic sounds offer what Pooja Rangan has called an "autistic counterdiscourse" that contrasts with the treachery of language. Soaba's fate inspires in the reader a distrust of verbal language as it is remapped in the struggle between the state and the insurgents against it.

Soaba's story sounds the English of the literary work through his prelinguistic sounds. By contrast, another of Ao's stories, "The Last Song," does so through its protagonist Apenyo's postlinguistic vocalities. Singing emerges as a sound of resistance and survival, a means to reclaiming agency. On the day that Apenyo's church is planning the dedication of a new church building, the Indian Army storms their way in to penalize the people for paying "taxes" to an underground government. As if on cue,

Apenyo—now the lead soprano of the choir—breaks into a song. As she is joined by the choir, the army officers read these sonic acts as acts of defiance that deserve "proper retaliation."[44] The army shoots and clubs the villagers at the gathering, but Apenyo keeps singing "as if to withstand the might of the guns with her voice raised to God in heaven."[45] The narrative suggests that it is not *what* Apenyo is humming—its linguistic meanings— but the very fact that she is singing that is powerful. Apenyo's voice does not obviously fight the perpetrators of violence. Instead, the narrator informs us, she invites the witness of god by singing. Apenyo sings even when the army men gang-rape her and her mother.

Indeed, Apenyo's singing does not even end when she and her mother are left to die. In contrast to her singing, Apenyo and her mother receive a "somber and songless funeral," while the army officer who raped Apenyo remains traumatized by the tune she sang as he "rammed himself into her virgin body, while all throughout, the girl's unseeing eyes were fixed on his face."[46] Apenyo's resistance does not arise from the words that she speaks. Indeed, she says nothing. Her quiet resistance is made possible by the embodied and affective aspects of her vocalization as she stares fixedly at the army men who rape her, demanding that they acknowledge her humanity. In the chaos of the army attack, Apenyo and her mother raise and claim their voice by singing and screaming. While the somber and songless funeral attempts to silence the women once and for all, their voices rise through memory and orality, as mediated in the English-language story.

It is the *description* of Apenyo's singing that inflects the English language of the narrative. In fiction, the language associated with violence is forced to operate on a different register and "speak" the voice of the unvoiced. The postscript of the story acknowledges the influence of the oral tradition of storytelling, a tradition that also seeks to memorialize the pain of a community for the community. In a world where forgetting is catastrophic, orality keeps historical memory alive. As the dominant literary medium in the region, the English language thus also becomes a site of remembering and unforgetting. The proposition to remember or remember in English is striking. As discussed earlier, in chapter 1, it is only by forgetting the colonial origins of English in India that it could be adopted as a viable language of the state. Indeed, in continued justifications of English, it is only by a daily plebiscite that its colonial formation is kept in abeyance. This new orality of literature—its surprising Anglophony—disrupts dominant relations to English as well as forms of representation to apprehend the precariousness of life.

At the end of story, in a postscript that is staged as an oral storytelling, an old woman tells her young skeptical audience about a hymn that originates from the graveyard on certain nights. "She tells them that youngsters of today have forgotten how to listen to the voice of the earth and the wind."[47] When they strain their ears, the young audience members catch "the low hum in the distance." They try again and can hear Apenyo's last song; the storyteller hums it herself. "Thus on a cold December night in a remote village, an old storyteller gathers the young of the land around the leaping flames of a hearth and squats on the bare earth among them to pass on the story of that Black Sunday when a young and beautiful singer sang her last song even as one more Naga village began weeping for her ravaged and ruined children."[48] As in Ibomcha's story earlier, the authority of the fictional world is very much oral. This orality strengthens the community, connects with nature, carries the memory of times and people past, and names the violence that has ruined the fictional world. In the process of mediating this orality, the written word itself becomes sound. Of course, any quest for immediacy, continuity, and community in language must necessarily be mediated in language. What is important here is not the possibility of that mediation. Instead, what is important is that in that mediation, the English-language work is a description or repetition, representing the unspeakability of trauma and inflecting the meaning of English in India.

In a discussion of Ao's "The Last Song," Amit Baishya notes that this story does not stage a class of orality and writing. Instead, the "dead letter of writing (the narration of Apenyo's life in the past tense) is reanimated and remembered through the vocal-aural act of oral storytelling that is added on as a supplement to the major diegetic space."[49] In this way, Baishya suggests, the story highlights the ethical imperative to listen carefully. I agree with this assessment of the story. The story, with its investment in acknowledging and witnessing the pain of those who have passed, does not reject writing in English, but, in fact, mediates that history through it and invites the audience to listen carefully.

In conflict zones across India, from Kashmir to the Northeast, the military-state apparatus has effectively recharted the territory. It has christened people and places in English as assets and targets, ironizing the mythologized and romantic autochthonous association of language with land. In discussions around indigenous language, affinity with land is often cast in positive terms as something to be recovered and preserved. Indeed, language and land have a strong relation in several literary traditions. Dante's *De vulgari eloquentia,* one of the earliest-known vernacular manifestoes, claims that regional dialects of the Italian language are distinctly shaped by the topography of the regions where they are found. In premodern India as well, *desi* and *margi* (roughly, local and global) literary traditions are distinguished by the geographical paths taken by the languages in which they are composed. As a corollary, the radical and contestatory borderland tongue explored in the work of Chicana poet and theorist Gloria Anzaldúa is also nourished by the land it straddles. Thus, those who speak from and speak for a land ravaged, prima facie, by the postcolonial state's use of the English language must also marshal the same language. In the Meira Paibis's protest, the vernacular resonances of English are clear. English assumes the most intimate relations of a people with their land, thrives in and through an oral culture of protest, and enables emancipatory aspirations. In the short stories by Ao and Ibomcha, as well as works by Mahasweta Devi and Arundhati Roy, English carries the sounds of a traumatized landscape and offers mediations of a counterhistory. Instead of conflating the language of resistance with the language of oppression, we must separate them to note the ways in which one puts pressure on the other and reflects the vernacular politics of English in postcolonial India.

CHAPTER 5

Sight

CINEMATIC ENGLISH AND THE
PLEASURES OF NOT READING

Seeing, Not Reading

"Do *you* read English?" snaps Balram Halwai as he stands by a pile of old English-language books on the sidewalk in Aravind Adiga's novel *The White Tiger*. Balram's characteristically confrontational question is a rebuff to his interlocutor—the bookseller. How dare the bookseller suggest that Balram has no business lurking around English-language books because he looks like someone who cannot read the language! This scene makes vivid what we have long known, that in postcolonial India, English shores up social distinctions and segregations. But, this snappy exchange is made more intriguing by the bookseller's brazen admission that he does not read English. Instead, he relies on the books' covers to identify them. The shared illiteracy of Balram and the bookseller levels the ground on which they stand. At the same time, it suggests a mode of reading where English becomes meaningful precisely by not being read. Literary and semantic meanings of English, of what is written, do not await unpacking by a rightful reader. Instead, the meanings of English rest, materially visible, on the surface of the book for anyone to apprehend. This act of non-reading is *jugaadu*, an act that demonstrates an entrepreneurial mindset and desire to make the most of one's available resources and know-how. It makes book covers into words, and transmutes words into the figural.

Numerous book vendors—like the one encountered by Balram—sell used and pirated English-language books in India. One such vendor, standing at another upmarket commercial address in New Delhi a mere

FIGURE 7. *Book Vendor I*. New Delhi, 2020. (Photo by the author.)

fifteen-minute drive from where Balram would have met his bookseller, was less assured about his lack of English. "अब हम लोग कैसे पढ़ सकते हैं," he had hurriedly responded when I asked him whether he read any of the books he sold. "Now, how can we read?" His rhetorical response made my question seem foolish. The pointed "how" challenged me to imagine the arguably impossible act of reading English in the face of its class and caste policing. Accordingly, when my sister and I asked him for a few titles, we had to point to what we wanted. But, surprisingly, the more well-known names like Haruki Murakami emerged without our guidance. I had wanted to ask again, how this self-professed nonreader of English knew Murakami in a stack of bestsellers, popular paperbacks, self-help bibles, and *Harry Potter*. I thought better of it, but it is a question that I turn to in this final chapter. Standing at the sidewalks of urban India—all underappreciated nodes in literary circulation—how do these real and imagined booksellers read the English-language wares they sell?

I raise this question here not to artlessly belabor the irony of the booksellers' illiteracy or their obviously loose interpretation of reading. But, I

FIGURE 8. *Book Vendor*. New Delhi, 2020. (Photo by the author.)

do want to probe the outrage and the humiliation—the shame and hope—of "how can we read" to extract the hermeneutic process that renders the English language visible in the first place: as a commodity, a literary masterpiece, or as something else entirely. Examples of booksellers who do not know English abound in Indian English literature. Imperial Book Depot in Vikram Seth's *A Suitable Boy* (1993) is run by two brothers, Yashwant and Balwant, who are "illiterate in English but so energetic and enterprising that it made no difference."[1] Rashmi Sadana traces one such bookseller as part of the economy of a "bestseller" in an eloquent discussion that opens *English Heart, Hindi Heartland*. In each example, there is a sense of irony and shock that English, English literature specifically, circulates through these paths. This is yet another instance of the salience of literacy in discussions of language and the ways in which nonacademic readers shape the meanings of language.

Today, English is an eminently readable language in the world. What we know as global English—the "simplified English" used in the software industry and prevalent in digital cultures—is called so because of the instant and universal legibility of its script, especially in digital media. This legibility is a contrast to the often-threatening illegibility of other non-European languages. Thus, *how* English is read is key to understanding the texture of its global dominance. The specifically ocular means by which the booksellers inventory their stock illuminates a visual rhetoric of the English language that constitutes English in seeing. The booksellers' reading is not conventional. It is not an act of interpretation that plumbs the depths of a text to reveal its hidden meanings. Instead, what the booksellers perform is a reading by nonreading that still renders the English language meaningful. Crowding in plain sight across sidewalks of urban India are not only junctures in global circulation but also networks of literary and linguistic meaning.

We have encountered the visual rhetoric of English in earlier chapters. The physical shape, form, and appearance of English have been "read" many times over. As brand names in *The White Tiger* or as text on the government poster in *Raag Darbari*, English words and phrases have been intelligible even to those who cannot read the language. As Modi's suit, English—or rather, the Roman script that, in India, is often associated with English—achieves visible form in mundane objects where its possession promises to confer elevation in race, class, and caste. Depending on where and how one *sees* it, what one *sees in* it, the English language has been abstracted in such a way as to stand for British colonialism and Indian bureaucracy, for oppression and freedom, for privilege and deprivation, for transgression and opportunity. These contradictory and concurrent meanings do not belong to the order of figuration. They are also not made accessible through a discursive knowledge of the language. Rather, the vernacular of English is legible to those people who—often passively and perforce—see the language as depthless, impenetrable, opaque, and repetitive.

Much of the reading of English today is really of the order of seeing. The presence of the Roman script—in digital transliterations or advertising—is apprehended primarily by sight, where it may not even be understood as the English language but visually apprehended as images. This transmutation is ironic because the colonial philological dichotomy of the rational Western discourse and the Oriental language is inverted as English—the rational language of the British Empire—is made into and read as a hieroglyph. Historically, Asiatic languages have been denied the status of language, reduced to pictograms or hieroglyphs. However, in the booksellers' compulsory reading, for instance, it is English that is understood visually and parsed through a visual vocabulary.

The universal translatability of English is global English. However, in seeing and not reading it, global English is itself richly encoded as a sight, a thing to see. Rita Raley has shown that transliterability of languages into the Roman script of English is actually one of its defining features that accounts for the hegemony of English in the world. It can be argued that the expansion of digital worlds does not strengthen the visual dominance of English but confounds and reauthorizes its meanings. The phonetic script of English has made it possible to encode other languages in it. As other languages are read in "English," which is to say the Roman script, by way of transliteration, English as a language recedes from the scene. The Roman script of English does not standardize and consolidate its hegemony. Even if the Roman script is not in fact English per se—text transliterated in the Roman script in India would be read as English. To build upon Michael Allan's examination of photographs of hieroglyphs in the essay "Picturing Other Languages" (2019), the encounter between cinema and language can illuminate the transmediality of language and destabilize not only the fantasy of monolingualism but also the fantasy of monomedium. Indeed, Lydia Liu has shown that the space key was the nonphonetic invention that made the reading of English possible and produced written text as an image.[2]

The global spread of English has led to anxieties about the destruction of other languages as well as the depletion of English itself. In *The Fall of Language in the Age of English*, Minae Mizumura argues that the growing spread of English is destroying Japanese literary culture and exhorts the government of Japan (and those of other countries and literary cultures similarly threatened) to establish strict policies to counter it. By contrast, David Damrosch in *What Is World Literature?* (2003) deplores the dampening of the linguistic richness of English. While Mizumura is concerned with the dilution of the languages that English comes into contact with, Damrosch is concerned about English itself. These apparently contradictory viewpoints not only perpetuate the jingoism of national languages, even though that language is threatened, but also fail to imagine moments of resistance or creative interaction between two languages. Instead of a deathly linguistic homogenization, we see a kaleidoscopic—a *cinematic*— proliferation of linguistic discourse.[3] In *The Sonic Color Line: Race and the Cultural Politics of Listening* (2016), Jennifer Stoever draws upon Kara Keeling's theorization of "the cinematic" as "a complicated aggregate of capitalist social relations, sensory motor arrangements, and cognitive processes" that are "at once political, material, sensory, affective, and bodily." Stoever uses "cinematic" to draw out the history of the materiality of technology as it related to the sensory politics flowing from and in tension with the (Black) body. I find "cinematic" productive as way to explore how the materiality of the film produces the materiality of the English language. Simultaneously, the cinematic also offers a reading practice that complements the ethnographic impulse of linguistic study that connects literary English to its lived experience beyond the screen.

How does the English language become visible, and what does it make visible? Following D. N. Rodowick in *Reading the Figural or, Philosophy after New Media* (2001), I use "visible" to mean that which is perceptible by sight as well as that which underwrites the conditions of visibility and legibility. The Roman script is the English language in this formulation even though in case of transliteration the language that is encoded might be very different from English. How can we elaborate a practice of reading that accounts for the ubiquity of English as a *sight?* In what follows, I turn to the audiovisual archive of film to propose cinematic signification as a point of departure for reading English in India today. Films reprise the lived experience of the English language in India by foregrounding and making inevitable the expectation of coercive mimeticism (the societal expectation that people within specific ethnic groups will "perform" their ethnic identity). With the visible world as their building block, films situate us first and foremost as their spectators. The logic of cinematic signification places image, text, and sound without according precedence to any of these. It thus reflects the circulation and objectification of English itself as a sight and sound that we have encountered many times over in the book. The realist claims of film in the image before the camera, in the narrative worlds of the film, and in the linguistic naturalism of its dialogues conjure the circulation of English as it becomes legible to those who cannot *read* it. Encounters with film, especially Bollywood films, in India are "inscribed on everyday spaces" and actually limn the uneven chronotopes of globalization.[4] Films from and about India provide opportunities to conceptualize sites where the English language circulates beyond privileges of urbanism, class, and caste.

Lying on tarp by the sidewalk, the piles of plastic-wrapped books locate the Anglophone world in vernacular spaces. Whether or not a willing and able reader is found, what is written demands that it be read. Two recent films present similar encounters and compulsions in English: Danny Boyle's and Loveleen Thadani's multiple-Oscar-winning *Slumdog Millionaire* (2008) and Zoya Akhtar's *Gully Boy* (2019, trans. *Boy from the Streets*). Set in Dharavi, one of the world's largest slums, located in Mumbai, the two films cinematically produce the slums as metonymy for India in the twenty-first century. With actual slum children as cast (*Slumdog*) and the actual slum as location (*Gully Boy*) both films strengthen the ontological referentiality of the filmic medium.

The films together challenge both what constitutes foreignness in film as well as the elements (song, language, location) that make Bollywood a globally legible category. *Slumdog*, a British film, was directed by a British director, adapted from the Indian novel *Q & A* (2005), filmed in India, inspired by Hindi films, and distributed by major media conglomerates the world over. *Gully Boy* was shot in Mumbai, was likely based on Eminem's *8 Mile* (2002), was produced and distributed by an Indian company, was executive produced by rapper Nas, and includes an eighteen-song soundtrack by fifty-four musical artists from India and abroad. While produced in different film industries, both films straddle the conventional world of Bollywood and global industries of production. For instance, *Slumdog* adopts the formal conventions and actors of Bollywood.[5] *Gully Boy*, despite its big-ticket Bollywood cast, conspicuously lacks many of the conventions of a Bollywood musical drama that *Slumdog Millionaire* boasts. *Slumdog* won eight Academy Awards (competing in the open category at the Oscars). *Gully Boy* was India's official entry to the Best International Feature Film category at the 92nd Academy Awards.

Slumdog Millionaire and *Gully Boy* fuel the tales of social ascent with, respectively, acts of nonreading and writing English. *Slumdog* tells the story of Jamal Malik, a young man from the slums who wins a popular trivia game show. *Gully Boy*'s Murad is also a young man from the slums, who becomes a successful rapper. Both films are located in the primarily vocal worlds of call centers and global hip hop. However, the act of speaking English is in tension with the sights of English, as speaking and seeing activate different representational and agential possibilities. The literal knowledge of English is either absent or deeply ineffective, and both films elaborate meaning through the mutual transmutability of denotative and figurative orders of sound, script, and image of English. *Slumdog* evokes the trope of the written text-as-image as being fated because all written instances of English, that the protagonist at best apprehends as hieroglyphs, prove to be useful information. This cinematic English also secures the film's association with the capitalist global order of brand names and currencies as the capitalist world emerges as inescapable. *Gully Boy* centers writing as the affectively charged act of narrative control. Reading and writing as modes of knowing resignify the abjection of the protagonists' slum life in urban India into their personal worth and fulfilment.

While the films share their location and a commitment to rags-to-riches stories, they present two different ways out of slum life. Murad Ahmed, the protagonist of *Gully Boy*, claims in a song that he does not want to become a slumdog millionaire (*nahin banna mujhe slumdog millionaire* / नहीं बनना मुझे स्लमडॉग मिलियनेयर) and rejects success that is given by others. *Slumdog* emphasizes the scale of slums, featuring many panoramic and bird's-eye-view shots that mesmerize us as audience and aestheticize the characters' destitution. The film shovels chocolate to create a literal mound of shit to impart the story authenticity—what Ajay Gehlawat has called the "shit narrative"—that Jamal must navigate.[6] These images of ersatz excrement are meant to characterize the dark underbelly of a developing nation and validate to the audience of *Slumdog* the verisimilitudinal claims of the film. *Gully Boy*, on the other hand, relies on uncomfortable close-ups that create for the audience the experience of living in the constricted quarters of Mumbai slums. In contrast to the open-air landscapes of *Slumdog*, *Gully Boy* largely uses indoor light (tungsten, naked bulbs) and has fewer shots of the open sky.

Montage, or Meaning Deferred in Slumdog Millionaire

Suspenseful music and game-show graphics in tow, *Slumdog Millionaire* opens with the suggestion that the protagonist Jamal Malik's destiny is tied to the written word. On the screen is a multiple-choice question about Jamal's win. The white typography of the question glows against the dark background of a bathtub full of thousand-rupee notes. There are only three options for answers: "he cheated," "he's a genius," and "he is lucky." Soon, a fourth option—"it is written"—fades into view. This same sentence reappears at the end to confirm and guide the audience's reading of the film. The simplicity of the image—in the proverbial black and white—distills the story to its essence before it has properly begun. The idea of the "written" unites a premodern logic of destiny, in which one's fate is cast at birth, with the more recent pervasiveness of English in media and markets. For those who are unable to read the writing on the screen, the still only confirms what they have perhaps known and feared. Their destiny, like Jamal's, is tied to the English language and its graphic and imaged forms, which Jamal is able to recall in response to questions on the game show. Indeed, as an adaptation, the film is itself (pre-)written.

While the film is about the victory of the underdog and the unlettered, the very crux of the film as expressed in this sentence is available and accessible only to the audience who can read (English). Most audiences not comfortable in English would most likely have watched a dubbed version and not actually relied on the subtitles, which shifts how English is read, lending English a kaleidoscopic quality. Towards the end of the game show, the host anticipates a question about literature by asking,

FIGURE 9. "Four Options." From *Slumdog Millionaire*, dir. Danny Boyle and Loveleen Thadani, Fox Searchlight Pictures, 2008.

"Big reader are you, Jamal?" Jamal's honest and disarming response "I can read" construes reading as literacy rather than literary. Jamal either misunderstands the question or willfully misinterprets it to share the skill he does have. In doing so, he also deflects the host's snide suggestion that Jamal is not learned and so is undeserving of his success thus far in the show. However, in the larger context of the film, this statement acknowledges that his "reading" of English prepares him to answer questions even as it does not necessarily help him arrive at any substantive understanding of the language or the material.

The montage that follows the question cinematically produces Jamal's mode of reading. He is asked to name all of Dumas's musketeers. As soon as the question flashes on the screen, the film cuts to a medium shot of his friend Latika and then to an over-the-head shot of Jamal and his brother, Salim, getting whacked by the teacher. Jamal and Salim are at school. The lesson for the day is Alexandre Dumas's novel *The Three Musketeers* in an English translation. As the boys struggle to keep up with the class (to which they are already late), the camera closes in on their tiny hands urgently flipping the pages till it freezes on the title page. This page takes up the entire frame and the screen space, highlighting its importance as a reading event. But then the scene cuts to a different time in their childhood, where Jamal convinces his brother to take in Latika because she could be their third musketeer ("she could be our third musketeer," वह हमारी तीसरी मुसकेतीर बन सकती है). This montage establishes the proximity of Jamal's life to English literature (in translation), and affirms the personal register into which Jamal translates literature to make sense of it.

FIGURE 10. "It Is Written." From *Slumdog Millionaire*, dir. Danny Boyle and Loveleen Thadani, Fox Searchlight Pictures, 2008.

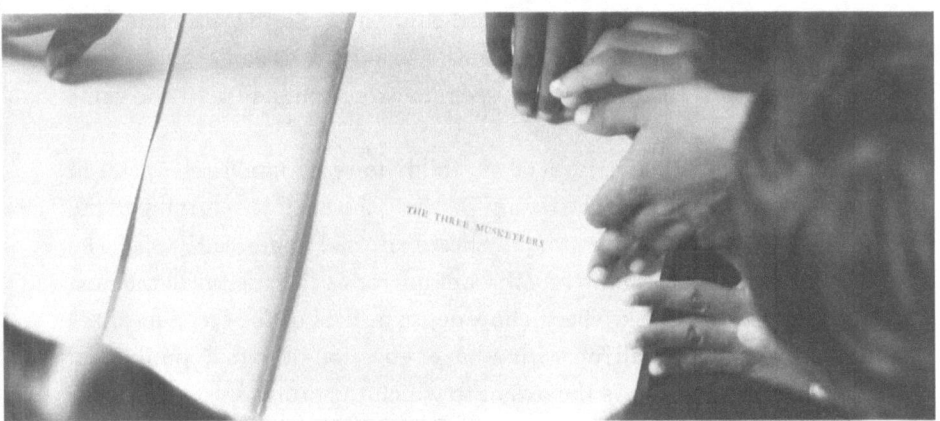

FIGURE 11. "The Three Musketeers." From *Slumdog Millionaire*, dir. Danny Boyle and Loveleen Thadani, Fox Searchlight Pictures, 2008.

The cut from the question in the studio to Latika's face establishes that, as far as Jamal is concerned, Latika is the third musketeer. He has no clue about the name of that character in the novel. Jamal uses his last "lifeline" on the show—an opportunity to phone someone who can give the answer. Knowing no one who could help him, he decides to call his estranged brother. Serendipitously (and comically), he finds on air that Latika has Salim's phone. At this point in the film, Jamal has won what he had wanted. He came on the show to get the attention of his lost love and to reach out to her. Still, reluctant to give up, he takes a stab at the answer anyway, which fortuitously turns out to be correct. Jamal's fluke answer

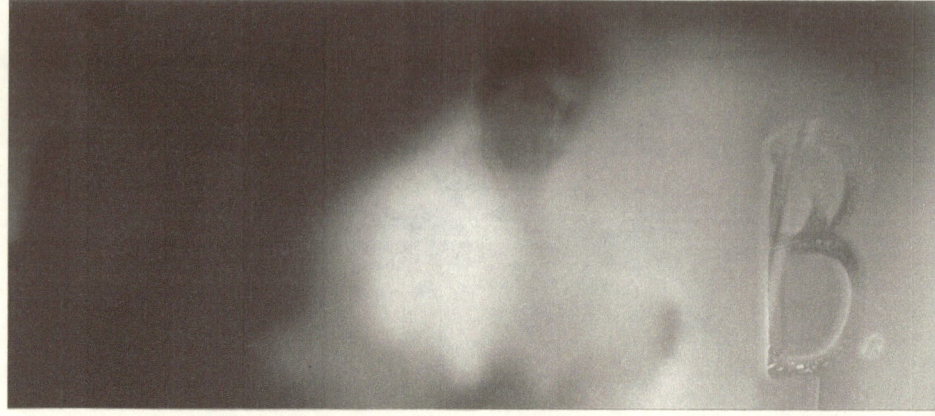

FIGURE 12. "B." From *Slumdog Millionaire*, dir. Danny Boyle and Loveleen Thadani, Fox Searchlight Pictures, 2008.

confirms what the opening scene of the film had told the spectator, "it is written." It also confirms the film's bias, which rewards Jamal for his hard life precisely because he does not seem to care about a reward and came to the show only for love.

In the cinematic portrayal of his ability to read, Jamal's character in fact undoes the script of the reality TV show. Just before returning to the studio and asking the question, the host had tried to mislead Jamal. The host traced the letter B on a bathroom mirror as the answer to the next question he would ask. The shallow depth of field of the scene focalizes the letter B on the mirror, with a hazy reflection of Jamal Malik in it. This composition shows the extent to which the protagonist's destiny—what he will "be"—is tied homophonically to a language he does not know. Jamal's initial "I can read" acknowledges also, then, the fact that he saw what the host was trying to tell him, though he may or may not act on it. "I can read" also affirms the fact that Jamal, as a middle-school dropout, can encounter texts, see English literature—although how he understands them may be quite different from how that same text might be traditionally read by those who know the language well.

The meaning of English language and literature for Jamal emerges in an interplay of different images—the sensory experience of the materiality of language—which is informed by memories of seeing those images. For each question, it is usually a *visual* memory that helps Jamal track the answer and eliminate options. In fact, for most of the questions, the flashback usually settles on an iconic or a graphic image. So when Jamal is quizzed on the geography of London, we see a sped-up flashback to the

FIGURE 13. "Dollar." From *Slumdog Millionaire*, dir. Danny Boyle and Loveleen Thadani, Fox Searchlight Pictures, 2008.

call center, the layout of which mimics the plan of the city of London. The film also shows reading as an experience of language in which one might exert senses beyond the visual. In response to one of the questions, the flashback shows Jamal's blind friend smelling, touching, and feeling a piece of paper to determine if the bill just handed to him is Indian or US currency. Once he realizes that it is indeed a dollar bill, he asks Jamal to "read" the bill for him—describe it to him—so that he can assess its dollar value. The reading of English that is remunerative is not a literal reading but one that combines tactile and olfactory modalities. The currency-like quality of written language is also clear in the episode where Salim sells a famous Bollywood actor's autograph. It foreshadows the many ways in which language and its script symbolically become tradeable like money in the film. This scene echoes the end of the film, where the words "it was written" appear against a background of a tub full of money.

Editing and cinematography augment the sensory perceptions, memories, and intersemiotic associations that synapse linguistic meaning simultaneously. The sights young Jamal takes in make little sense to him then—he barely registers them—but they become meaningful when he encounters the same words and sounds in the questions asked on the game show. Montage sequences between the questions and the unexpected paths Jamal traces to get to the answers illuminate the production of meaning for the English-language images and the English language as image. In montage, the meaning is deferred to a future event—the next shot, the next sound—rather than being inherent in what is seen in the moment. The meaning is also not the sum of the parts but is actually usually different from both. Likewise, the social, political, economic, and especially literal meanings of English become clear over time. It is not as if the written language gives meaning to images; rather, the written language itself becomes meaningful as an imaged hybrid form. By repeatedly establishing the image as something to be read, but not literally, the film highlights the poetic quality of cinema and the cinematic quality of language.

The English language of the film recedes into a graphic puzzle to be solved, whether one knows the language or not. It appears in the questions and in shots of the cities, in the writing on trains, on buildings, posters, cellphone and television screens, and on billboards. If the film privileges linguistic mediation, it also highlights the performative, temporary, and mediated quality of language. Public signages and graffiti make the city of Mumbai legible. As Jamal waits for Latika in the final scene, the camera zooms in on the plaque commemorating Fredrick W. Stevens as the colonial-era architect of the Victoria Terminus station where Jamal is sitting. The plaque is a hat tip to the city's British colonial past and to the historical landmark markers that give it identity. But, such scriptural cues also help to translate and transliterate the geopolitical scene for an international audience. They render the local languages and landscape into English for nonlocal audiences everywhere to follow.

Such a spatial organization of the English language, to borrow Ian Garwood's words from a different context, "self-consciously establishes" it as "a visually pleasurable object to the viewer."[7] As animated subtitles flit across the screen, English becomes an actor and a translator that brings pleasure to the characters and to the viewer. It is aesthetic and it aestheticizes. Subtitles, in particular, assume a life of their own. *Slumdog* moves from a static, bottom-screen, predictable placement of "subtitles as plain white lines of text tethered to the bottom of the screen" to dynamic, floating subtitles unpredictably appearing on the screen.[8] Many of the subtitles for dialogues spoken by young Jamal, Salim, and Latika appear in jewel tones against an otherwise brown-toned shot. These animated words and sentences, against the background of a squalid (and thus "real," "dirty," and "underdeveloped") India, create a powerful impression of the translational power of the English language. The jewel tones turn the English language into shiny, colorful, and precious objects that not only feel luxurious but hold immense promise of social mobility. In an interview, codirector Danny Boyle said that he wanted the subtitles, in fact, "to be read like a comic book," making the film an experience to be read as much as seen.[9] Ironically, Boyle explains that he wanted the subtitles to be easy to take in, so that the audience could *watch* the film and not *read* the subtitles. Boyle's words suggest that he wanted the image and the text to be one and not to clash with each other.

Slumdog, as a film, invites its audience not to read but to watch, as part of the moving image, what is written. It situates the Roman script as part of the figural order that disrupts the flow of meaning from text to image. The text of the subtitle does not translate the image and action but becomes a part of its audiovisual modality and the visual field. Such a hybrid written and imaged form of "figural activity," Rodowick has argued, "confounds the phonocentric model of signification ... the literal shape of writing, when inserted into the field of the image, denies any stable meaning. The shape of its lines enhances the image, but its traces of script change the narrative that is engaged."[10] In a relation that invokes the arrival of English in India, the dynamism and color of the subtitles make the English a part of the scene without drawing direct meaning from it. In this instance, it is not the externally imposed language that gives the space meaning; instead, the language becomes one with the scene.

While *Slumdog* emphasizes the written English word, it also primes its audience not to read but to see and watch that written form. In this visual experience, English approximates its familiar and iconic experiences in India: "It is both *naturalized* (everyone in the film is comfortable with it) and *elevated* (it is prized as the language of education)."[11] For audience members who know the language, this book-like organization of English subtitles only reinforces the pervasiveness of English in the postcolonial Indian milieu of the slum. The readerly quality of the film only magnifies the way in which audiences in India would be attuned to reading English around them on billboards, storefronts, advertisements, et cetera. For audience members who may not know the English language, these subtitles remind them of the visual experience of English in present-day India. The subtitles intensify the interdiction (the tragic paradox of prohibition and incitement) to read, learn, and speak the language, and in turn, also function like interactive pedagogical tools to aid that task.

As an icon, the English language also immediately points to a dominant Anglophone culture that has made inroads into the most underprivileged enclaves of urban India. As an icon, English stands for itself—as a language of global markets, media, and diplomacy. However, at the same time, as it translates the dialogues of the young slum children and occurs in their dialogues, it also becomes the most underprivileged enclave of urban India. In *Slumdog Millionaire*, the depiction of life in slums was so unsavory that several international businesses such as Mercedes-Benz and Pepsi did not want to be associated with the film, and their brand icons were concealed. In the absence of these brands, the English language itself appears as a brand. As in Modi's use of English in the "Idea of India" address mentioned in the preface, English as a brand signals desirable and aspirational values.

These two levels of meaning—as an icon and as an index—anchor the verisimilitudinal claims of *Slumdog* in a way that its English dialogue does not. Despite its tremendous critical success, many reviews from India dismissed *Slumdog* as "inauthentic" and "unrealistic." Ironically, while commercially produced films in India regularly demand a generous suspension of disbelief, *Slumdog*, a film about India, received criticism for not being realistic and accurate enough. According to these critics, it represented India in an unflattering light and was called out as slum slam and poverty porn. For the Indian audiences accustomed to Bollywood films, the portrayal of slums was shocking because it came after the gentrification of Bollywood, when, as Tejaswini Ganti writes, not only had "all signs of poor people . . . disappeared," but also "no one in the industry [wanted] to show a slum anymore" and "slum [had] become a really bad word."[12] The film was made even less compelling by its sounds. Indeed, the biggest challenge to *Slumdog* came from the English spoken in it.

The first third of the film features young Jamal and Salim, and they speak Hindi with a mix of English words like "sorry," "urgent," "time pass," "border," "customer," "time," "limit," "helicopter," "autograph," "double," and "triple." At this point, there is greater coincidence between the actors and the characters. Yet again, the use of English is strategic so that the audience not familiar with Hindi can follow, and is a means to speak to audiences outside of India. At the same time, these words—appearing in discussions of business transactions—perform a mimetic function. They show that India's openness to the world has not only brought in foreign money but also brought English as the language of global capitalism. This knowledge of English has remunerative potential. The mimetic bilingualism of the film promises an unmediated, authentic glimpse of India (remember the actors are children from the slum) that dissolves the binaries of global and local, of English and its others.

As they grow older, however, the fluent English spoken by Jamal and Salim subverts the realism of the "shit narrative." When young, the characters of Jamal and Salim evoke the figure of the *tapori* (vagabond) and are legible within that convention. The figure of the *tapori*, as it gained prominence in the 1990s, also used English as part of a noticeably mixed urban idiom of English, Hindi, and Marathi (the language spoken in the state of Maharashtra of which Mumbai is the capital). The *tapori* is often understood as a rebellious figure from the lower class who uses a characteristically urban hybrid tongue, Bambaiyya. He is "a figure of transgression" who "borrows gestures and language toward a bodily resistance in the public spaces of the city."[13]

It is when Salim and Jamal continue to live on the streets but begin to speak grammatically correct and impeccably accented English that they become confusing. At this point, the characters disrupt the way English is supposed to index class position in Hindi and other Indian-language cinema. The switch to English can be traced to the brief period when Salim and Jamal worked as tour guides at the Taj Mahal and had to extemporize in the English language to lure the richer international tourists, or perhaps when Jamal worked at the call center. This access to English would confirm the multiple language geographies of English across the world. However, even at the Taj, their knowledge of the historical site and their knowledge of English are both shaky, which lends them credibility as characters if not as tour guides. At the level of the narrative itself, it is unbelievable that from speaking falteringly in English at the Taj Mahal, Jamal speaks English so perfectly later.

What is further disconcerting, beyond the fact that Jamal speaks in English, is how he does so. The representative capacity of English is now more or less accepted in Anglophone novels but not in films, where it must be explained by privileges of class and location. The accent of a character must translate their skin color as well as their class and regional affiliation. Thus, in *Slumdog Millionaire*, the discomfort for a spectator like historian and essayist Mukul Kesavan, as he writes in "Lost in Translation," does not arise from the presence of English per se but from the fact that the language is spoken flawlessly by a young man of no education.[14] The presence of English in films demonstrates the ways in which the language is understood differently in its spoken and written forms. English spoken incorrectly by an unlettered slum dweller is not as uncanny as its grammatically correct use by the same figure. Indeed, this uncanniness comes down to the character's lack of formal education, which was precisely also the factor that delegitimized the narratives of low-caste and low-class characters like Balram Halwai in *The White Tiger*, discussed in chapter 3. It is because Jamal did not complete his formal education—not even through the informal means available to the protagonist in the original novel—that his portrayal risks appearing unforgivably unrealistic.

The spoken word appears de-emphasized and invalidated as it clashes with the visual order of meaning. For instance, the call center scenes—where Jamal works when he goes on the quiz show—may be the most glorified site of interpellation into a global economy of cheap international labor. Rey Chow has called the offshore call center "the scene of literal calling and vocation, [which] embed[s] in its smooth operability the memory of that earlier scene, whereby the colonized were recruited into the ideological state apparatus that was English."[15] But, if the call center evokes the memory of Thomas Babington Macaulay's 1835 "Minute on Indian Education," in *Slumdog Millionaire*, Jamal's interpellation is aborted and incomplete. When another employee slips away for a break, Jamal takes a call for him and, per Althusser's example of interpellation, finds himself responding to the "hey" from the other side. While Jamal is able to improvise a little bit and talk to the customer (thus, not lose the call), he is shown to be comically ill equipped to actually help. Instead, once the caller irately disconnects the call, Jamal uses that opportunity to look up his brother, with whom he has lost contact. Ironically, Jamal uses his knowledge from the call center not to serve the callers or the business but himself—by locating his brother and later by answering questions about British culture on the quiz show. Once again, as in the case of Macaulay, Jamal's "education" in English is not a deep immersion into another culture. It is only as a matter of picking up enough trivia and knowledge that Jamal is, for practical purposes, both English and not English.

The Ordinariness of English in Gully Boy

In contrast to the visual abundance of *Slumdog Millionaire*, English in *Gully Boy* is neither iconic nor familiar, and certainly not stunning. It just is—always present in plain sight, such that it often does not even register as English. An early example appears in the opening credits with a typography that is a mash up of Roman and *devanagari* scripts. The title of the film is also a transliteration of the Hindustani word *gully*, which means street. These linguistic and scriptural hybrids prepare us to read the Roman script as Hindi and erase English. The English language can be found in both public and private spaces, as Murad, the eponymous *Gully Boy*, navigates the urbanscape of Mumbai. In private moments, the script is instrumentalized as Murad pens his innermost thoughts in poetry and later performs from the notebook.

In the opening scene, Murad and his friend Salman literally jump out of one of the inscribed-upon arcades of Art Deco Mumbai. A medium-long shot frames the scene such that buildings and their English-language signages tower over these young men as they walk. Murad appears conspicuously uncomfortable, his head down and face concealed by a hoodie. Murad's general sense of vigilance and discomfort as he reluctantly follows his friend to steal a car mirrors how he—a young Muslim man from the slums of Mumbai—navigates the social world in which he lives. Murad's relation to this world changes when he chances upon the hip-hop subculture in the city. Hip-hop is just the outlet Murad needed for his poetry and frustration, and he soon blossoms into a powerful voice on the scene.

In several scenes, Murad's writing and typing make his poetry visible. However, as his metaphorical and literal voice gives sound to the written word in voice-overs, it also fractures the linguistic sign of English on the page into the signifier (script) and the signified (sound). For instance, writing is an outlet for Murad's frustrations, a fact established through multiple shots of Murad writing in his notebook deep into the night. However, writing in *Gully Boy* is always transliteration. The script that Murad traces is always Roman script, while the voice-over reads the Hindi poetry. As Murad writes, the cut from a shot of the notebook where he is writing to a close up of his face makes the Roman script disappear before most bilingual viewers would explicitly think of its association with English. This kind of editing elevates poetry to the most authentic form and medium of expression, one that circumvents mediation. But, it also makes the Roman script appear and disappear before viewers can even consciously register it as the script of English.

In the tradition of hip-hop, the use of language is understood as affective, immediate, pliable, and improvisable. Murad's poems, his literal and figurative writing, are shaped by his life and body. Before beginning his performance at a rap battle, Murad first puts the microphone to his chest so that the sound of his heartbeat reverberates. In any situation, he first feels and responds bodily, for instance, with a twitch or by closing his eyes. Murad's art dramatizes his mentor's philosophy that "poetry stems from the 'storm inside.'" This political and affective response in poetry likens the process of "exporting" a music file to an "explosion." The ability to articulate one's pain is a transformative experience both psychically and politically; as Murad writes in one of the poems, "the lava of words will melt my shackles." The film's romantic notion of writing is mediated by technology and by English as a technology.

Life's inequalities move Murad to write, and technological media forms become prosthesis that assume somatic charge. Devices like the iPad and cell phone help Murad find a community of artists in Mumbai and later disseminate his music widely. The pen with which he writes and the sieve

FIGURE 14. "Murad Writing in a Notebook." From *Gully Boy*, dir. Zoya Akhtar, Tiger Baby Films, 2019.

into which he speaks to modulate his voice literally and metaphorically help him claim his voice and direct his life. As Murad claims proudly to his father towards the end of the film, he writes his own story himself (मैं अपनी कहानी खुद लिखता हूँ). In a scene that follows Murad's early success, a shot of him writing exemplifies the importance of technology. As hip-hop groups have long done to reach a wider audience and boost their popularity, Murad goes with his friends to paint graffiti at night. Atop a postered wall, Murad traces a new equation of modern India: "*roti, kapda, makaan* + Internet." The first three words are written in the *devanagari* script and name the bare necessities of modern life: "bread, clothing, and shelter." The Hindi words were a catchy election slogan in the 1960s for Indira Gandhi, a former prime minister of India. Murad updates this slogan with "Internet," thus playing with the idea of the "bare essentials" of life.

The addition of "Internet" brings to mind Chandrabhan Prasad's Goddess English, who stands on the computer to signal her potential to circumvent national caste-based paths and effect change through technology. In *Gully Boy*, the use of English/Roman script to write the word "Internet" transmutes the value of one onto the other—English is only a communicative technology. Graffiti, as one of the characters says in the film, "is not art, it is war." It is a class war. Graffiti does not seek permission. It begins in transgression, by inscribing on what is already written. In *Unlearning the City* (2012), Swati Chattopadhyay writes that political wall writings and political posters serve as examples of a spatial imagination that "link[s] the body, city space, and the body politics, turning on the attempt to open a

FIGURE 15. "Roti, Kapda, aur Makaan + Internet." From *Gully Boy*, dir. Zoya Akhtar, Tiger Baby Films, 2019.

space between freedom and violence."[16] This spatial imagination reveals that the materiality of the walls can always be read differently—that there is always what Chattopadhyay calls a "different order of legibility"—that can challenge the spatial imagination of the state. As a metaphor for a contestatory English, the act of inscribing the city is a rebuttal to the English under which Murad and his friends shuffled earlier in the film. It does not erase what is written, but builds upon—and derives its critical power through—an antagonistic relation to it.

The editing of *Gully Boy* renders English words and phrases, or even full sentences, a part of its visual landscape. Early in the film, when Murad is still only a listener of rap and not its singer, he raps a bit of Nas. A white tourist is in his house, "touring" the slums, as Murad is sitting on his bed, eating his lunch. The tourist wears a white T-shirt with Nas's face on it. This prompts Murad to rap a little in recognition. The tourist exclaims in disbelief, surprised that this young man knows about Nas and can rap in English, and asks if he can take his photo. Murad covers his face for the photo and continues eating his lunch while other tourists mill around him. The English of his rap prompts surprise because it is incongruous and unexpected to the tourist. But, as Murad covers his face for the photo, the crossed-out sign re-sounds Murad's voice as erasure, and returns the meaning of the song back to Nas on the T-shirt as an echo. There are a handful of other times when Murad speaks English. Most of these are part of the language of the hip-hop subculture—expressions like "*bhot hard*" (very hard) to convey admiration for a composition/performance or "rhythm and tempo" to talk about music. Murad also learns English expressions as part of his education in college and as a salesman, but quits his job and never uses that knowledge. If the knowledge of English led to transformative effects in *Slumdog Millionaire*, such effects are thwarted in *Gully Boy*; English leads to little monetary reward.

By so juxtaposing the visual, sonic, and literary registers, *Gully Boy* forges a new language of creative expression. The film is inspired by the lives of two real-life young hip-hop artists from India, Naezy and Divine, calling itself a "shout out" to these artists in the opening credits. Through Murad's story, it brings attention to the thriving hip-hop scene in India and to a growing interest in poetry across Hindi, Urdu, and English languages.[17] This emergent literary scene—of which the Sahitya Akademi poets discussed in chapter 2 are an important part—is made possible by access to the Internet, where one can upload one's art or reach out to other like-minded artists. The novel form has long dominated conversations about Indian, South Asian, and global literatures. However, over the past decade, there has been much exciting work and popular interest in poetry from different corners and in a range of languages. There is a veritable generation of first-time young poets (especially Dalit and Urdu-language poets) who share their works on social media, as discussed in chapter 2. At the same time, poetry rivals prose fiction in traditional publishing today, with writers such as Tishani Doshi, Akhil Katyal, and Ravish Kumar. We see a number of poetry circles and poetry events across cities. As Cyrus Oshidar says about Indian hip-hop, "With internet has come a newfound confidence for the youth to say: I live here, too."[18] If global English is specifically tied to the presumably dull and dulling language of digital worlds, then these artists offer the reminder that they live in these worlds, too, and English lives with them and through them.

When we first meet him in the film, Murad is a shy, timid, and quiet young man. His cautious personality and powerlessness against an authoritarian father are heightened in the face of a more generalized sense of his father's powerlessness as a working-class Muslim man in India. While Murad finds solace in writing and listening to music in the quiet of the night, we are also made aware that a life of letters is not for him. When Murad's father meets with an accident and asks his employer to hire Murad in his stead, Murad works part-time as a driver. This episode is reminiscent of *The White Tiger*, and as it does for Balram, it heightens Murad's ability and interest in driving his own life. The film is attuned to class and religious differences in India and centers art as a way to address and redress them. It focuses on Murad's transformation from a diffident young man at the beginning of the film to a rap artist who takes an entire auditorium by storm as he opens for Nas. Hip-hop and poetry help Murad find meaning and pride—voice—in his experiences.

To voice Murad, the film does not favor one language or another. The language privileged by the film is the political language of speaking truth to power. It is not a language like English or Urdu or Hindi. Like other real-life artists, Murad is also shown rapping in a hybrid tongue of many different languages that coexist in the urban slums of Mumbai. Many contemporary rap artists sing in Indian languages like Punjabi, Kashmiri, and Haryanvi, and often switch to English during the song. Their use of Indian languages is strategic as it allows them to distinguish their work and tap into a market beyond the English-speaking pockets of the country. The limited use of English is a political statement in itself: "For the first time people are saying to the moneyed class: 'We don't want your money; we don't want to be like you [upper middle class, English speaking].'"[19] This rejection of speaking English—but not writing it—is implicit in the line "I don't want to be a slumdog millionaire" (नहीं बनना मुझे स्लमडॉग मिलियनेयर) in *Gully Boy* that constitutes one of its self-proclaimed differences from *Slumdog*.

Indeed, Murad and his friend do not talk in English in *Gully Boy*. Only one of the characters speaks in English. Sky is an aspiring music producer from the Berklee School of Music who collaborates with Murad and his mentor. In one of the few scenes that take place under the open sky, Murad and Sky are sitting in the latter's car, windows rolled down, and smoking. In a rare moment of quiet, Murad marvels at the recent success of his first video: "I can't believe I am in a professional music video" (*mereko toh yaqeen nahin ho raha main* **proper video** *mein hoon* / मेरे को तो यकीन नहीं हो रहा मैं प्रॉपर विडियो में हूँ). When Sky exclaims that she cannot believe he was planning to do something besides singing, Murad continues, "It is not that simple, madam. One needs to earn money too" (*aisa nahin hota* **madam, simple** *nahin hai, paisa bhi kamana hota hai* / ऐसा नहीं होता मैडम, सिंपल नहीं है पैसा भी कमाना होता है). Sky gives Murad the neoliberal advice to "follow his passion," which will (magically!) bring money. Murad looks at her directly and repeats the word "passion" with a scoff. Sky's use of the English word and her weak grasp of Hindi indexes her class and cosmopolitan location. As she struggles to explain her sentiment in Hindi, Murad supplies the translation. Upon hearing the Hindi word for passion (*junoon*, and so more accurately, an Urdu word), she claims that she likes the sound of the word. Murad teases her in English by saying, "You like it? You like the word?" This scene might suggest that English is the language of those who have the luxury of following one's passion, whereas Hindi is the language of those who worry about their next meal. But, this would be a weak reading of the scene. While English does have a place in the film, it is not fetishized or distinguished in any way. Murad approaches English as a means to an end. As he teases Sky for fetishizing the Hindi/Urdu word and its sounds, he takes power away from the world view in which Hindi is romanticized and English shown to be a choice. Indeed, Sky's fetishization of the word contrasts the fetishization of English often encountered in this book's examination of English in India.

In *Slumdog Millionaire* and *Gully Boy*, English has to be made intelligible between the worlds of the slums and its global spectators. To solve this problem, the films cinematically produce the slums of Mumbai as an Anglophonic habitus. The characters, Jamal and Murad, along with the audience, encounter English as part of the landscape, the set, and the mise-en-scène. To those in the audience who—like Murad—know English, the language appears self-evident in advertisements, graffiti, technology, poetry. To those in the audience who—like Jamal—may not know English, the written English language recedes into the figural. As both types of readers read this English, the films produce a cinematic mode of linguistic signification.

Materiality of English in Hindi-Urdu Cinema

Film, as a medium that deals with the conjunction of sound and image, pries open different experiences of language. Such a cinematic English complements the ethnographic approach of reading English through its lived experience. In *Gully Boy* and *Slumdog Millionaire*, what gets read under the sign of English expands through a tension between sound and script. This mode of cinematic signification has implications for film studies more broadly, as it calls attention to the shifting meanings of English within the corpus of Hindi-Urdu cinema.

It is a well-regarded argument that the Hindi film industry based in Bombay is the last bastion of Hindustani and Urdu in India. Scholars of Hindi-Urdu film noted a gradual replacement of Urdu with English in these films. What seemed like a decline of Hindi-Urdu and related "Muslimness" was attributed to the transnational modalities of film production, expanding audiences outside India, and the ascension of Hindu nationalism. Indeed, the broader political and economic changes affected the film industry as well. The 1990s was the decade when Bombay cinema became globally recognizable as "Bollywood." The word "Bollywood"—as a hybrid of Bombay and Hollywood—first appeared "as a joke" in *Screen Weekly*, a popular English-language film magazine.[20] Over time, the playfulness of the term "Bollywood" has come to refer to a trend, a culture, and exotica as much as the film industry based in Mumbai. Ravi Vasudevan, in his essay "The Meanings of Bollywood" (2008), identifies in the moniker the "displacement of nation as art form with nation as brand."[21] As a broader cultural trend on a global scale, Bollywood filmmakers fashioned their films in a global vernacular that was easily translatable within the multilingual context of India as well as outside it. English played an important role in this reinforced visibility, intelligibility, and popularity of Bombay cinema.

Up until then, English had been represented as and been representative of a predictable catalog of values and attributes in Hindi films. The language was spoken incorrectly by lower-class characters for comic effect and to convey their earthiness; conversely, it was spoken correctly by villains and by upper-class and cosmopolitan characters. When spoken by villains or characters from outside India, the English language indexed a divergence from patriotic sentiments and conservative patriarchal (glossed as "Indian") values, even an out-of-placeness. "Correct" English, then, became an index of national, moral, and class-based inauthenticity. This logic persisted for a long time, well into the 1990s, where diasporic Indian characters in Hindi films typically spoke in English to convey their "Westernization," but only until they truly became conscious of their Indian sensibilities.

M. Madhava Prasad has argued that Hindi and English represent the entirety of Indian linguistic diversity in Bollywood, which shares the structural bilingualism of the Indian nation-state.[22] Like the state machinery, Bollywood also uses a language—"metalanguage"—to secure the entirety of linguistic diversity without which the nation cannot be articulated. Hindi-Urdu cinema had used Hindustani written in both *nastaliq* (Urdu) and *devanagari* (Hindi) script in film credit sequences as well as its own script- and song-writing practices. But, the "ideological work" of Urdu—its evocation of a pre-Partition composite culture and business practices—"has now been challenged by English, which provides the ideological coordinates of the new world of the Hindi film."[23] But perhaps the metalanguage is itself structurally bilingual as in the Constitution: Hindi and English together function as the metalanguage in which a specious "national" ideology is articulated. In fact, rarely does the use of the English language make a Hindi film an English film, or vice versa. The monolingualism that Prasad attributes to English in Bollywood is in fact a bilingualism made possible by a structural forgetting that the likes of C. Rajagopalachari at the cusp of India's independence had demanded of the Indian people—a structural forgetting in which English is reimagined as an Indian language. The super-sign of Hindi and English set in motion by the Indian Constitution also girds the film industry and makes it legible as "Indian."

Let me give an example. In the Hindi patriotic film *Purab Aur Paschim* (East and West) (dir. Manoj Kumar, 1970), the meaning of the English-language lyrics become legible through the bodies and movements of the actors. Through an emphasis on accent and diction, the English language stands for both foreignness and authenticity to India. Titled "Twinkle, Twinkle, Little Star," the lyrics of the song are rather basic—nursery rhymes interspersed with a few other lines in English and Hindi. The song opens with a frontal shot of a stage with two puppet dolls that are meant to resemble the film's hero and heroine. The hero is dressed in traditional Indian clothes, and the heroine in a short dress and blonde wig, holding a whiskey and a cigarette. They epitomize the East and the West respectively. Regular cutting from the stage puppet show to close ups of the actual hero and heroine further emphasize the relation. This mise-en-scène, along with the voice-over that supplies all the spoken sounds, heightens the performative and staged quality of the English language in the film.

The premise of the song rests on the heroine's request that the hero sing an English song for her. The hero claims to not know one, after which the heroine proceeds to teach him. The hero's efforts to bring the heroine back from her errant "Western" ways are an important part of the film narrative, and this song dramatizes their mutual instructional impulses. As the camera pans out to involve the real actors, the song performs a parable of reform through the puppets. As one teaches and the other repeats, both the hero and the heroine sing the same words, but their pronunciations are entirely different. Careful enunciation and an incorrect Hindi grammar as she sings in Hindi mark the heroine as the Londoner she is supposed to be. The hero, on the other hand, speaks fast, flattening his English *w*'s and singing the English rhymes to a folk Indian tune. The hero clearly knows English, as he is able to formulate sentences in English ("I want a chance, baby") and pun on the heroine's lines as she calls him a "fool." However, his pronunciation and the music to which his part is set distinguish him from someone who speaks "standard" English, marking him as "authentically" Indian. When the heroine calls the hero a "fool," he riffs-off on the English word "fool" with its Hindi homophonic equivalent *phool*, which means "flower." He then makes a philosophical argument about flowering and maturity to say that everyone is a "fool" (the English word) in their youth. This is, obviously, a reference to what he sees as the heroine's degenerate ways in her youth, and the possibility that she may be able to mend those ways after all. In a repetition with difference, the English nursery rhyme emerges as the very epitome of the "West" as well as the declaration of an incorruptible "Indian-ness."

In "Twinkle, Twinkle, Little Star" the English language—in its repetition with difference—is already bilingual. English sustains a nationalist vision by being spoken by the Indian hero (to establish its equivalence with Hindi) and by the London-returned heroine (to emphasize its foreign Englishness). Thus, English is associated with two opposing ideological realms that constitute a structural bilingualism of the metalanguage. Films in India are not only enactments of the visual circulation of English in India; they are also a part of that visual economy. Beyond narrative analysis and dialogue, Bollywood offers a topos to visualize the encounter between English and the vernacular. While English plays an important role in the reinforced visibility, intelligibility, and popularity of Bollywood, the aesthetic excess of Bollywood also shapes the meanings of English.

Additionally, the English language enjoys a sonic materiality in the film ecology that extends beyond the screen. English words appear in film titles, songs, and film scripts, where it circulates untethered to the image. In songs especially, English becomes a part of what Budhaditya Chattopadhyay has called "the auditory spectacle" of the film.[24] Particularly since the 1990s, many popular Hindi film songs include a few English words and phrases in the chorus. As part of catchy songs, these words usually penetrate the colloquial vocabulary of the audiences who may not be considered as users of English as a first language. Beyond subtitling, dubbing is a sound practice that can provide audiences access to English-language films. When, as a result of economic liberalization in the 1990s, more and more international films were first released in India, the state was very closely involved in controlling the content and viewership of films. The *Report of the Working Group on National Film Policy* (1980) noted that the "audio visual medium had immense potential to mould [*sic*] the mind of man."[25] That cinema was an instrument of social change and not only a "luxury to be tapped into for tax resources."[26]

The heightened censorship practices of the time were concerned with policing the foreign and so shaping the foreign. In the case of foreign-language films (mainly English), examining committees and censor boards presumed that the necessary foreignness of their practices would make these unintelligible to audiences. However, the problem arose when these supposedly foreign practices appeared not performed by a foreign body. For instance, one of the reports of the Indian Cinematograph Committee argued that Hollywood films with explicit intimacy scenes were not as harmful because most Indian audiences did not understand, did not like, and did not go to see such films.[27] The release of Mira Nair's *Kama Sutra* in 1998 in India is an important example here.

Nair's film is based on an Urdu short story "Uttaran" (Hand-me-downs; 1977), by Wajidah Tabassum, and it is a feminist take on Vatsyayan's third-century text, *Kama sutra*. It is set in sixteenth-century India and features two female leads, Maya and Tara. Tara is a princess and Maya the servant who grows up wearing Tara's hand-me-downs. Maya resents this unfairness and on the eve of Tara's marriage to the king, seduces him to avenge her humiliation. The rest of the narrative follows the rivalry between the two heroines and the king's growing attachment to Maya.

At the time of its release in English, the film did not create a stir, and received only minimal cuts and deletions. It met with a lukewarm response despite the controversy and the anticipation around it. While many viewers found the plot unengaging, far more people commented on the film's use of the English language. Sample these reviews published in *Screen Weekly*, which reflect the dominant reception of the film: "A factor that takes away from the charm of watching the film is to hear an Indian story with Indian actors mouthing English dialogues. 'Do not surrender to despair,' says Rekha [one of the actresses]. It does sound a little too heavy for easy handling."[28] The writer's comment calls attention to the ponderous and archaic tone of the language, which seemed incommensurate to intimate discussions of love and despair. The article seemed to say that the English language was not only not the lingua franca of sixteenth-century India it was also not "light" enough to assume the spokenness and ease of conversation in a film.

This reception of English was in contrast to Hindi-Urdu films where English assumed an iconicity by virtue of its "topological similarity,"[29] or where, as in *Purab Aur Paschim*, English was heard as Hindi. In *Kama Sutra*, the English language fails to assume this role. If anything, English works against the narrative. For example, the word *maya* in Hindi refers to the world as an illusion, as well as the powers by which the phenomenal world becomes manifest. In the film, Maya represents an "illusion" and a temptation to the king. In an important dialogue, the king remarks on the *maya*-like quality of Maya. However, in the English-language dialogue, that comment is not meaningful at all. English is lacking its usual desirable and aspirational associations in *Kama Sutra*.

It is fair to say that thus far, the journey of *Kama Sutra*, Mira Nair's English film in India had been unremarkable. Interestingly, however, as soon as there were talks about dubbing the film into "vernacular languages,"[30] writes Monika Mehta, the Central Board of Film Certification suggested more deletions and edits than it had suggested for the English language. This decision was guided by the argument that "the audiences who would view these films lacked 'proper' education, making them more inclined to imbibe and spew vulgarity."[31] This incident exposed the class pretensions and presumptions that confuse education with speaking English and being upper middle class. In fact, the chairman of the Central Board of Film Certification from 1991 to 1997, Shakti Samanta, said that "the psyche of the audience who watches English and Hindi films is different."[32]

The script with the cuts recommended by the Central Board of Film Certification (CBFC) as found at the National Film Archive of India in Pune shows that only three cuts were recommended by the examining committee to the Hindi dubbed version. Of the three excised sounds, the first is a set of expletives that translate to "whore" and "bitch." The second cut occurs when a doctor comes to examine Tara, who is wasting away because she is deprived of physical intimacy. Doctor Mani is putting his hands inside a hole cut into a piece of embroidered fabric to examine Tara, who is "sick." In the Hindi version the image on the screen is not excised but the dialogue "जाँच रहे हैं, जाँच रहे हैं" ("examining, examining") is. The scene itself presents complex dynamics of the seen and the unseen. The doctor is brought blindfolded into the women's quarters and has to resort to examining his patient through a sheet because the queen must not be seen, even though the audience can see everything. In the English version, the repetition of the word "examining" is supposed to reassure the audience of the scene that the doctor is only performing his professional duties. However, the audience outside the scene can see that Tara is using the doctor's fingers to pleasure herself.

Finally, the last cut is a line spoken by the king to Maya in praise of her art of seduction as they are having sex. The king says: "यह अदा मुझे बहुत पसंद है" (lit., "I like this style a lot" though in the English original it is rendered as "God's grace is in you") invoking a feudal Islamicate tradition. All of these cuts are sound only. No scenes of nudity were required to be cut, and indeed, *Kama Sutra* received a lot of praise for its cinematography and its use of color in India and abroad. In addition, the Hindi script of *Kama Sutra* lists some "voluntary" deletions made by the applicant, the director, which include cutting out visuals of Tara's and Maya's bare bodies at three different points. While the applicant assumed that the images of naked bodies would be unacceptable to a Hindi-speaking audience or to an examining committee acting on its behalf, the division of the sound from the image in the decisions seems to suggest that what is said and heard holds greater impact than what is shown and seen.

If the dialogues parse the images, translate them for the audience, then silencing the audio is akin to arresting that process of intersemiotic translation. All the English words of the dialogues are easily translated into Hindi equivalents, but are rendered untranslatable by being silenced. The examining body of the Central Board of Film Certification quiets the Hindi dialogues because they risk being understood and animating the presumably erotic images. Without the Hindi "sounds," the images, the values of feudal Islamicate culture, and the actions in a diasporic film dubbed from English, it is hoped, remain unintelligible. Ironically, however, the audience's dissatisfaction with the English dialogues arises from the fact that they were discordant and unsuitable, that is, they were not commensurable translations.

In suggestions for censorship in *Kama Sutra*, the overall message seems to have been translated as the unintelligible—the message that the Hindi-speaking audience receives is that the original English dialogues are unintelligible (or even, irrelevant). A Hindi-dubbed version of the film would also not include English subtitles as part of the image on the screen. In their (linguistic and interlingual) untranslatability and inaudibility, these specific scenes in *Kama Sutra* are rendered as not belonging to the cultural context of the film and the audience. The examining committee's suggestion to only silence the dialogues is really an invitation to separate the written/graphic English from its cultural associations. By separating scenes of sexual explicitness from dubbed dialogues, the state is inviting the audience to imagine an English that is not immediately associated with the vulgarity of foreign provenance or the decadence of a feudal culture. For instance, the excised Hindi dialogue of "I like this style a lot" is racy and presumably just as inappropriate for consumption by a nation-building family unit as the original English rendering—"God's grace is in you"—that might, according to the same conservative Hindutva ideas, uncomfortably join a devotional register to a sexual one. Instead, sterilized by removing all dialogues, we have an English that does not translate feudal Islamicate culture but is fit for a national audience and ripe for its role in the structural bilingualism of the state's metalanguage.

This strategic un/translatability of English—its translation by suggesting that it is not translatable—in both the intersemiotic and interlingual senses—locates English as a nationalized vernacular through censorship. Film censorship at the levels of the state and of reception betrays a preoccupation with policing the foreign. But English is not, as a matter of course, deemed foreign. In fact, its different visible, audible, and legible forms often cast it as "Indian" and familiar. Both for the postcolonial state and an aspirational audience, films are valuable in their instructional capacity, and the use of English is understood within this context. In its liberal guise of formal education, English legitimates the audience's ability to appreciate films. English also of course itself emerges as knowledge worth gaining through films.

As part of the cinematic infrastructure, English expands through citations and invocations. The language materializes in networks of circulation, in technologies of information and communication, in brand names, in "alphabetical and iconic writing in the field of moving image,"[33] and in moments where English does not even register as English. The transformative power of reading, especially a kind of reading that often wouldn't be categorized as reading, fractures the authority we may be tempted to impute to the written word. In a world of digital technology and social media, the characters exert their visual, haptic, and auditory senses to read. In this compulsory and creative reception, we find, once again, that globally circulating English is always vernacular English. The multimodal and multisensorial answers of Jamal Malik, for instance, are a result of new linguistic habits that put the written and the spoken language in tension and allow him to read without any prior or subsequent knowledge at least in the traditional sense. As in Balram Halwai's phonic letter and the Meira Paibis's protest, this tension reminds us that the script of Anglophonic globality is repeatedly disrupted by its own sounds. It invites us as scholars to pay attention to the literal and metaphoric voices of the Anglophone world and the conditions of speaking and listening.

CODA

Radical Anglophony, or The Ethics of Attunement

SO, HOW SHOULD we read Anglophone literatures? Should we read them as palimpsests of a multilingual culture or as the culture's vanishing point? By turning to the defining feature of Anglophone literature—the English language itself—this book proposes that we detach the word "Anglophone" from its popular epithet "global." The compulsory yoking of these terms has produced only anxiety and confusion as "Anglophone" has consistently emerged inadequate to the "global," and the "global" has claimed questionable teleologies for the "Anglophone." Instead, this book uses "Anglophone" to draw attention to the eponymous English-speaking people and the processes of mediation, translation, and embodiment that make English heard.

The disciplinary nomination of "literatures in English other than British and American" as global/world Anglophone literature places a productive, if unwitting, emphasis on the *speakers* and *speaking* of English. A heteronymic understanding of "speaker" brings to auditory attention the different kinds of speakers of English as well as the fundamental role of *tekhne* in the inflection of what is said (the phonic) and what is heard (the sonic). In the present global conjuncture, especially, performances of racialized voices, accents, and "skin tones" materialize in a fundamentally biopolitical terrain of listening.

But while scholarship has thought much and very carefully about the empire's gaze in/and its word, sounds of English from erstwhile colonies are fraught with interpretive dissonance. A brown body sounding the English language is inevitably heard as making audible a colonial trace. With little attention to what they say or where, why, and to whom, the act of speaking English—a colonial and global language—is usually understood to be tinged with loss or nostalgia or humiliation. Perhaps because the call centers seem to legitimize this trace, they have become the leading stereotype guiding how postcolonial English literatures are read in Anglo-American academies. The telemarketer sitting somewhere in India or the Philippines embodies not only the violence of exploitative global economies but also the continued humiliation of those previously colonized. Together the call center and the telemarketer conjure a familiar narrative of bodies and minds being disciplined in the service of one empire or another.

But, even call center employees—with their stereotypically awkward performances of identity and deceiving accents—do not just talk to presumably monolingual English-speaking customers in the United States or the United Kingdom. Those call center telemarketers also step out of their cubicle farm without always shedding their work accent. In India that accent and the very act of speaking English will have a variety of different meanings. Since the knowledge of English is often a result of privileges of education, an English speaker may be read as upper caste, upper class, and educated. It has been argued that traditional hierarchies of class and caste have dissolved, and English speakers today are a class of their own. Yet, these tantalizing assumptions about a new linguistic order conceal the psychodynamics of speaking English and belie the difficulty of being heard. Think back to the cast of characters we have encountered in the book. For many like Narendra Modi, India's current prime minister, and Balram Halwai in *The White Tiger*, speaking English is an imperative as well as an impossibility. The inability of untrained vocal cords to produce the correct pronunciation can seem like a betrayal of one's very body.

In the biopolitically fraught soundscape of the Anglophone world, the Sahitya Akademi Dalit poets, the Meira Paibis, and the writers from Northeast India remind us how vast the Anglophone world is, how different its speakers, and how deeply political are its sounds. Scholarly criticism on Anglophone writing is shaped by a broader cultural emphasis on speaking, where we have been concerned not only with what is said but who has been able to say it. But, how do we know what is said? Thus far, criticism on Anglophone literatures is restricted to—indeed, restricted by—what has long been known about the English language and forms of empire. How do we as scholars of global Anglophone literature practice a radical listening that tells us more than what we already know? No one just uses words, English or otherwise, when they speak. People use the sound of their voice, the movement of their hand, the expression in their eyes. They speak with their whole bodies and hear what is said with their whole bodies as well. As practitioners who are often concerned with the voice of the character, our ability to *listen* itself is an embodied and mediated intersubjective relation.

The phonological debt of the category of "Anglophone" literature demands what Lisbeth Lipari has called an "ethics of attunement." Listening is a profoundly mediated modality of relation. In Lisbeth Lipari's words, it brings others to speech. It is a risk that "requires the courage to listen for the not-already-known, and in so doing, reveal our own particular vulnerability and weakness."[1] Listening requires us to implicate ourselves and allows us to access what we do not yet know. In my listening, I propose the Anglophone as an experience of the promised commonality of English, which may confirm the violence of the English language but which also constantly challenges its normativity via a counterdiscourse. These counterdiscursive meanings of English—what I am calling vernacular English in this book—become audible in the acknowledgement of the embodied, affective, and material sounds of the Anglophone. This is not the romance of a phonocentric recidivism but a commitment to linguistic meaning as it becomes sensible between sound and script. It is a commitment to the conviction that the story of English in India and the Anglophone world cannot simply be the story of oppression.

NOTES

Preface. On the Grounds

1. Based in the different texts that it brings together, this book uses a few different caste-based categories. These include untouchable, outcaste, Dalit, and *shudra*. The caste system divides Hindus into four main categories—Brahmins, Kshatriyas, Vaishyas, and the Shudras. At the bottom of the hierarchy are the Shudras, who were said to come from the Hindu god Brahma's feet and who were responsible for common labor. The main castes were further divided into other castes and subcastes, each based on their specific occupation. Outside of this Hindu caste system were the *achhoots*, the outcastes, the untouchables. Gandhi popularized the word *Harijan* (children of God) in place of "untouchables." Many saw it as Gandhi's misdirected attempt to advance the social position of the Dalits without abolishing the caste system. The term "Dalit" (literally meaning "scattered" or "broken") was first used by B. R. Ambedkar in 1928 in his newspaper *Bahishkrut Bharat*. In an editorial, he characterized being Dalit as an experience that consisted of deprivation, marginalization, and stigmatization, and positioned it against Gandhi's appellation for Untouchables, *harijan*, a term Ambedkar found "patronizing".

2. Modi has claimed he belongs to a socially disadvantaged class of society. After his recent election win, he claimed, in a way that will resonate with Aravind Adiga's *The White Tiger*, that there are two castes in India: the caste of the poor and the caste of those who will fight poverty. See Sagar, "Narendra Modi's 'Two-Caste Society' Is a Façade to Hide the BJP's Casteist Politics," *Caravan Magazine*, June 21, 2019, https://caravanmagazine.in/politics/narendra-modi-two-caste-society-casteist-bjp.

3. Praseeda Gopinath, "Modi Speaks the Nation: Masculinity, Radio, and Voice," in *Indian Sound Cultures, Indian Sound Citizenship*, ed. Laura Brueck, Jacob Smith, and Neil Verma (Ann Arbor: University of Michigan Press, 2020), 152–73.

4. "Modi 'Actually Speaks Very Good English,' Says Trump," *The Hindu*, August 26, 2019, https://www.thehindu.com/news/international/modi-actually-speaks-very-good-english-says-trump/article29260893.ece.

5. Chanda Nandy, "Modi's Monogrammed Suit: Rise of the Narcissistic Parvenu," Nandygram-Times of India Blogs, *The Times of India*, January 27, 2015, http://blogs.timesofindia.indiatimes.com/nandygram/modis-monogrammed-suit-rise-of-the-narcissistic-parvenu/.

6. In an article titled "English Speaking Curse," with a wordplay on the numerous courses teaching conversational English that are mushrooming across the country, Anjali Puri writes about the many students of lower-caste and poorer backgrounds who have died by suicide when unable to cope with the burden of learning English in schools and universities. See Anjali Puri, "English Speaking Curse," *Outlook India*, March 24, 2008.

7. Tony Kurien and Suraj Gogoi, "Reclaiming Academia: Understanding the Student Movement of Our Time," *Kafila*, January 31, 2016.

8. "My Birth Is My Fatal Accident: Full Text of Dalit Student Rohith's Suicide Letter," *The Indian Express*, January 19, 2016.

Introduction. Vernacular English: Reading the Anglophone

1. In "Postcolonial, Still" (2019) Yogita Goyal notes that she encountered "a very conservative 'great books' curriculum" at the University of Delhi in the 1990s with an exclusive focus on British literature." Indeed, the 1990s saw an especially anxious discussion on the relevance of English literary education and the curriculum was revised shortly after to reflect a postcolonial approach. See Rajeswari Sundar Rajan, ed., *The Lie of the Land* (Delhi: Oxford University Press, 1992); Svati Joshi, ed., *Rethinking English: Essays in Literature, Language, History* (New Delhi: Trianka, 1991); Sudhakar Marathe, et al., *The Teaching of English Literature in India* (Madras: Sangam Books and British Council, 1993); and Susie Tharu, ed., *Subject to Change: Teaching Literature in the Nineties* (New Delhi: Orient Longman, 1998). See also Yogita Goyal, "Postcolonial, Still," in "Forms of the Global Anglophone," *Post45 Contemporaries*, February 22, 2019, https://post45.org/2019/02/postcolonial-still/.

2. In "English Studies: A Personal Journey" (2013), G.J.V. Prasad writes, "It seemed that to have tertiary education in English was perpetuating (and creating further) two Indias—one with access to power and one without, one of elites and one of disenfranchised masses. Nobody believed this more than English teachers themselves." See G.J.V. Prasad, "English Studies: A Personal Journey," *Australian Literary Studies* 28, nos. 1–2 (May 2013): 40–49.

3. Simon Gikandi, "Editorial: Provincializing English," *PMLA* 129, no. 1 (January 2014): 7–17; Srinivas Aravamudan, *Guru English: South Asian Religion in a Cosmopolitan Language* (Princeton, NJ: Princeton University Press, 2005); Jonathan Arac, "Anglo-Globalism?," *New Left Review* 16 (July/August 2002): 35–45; Gaurav Desai, "Rethinking English Studies," in *A Companion to Postcolonial Studies*, ed. Sangeeta Ray and Henry Schwarz (Malden, MA: Blackwell, 2005), 523–39; and Rey Chow, "In the Name of Comparative Literature," in *Comparative Literature in the Age of Multiculturalism*, ed. Charles Bernheimer (Baltimore: Johns Hopkins University Press, 1994), 107–16.

4. Rashmi Sadana, *English Heart, Hindi Heartland: The Political Life of Literature in India* (Berkeley: University of California Press, 2012).

5. Moradewun Adejunmobi, *Vernacular Palaver: Imaginations of the Local and Non-Native Languages in West Africa* (Cleveland: Multilingual Matters, 2004), 119. See also Nasia Anam, "Bangladeshi Anglophone Literature: Rerouting the Hegemony of Global English," *Interventions: International Journal of Postcolonial Studies* 20, no. 3 (2018): 325–34; Sumit K. Mandal, "Reconsidering Cultural Globalization: The English Language in Malaysia," in "Capturing Globalization," special issue, *Third World Quarterly* 21, no. 6 (December 2000): 1001–12.

6. See Minae Mizumura, *The Fall of Language in the Age of English* (New York: Columbia University Press, 2015).

7. Tobias Warner, *The Tongue-Tied Imagination: Decolonizing Literary Modernity in Senegal* (New York: Fordham University Press, 2019), 4.

8. In "Call Center Agents and Expatriate Writers: Twin Subjects of New Indian Capital," Ragini Tharoor Srinivasan makes a simple but very astute observation. She writes that Rey Chow (and many scholars of call center economies) erroneously assume that the call center agent is only speaking to the customer located in the United States or United Kingdom. This is obviously not the case and would change how we

understand the labor of the call center agent. See Ragini Tharoor Srinivasan, "Call Center Agents and Expatriate Writers: Twin Subjects of New Indian Capital," *ariel: A Review of International English Literature* 49, no. 4 (2018): 77–107.

9. See Aarthi Vadde, *Chimeras of Form: Modernist Internationalism beyond Europe, 1914–2016* (New York: Columbia University Press, 2018); Madhumita Lahiri, *Imperfect Solidarities: Tagore, Gandhi, Du Bois, and the Global Anglophone* (Evanston, IL: Northwestern University Press, 2020).

10. Aatish Taseer, "How English Ruined Indian Literature," *New York Times*, March 19, 2015, https://www.nytimes.com/2015/03/22/opinion/sunday/how-english-ruined-indian-literature.html.

11. Rukmini S., "In India, Who Speaks English, and Where?," *Mint*, May 14, 2019, https://www.livemint.com/news/india/in-india-who-speaks-in-english-and-where-1557814101428.html.

12. See Gauri Viswanthan, *The Masks of Conquest: Literary Study and British Rule in India* (1989; repr., New York: Columbia University Press, 2014), 43; Homi Bhabha, "Signs Taken for Wonders: Questions of Ambivalence and Authority under a Tress outside Delhi, May 1817," in "'Race,' Writing and Difference," special issue, *Critical Inquiry* 12, no. 1 (Autumn 1985): 144–65; and Shefali Chandra, *The Sexual Life of English: Languages of Caste and Desire in Colonial India* (Durham, NC: Duke University Press, 2012).

13. Fiona Somerset and Nicholas Watson, *The Vulgar Tongue: Medieval and Postmedieval Vernacularity* (University Park, PA: Penn State University Press, 2003), x.

14. Ibid.

15. In *Strange Vernaculars*, Janet Sorenson notes that the observation of unfamiliar or defamiliarized words is a mode of Enlightenment Orientalism. See Janet Sorenson, *Strange Vernaculars: How Eighteenth-Century Slang, Cant, Provincial Languages, and Nautical Jargon Became English* (Princeton, NJ: Princeton University Press, 2017).

16. See Paula Blank, *Broken English (The Politics of English)* (Oxfordshire: Routledge, 1996); Daniel DeWispelare, *Multilingual Subjects: On Standard English, Its Speakers, and Others in the Long Eighteenth Century* (Philadelphia: University of Pennsylvania Press, 2017); Sorensen, *Strange Vernaculars*.

17. Alexander Beecroft, *An Ecology of World Literature: From Antiquity to the Present Day* (New York: Verso, 2015).

18. Shaden Tageldin, "Beyond Latinity, Can the Vernacular Speak?," *Comparative Literature* 70, no. 2 (2018): 114–31.

19. See Simon Gikandi, "Contested Grammars: Comparative Literature, Translation, and the Challenge of Locality," in *A Companion to Comparative Literature*, ed. Ali Behdad and Dominic Thomas (Oxford: Wiley Blackwell, 2011), 254–72; Ngũgĩ wa Thiong'o, *Decolonising the Mind: The Politics of Language in African Literature* (Portsmouth, NH: Heinemann, 1986); Brian T. Edwards and Dilip Gaonkar, *Globalizing American Studies* (Chicago: University of Chicago Press, 2010).

20. Susan Koshy, "Minority Cosmopolitanism," *PMLA* 126, no. 3 (May 2011): 592.

21. Daniel DeWispelare, "What We Want in Elegance, We Gain in Copiousness: Eighteenth-Century English and Its Empire of Tongues," *The Eighteenth Century* 57, no. 1 (Spring 2016): 127.

22. See Ben Tran, "Negative Paradise: Rethinking Anglophone and World Literature as Literary Dubbing" in *Modern Fiction Studies* 64, no. 1 (Spring 2018): 153–75.

23. Subramanian Shankar, *Flesh and Fish Blood: Postcolonialism, Translation, and the Vernacular* (Berkeley: University of California Press, 2012), 138.

24. Charu Gupta, Laura Brueck, Hans Harder, and Shobna Nijhawan, "Literary Sentiments in the Vernacular: Gender and Genre in Modern South Asia," *South Asia: Journal of South Asian Studies* 43, no. 5 (2020): 803–16; Anirban K. Baishya and Darshana S. Mini, "Translating Porn Studies: Lessons from the Vernacular," *Porn Studies* 7, no. 1 (2020): 2–12; Subramanian Shankar, "The Vernacular: An Introduction," *South Asian Review* 41, no. 2 (2020): 191–93.

25. Amit Chaudhuri, *Picador Book of Modern Indian Literature* (New York: Pan Macmillan, 2001), xxii.

26. Vikram Chandra, "The Cult of Authenticity," *Boston Review*, February 1, 2000, http://bostonreview.net/vikram-chandra-the-cult-of-authenticity.

27. Tageldin, "Beyond Latinity," 118.

28. Donald Winford, "The Origins of African American Vernacular English: Beginnings," in *The Oxford Handbook of African American Vernacular* (New York: Oxford University Press, 2015), 85–104.

29. Bernard Cohn, "The Command of Language, the Language of Command," in *Colonialism and Its Forms of Knowledge: The British in India* (Princeton, NJ: Princeton University Press, 1996), 16–56.

30. See Lisa Mitchell, *Language, Emotion, and Politics in South India: The Making of a Mother Tongue* (Bloomington: Indiana University Press, 2009); Aamir Mufti, *Enlightenment in the Colony: The Jewish Question and the Crisis of Postcolonial Culture* (Princeton, NJ: Princeton University Press, 2007); Francesa Orsini, *The Hindi Public Sphere, 1920–1940: Language and Literature in the Age of Nationalism* (Oxford: Oxford University Press, 2002); Sravanthi Kollu, "On Common Speech: 'Real Vernacular,' Unchaste Woman and the Lure of One's Own Language," *Comparative Studies of South Asia, Africa and the Middle East* (CSSAAME) 41, no. 3 (2021): 485–98.

31. Subramanian Shankar, "Vernacular," *ACLA State of the Discipline*, March 12, 2014, https://stateofthediscipline.acla.org/entry/vernacular.

32. Farina Mir, *The Social Space of Language: Vernacular Culture in British Colonial Punjab* (Berkeley: University of California Press, 2010).

33. Henry Louis Gates Jr., *The Signifying Monkey: A Theory of African-American Literary Criticism* (New York: Oxford University Press, 1988), xxiii.

34. Steve Botterill, introduction to *Dante: De Vulgari Eloquentia*, ed. and trans. Steve Botterill (Cambridge: Cambridge University Press, 1996).

35. Franz Fanon, *Pour la révolution africaine. Écrits politiques* (Paris: Maspero, 1979); Fanon, *Toward the African Revolution*, trans. Haakon Chevalier (New York: Grove Books, 1994), 37.

36. Ragini Tharoor Srinivasan also notes that English is treated as if it is not a language at all. See Ragini Tharoor Srinivasan, "Introduction: South Asia from Postcolonial to World Anglophone," *Interventions* 20 (2018): 309–16.

37. Annette Damayanti Leinau, "Introduction: Vernacular Comparisons beyond the Europhone," *Comparative Literature* 70, no. 2 (2018): 106.

38. Sheldon Pollock, "Future Philology? The Fate of a Soft Science in a Hard World," *Critical Inquiry* 35, no. 4 (Summer 2009): 931–61; Edward Said, "The Return to Philology," in *Humanism and Democratic Criticism* (New York: Columbia University Press, 2004); Siraj Ahmed, *Archaeology of Babel: The Colonial Foundations of the Humanities* (Stanford, CA: Stanford University Press, 2017).

39. Gikandi, "Editorial: Provincializing English," 10.

40. Ibid., 11.

41. Ibid., 13.

42. Chow, "In the Name of Comparative Literature," 108.

43. Gikandi, "Editorial: Provincializing English," 13, my italics.

44. Ulka Anjaria, "New Provincialism," in *Reading India Now: Contemporary Formations in Literature and Popular Culture* (Philadelphia: Temple University Press, 2019).

45. Rita Raley, "A Teleology of Letters; or, From a 'Common Source' to a Common Language," *Romantic Circles Praxis Series* (2000), https://romantic-circles.org/praxis/containment/raley/raley.html.

46. Geeta Patel, "Vernacular Missing: Miraji on Sappho, Gender, and Governance," *Comparative Literature* 70, no. 2 (2018): 132–44.

47. See B. Venkat Mani, "Multilingual Code-Stitching in Ultraminor World Literatures: Reading Abhimanyu Unnuth's *Lāla Pasīnā* (1977) with Amitav Ghosh's *Sea of Poppies* (2008)." *Journal of World Literatures* 3, no. 3 (August 2018); and Jahan Ramazani, "Code-Switching, Code-Stitching: A Macaronic Poetics?," *Poetry in a Global Age* (Chicago: University of Chicago Press, 2020).

48. Jawaharlal Nehru, "Tryst with Destiny," August 14, 1947, https://www.americanrhetoric.com/speeches/jawaharlalnehrutrystwithdestiny.htm.

49. Raley, "Teleology of Letters."

50. Both Nehru and Gandhi, along with other political leaders, agreed that English was needed to speak to the world, which was increasingly important to assert India's emerging place in the international arena.

51. In a different vein, Jinnah's Anglophilia can also be read as an instrumental mobilization of Englishness. Both Ambedkar and Jinnah performed their Anglophilia through English sartorial and material choices. But they have a metonymic relationship with the English language that they both used rather self-consciously. Jinnah cultivated a remarkably English appearance even though he could not imagine a language besides Urdu as the national language of east and west Pakistan. His sartorial style indexed his rationality as a lawyer. Ambedkar dressed in Western-style clothes to defy caste strictures about clothing. In each of these cases, no matter their stance, what is common is this instrumental mobilization of the English language.

52. See more in Rohit De, *A People's Constitution: The Everyday Life of Law in the Indian Republic* (Princeton, NJ: Princeton University Press, 2018).

53. Naoki Sakai, *Translation and Subjectivity: On "Japan" and Cultural Nationalism* (Minneapolis: University of Minnesota Press, 1997), 4.

54. Aamir Mufti, *Forget English! Orientalisms and World Literatures* (Cambridge, MA: Harvard University Press, 2016), 171.

55. Rebecca Walkowitz, *Born Translated: The Contemporary Novel in an Age of World Literature* (New York: Columbia University Press, 2015), 4.

56. See Shankar, *Flesh and Fish Blood*; David Damrosch, *What Is World Literature?* (Princeton, NJ: Princeton University Press, 2003); Ragini Tharoor Srinivasan, "South Asia: From Postcolonial to World Anglophone," *Interventions* 20, no. 3 (2018); Nasia Anam, "Forms of the Global Anglophone," *Post45 Contemporaries*, February 22, 2019, https://post45.org/sections/contemporaries-essays/global-anglophone/.

57. In her short essay, "What's in a Name? The Global Anglophone, the Anglosphere, and the English-Speaking Peoples," Marina Bilbija writes, "There is no such thing as an Anglophone world." See Bilbija, "What's in a Name? The Global Anglophone, the Anglosphere, and the English-Speaking Peoples" in "Forms of the Global Anglophone," *Post45*, February 22, 2019, https://post45.org/2019/02/whats-in-a-name-the-global-anglophone-the-anglosphere-and-the-english-speaking-peoples/.

58. See Madhumita Lahiri, *Imperfect Solidarities: Tagore, Gandhi, Du Bois, and the Global Anglophone* (Evanston, IL: Northwestern University Press, 2020).

59. Snigdha Poonam, "The English Man," in *Dreamers: How Young Indians Are Changing the World* (Cambridge, MA: Harvard University Press, 2018), 31.

60. Poonam writes that the English that is taught in the many "English-speaking schools" is "not the English of English literature or that of official project reports, but a cut-price version called, simply, Spoken English. It required of its user barely the ability to speak a set of sentences to get through basic communication in a globalizing India. Spoken English was going to be the operative language of the new India, the currency of communication at 'multi-cuisine resto-bars' [a fusion name for a restaurant and bar that serves several different cuisines], shopping malls, airport check-ins" (Ibid., 29).

61. I borrow the vocabulary of "flipping the gaze" from Laura Brueck who repositions Premchand's representation of caste violence through Dalit reading and writing on it. See Brueck, "Questions of Representation in Dalit Critical Discourse: Premchand and Dalit Feminism," in *Dalit Studies*, ed. Ramanarayan Rawat (Durham, NC: Duke University Press, 2016), 193–214.

62. Michael Lucey and Tom McEaneny, "Introduction: Language-in-Use and Literary Fieldwork," *Representations* 137, no. 1 (2017): 1–22.

63. As literary scholars, we are used to asking "who speaks" but rarely "who listens?" or "how?" These latter questions motivate Julie Beth Napolin's book, *Facts of Resonance: Modernist Acoustics and Narrative Form*, which explores the "acoustics" of the modernist novel. Napolin pointedly notes that the presence of a linguistic difference—be it a foreign language or dialect—in a literary work requires description, transcription, and translation. Each of these practices is marked by cultural power relations that "focalize" or home in on an ethnographic difference. See Napolin, *Facts of Resonance: Modernist Acoustics and Narrative Form* (New York: Fordham University Press, 2020).

64. François Noudelmann, "Philosophical Aurality," *PMLA* 135, no. 2 (March 2020): 418.

65. Rita Raley, "Machine Translation and Global English," *The Yale Journal of Criticism* 16, no. 3 (Fall 2003): 291–313.

66. Damrosch, *What Is World Literature?*, 225.

67. See Mũkoma wa Ngũgĩ's *The Rise of the African Novel: Politics of Language, Identity, and Ownership* (Ann Arbor: University of Michigan Press, 2018); and John Mugane, "Contemporary Conversations: Is English an African Language?," *Journal of African Cultural Studies* 30, no. 2 (2018): 121–23.

68. Ada Uzoamaka Azodo, "Interview with Chimamanda Ngozi Adichie: Creative Writing and Literary Activism," https://citeseerx.ist.psu.edu/viewdoc/download?doi=10.1.1.551.6641&rep=rep1&type=pdf.

69. Adichie in Azodo, "Interview," 2.

70. J. Daniel Elam, "The Form of Global Anglophone Literature Is Grenfell Tower," in "Forms of the Global Anglophone," *Post45 Contemporaries*, February 22, 2019, https://post45.org/2019/02/the-form-of-global-anglophone-literature-is-grenfell-tower/.

71. Five years ago, in the new "Preface to the 25th Anniversary Edition" of *The Masks of Conquest: Literary Study and British Rule in India*, Gauri Viswanathan returns the colonial origins of English literary studies to claim that its current and future shape will be as diffuse. See Gauri Viswanathan, *Masks of Conquest: Literary Study and British Rule in India* (Twenty-Fifth Anniversary Edition) (New York: Columbia University Press, 2014), xii.

Chapter 1. Law: Democratic Objects in Postcolonial India, or India Demands English

1. Walter Hakala, *Negotiating Languages: Urdu, Hindi, and the Definition of Modern South Asia* (New York: Columbia University Press, 2016).

2. Commission for Scientific and Technical Terminology, Government of India, http://www.csttpublication.mhrd.gov.in/english/overview.php.

3. Akhil Gupta, *Red Tape: Bureaucracy, Structural Violence, and Poverty in India* (Durham, NC: Duke University Press, 2012).

4. Lisa Gitelman, *Paper Knowledge: Toward a Media History of Documents* (Durham, NC: Duke University Press, 2014).

5. Emma Tarlo, "Paper Truths: The Emergency and Slum Clearance through Forgotten Files," in *The Everyday State in Modern India*, ed. C. J. Fuller and Veronique Benei (London: C. Hurst, 2001).

6. Aijaz Ahmad, *Disciplinary English: Theory, Third Worldism, and Literary Study in India*, Occasional Papers on History and Society 43 (New Delhi: Centre for Contemporary Studies, Nehru Memorial Museum and Library, 1991), 60.

7. John Durham Peters, *Speaking into the Air: A History of the Idea of Communication* (Chicago: University of Chicago Press, 2001).

8. See Aamir Mufti, *Enlightenment in the Colony: The Jewish Question and the Crisis of Postcolonial Culture* (Princeton, NJ: Princeton University Press, 2007).

9. M. K. Gandhi, *The Collected Works of Mahatma Gandhi*, vol. 9, September 1908–November 1909 (The Publications Division, Ministry of Information and Broadcasting, Government of India, 1963), 177–78.

10. Ibid.

11. Ibid.

12. Ibid.

13. Gandhi in "A Sad Spectacle" (1948), in *Our Language Problem*, ed. Anand T. Hingorani (Bombay: Bharatiya Vidya Bhavan, 1965), 34.

14. In the January 25, 1948, issue of *Harijansewak*, Gandhi justified publishing his weekly journal, *Harijan*, in English by strategically delinking the empire of the

English language from the British Empire: "The British empire will go because it has been and still is bad; but the empire of the English language cannot go." Gandhi in Hingorani, 131.

15. Tagore in Gandhi, *Collected Works* (1909), 178.

16. Mufti, *Enlightenment in the Colony*, 144.

17. Sandipto Dasgupta, "'A Language Which Is Foreign to Us': Continuities and Anxieties in the Making of the Indian Constitution," *Comparative Studies of South Asia, Africa and the Middle East* 34, no. 2 (2014): 231.

18. *Constitution of India*, https://www.mea.gov.in/Images/pdf1/Part17.pdf.

19. Lydia Liu, *The Clash of Empires: The Invention of China in Modern World Making* (Cambridge, MA: Harvard University Press, 2006), 38.

20. Ibid., 37.

21. Ibid., 34–35.

22. Mufti, *Enlightenment in the Colony*, 146.

23. B. R., Ambedkar, *Thoughts on Linguistic States* (1955), http://drambedkar.co.in/wp-content/uploads/books/category2/9thoughts-on-linguistic-states.pdf.

24. Ambedkar writes, "How can this danger be met? The only way I can think of meeting the danger is to provide in the Constitution that the regional language shall not be the official language of the State. The official language of the State shall be Hindi and *until India becomes fit for this purpose English*. Will Indians accept this? If they do not, linguistic States may easily become a peril" (Ambedkar, *Thoughts*, 8, my italics).

25. Dasgupta, "'A Language Which Is Foreign to Us,'" 231.

26. Isaac Mathai, ed., *India Demands English; The Speeches and Writings of C.P. Ramaswami Iyer [and Others]* (Bombay: Mathai's Publications, 1960), 4.

27. Gupta, *Red Tape*, 182.

28. Adib, "Life and Letters" in Mathai, *India Demands English*, 55.

29. See also Chandra, *Sexual Life*.

30. Mathai, *India Demands English*, 58.

31. C. Rajagopalachari, "Five Fallacies about Hindi," in Mathai, *India Demands English*, 66–67, my italics.

32. Mirza Ismail, "Wanton Destroying of National Asset," in Mathai, *India Demands English*, 68, my italics.

33. Ibid., 48.

34. Ibid., 68.

35. Ibid., 29.

36. Elspeth Probyn, "Writing Shame," in *Affect Theory Reader*, ed. Melissa Gregg and Gregory J. Seigworth (Durham, NC: Duke University Press, 2010), 71–92.

37. See Akshya Saxena, "Pushing Hindi as Politics, Not Hindi as Language." *The Wire.* June 13, 2019. https://thewire.in/education/national-education-policy-hindi-language.

38. Upamanyu Chatterjee, *English, August: An Indian Story* (1988; repr., New York: New York Review of Books, 2006), 10.

39. Srilal Sukla, *Raag Darbari* (1968; repr., New Delhi: Rajkamal Prakashan, 2013), 137.

40. Mufti, *Enlightenment in the Colony*, 134.

41. Sukla, *Raag Darbari*, 19.

42. Jyotindra DasGupta, *Language Conflict and National Development* (Berkeley: University of California Press, 1970), 141.

43. Ibid., 140.

44. Viswanathan, *Masks of Conquest*, 22.

45. Sukla, *Raag Darbari*, 178.

46. Ibid.

47. Ibid., 260.

48. Ibid.

49. Ibid.

50. Ibid., 60.

51. Ibid.

52. Ibid., 148.

53. Ibid., 59.

54. Ibid., 60.

55. Upamanyu Chatterjee, *Mammaries of the Welfare State* (New Delhi: Penguin, 2001), 133.

56. Nehru in Selma Sonntag, *Local Politics of Global English: Case Studies in Linguistic Globalization* (Lanham, MD: Lexington Books, 2003), 62.

57. Ibid.

58. Nehru in Mathai, *India Demands English*, 59.

59. Ibid.

60. Rey Chow, *Not Like a Native Speaker: On Languaging as a Postcolonial Experience* (New York: Columbia University Press, 2014), 14.

61. Ibid.

62. Jacques Derrida, *Monolingualism of the Other, or The Prosthesis of Origin*, trans. Patrick Mensah (Stanford, CA: Stanford University Press, 1998), 5, emphasis original.

Chapter 2. Touch: Dalit Anglophone Writers and a Language Shared

1. For instance, the now famous Jaipur Literary Festival did not feature Dalit writers in its early years. While underrepresentation of Dalits has changed in recent years, Dalit writers and activists (as part of the Ambedkarite Writers' Society) have also hosted a separate festival in Delhi called the Dalit Literature Festival.

2. Dhrubo Jyoti, "A New Horizon in Dalit Writing," *Hindustan Times*, August 4, 2018.

3. The poets' demand to be hosted at the Sahitya Akademi speaks to possibilities of a nationwide and pan-Dalit representation in English. There already exists a Dalit Sahitya Akademi, which is supposed to be the Dalit equivalent of the state institution that is Sahitya Akademi. See more in Laura Brueck, *Writing Resistance: The Rhetorical Imagination of Hindi Dalit Literature* (New York: Columbia University Press, 2016).

4. Personal conversation, May 20, 2019.

5. Christoph Jaffrelot, *Religion, Caste, and Politics in India* (Delhi: Primus Books, 2010), xvi.

6. See Manoranjan Byapari, "How Important Is English for Dalits?," *RAIOT*, http://www.raiot.in/how-important-is-english-for-the-dalits/.

7. Anupama Rao, *The Caste Question: Dalit Politics and the Making of Modern India* (New York: Columbia University Press, 2000), xi.

8. Subramanian Shankar and Charu Gupta, "'My Birth Is My Fatal Accident': Introduction to Caste and Life Narratives," *Biography* 40, no. 1 (2017): 2.

9. Luis Cabrera, "'Gandhiji, I Have No Homeland': Cosmopolitan Insights from BR Ambedkar, India's Anti-Caste Campaigner and Constitutional Architect," *Political Studies* 65, no. 3 (October 2017): 576–93.

10. In *Sexual Life of English*, Shefali Chandra shows that English was always regulated by caste in India but still not defined by it.

11. Neerav Patel, "The Remains of the Name," *Gujarati Dalit Literature* (blog), http://gujaratidalitsahitya.blogspot.com/2009/08/poems-by-neerav-patel.html.

12. Rita Kothari, "Caste in a Casteless Language," *Economic and Political Weekly* 48, no. 39 (September 28, 2013): 60–68.

13. Laura Brueck and Christi Merrill, "Beyond Untouchability: Dalit Literature in Hindi," *Words without Borders*, October 2018, https://www.wordswithoutborders.org/article/october-2018-dalit-writing-beyond-untouchability-dalit-literature-in-hindi.

14. Ibid.

15. Kandasamy in Pallavi Singh, "Dalits Look upon English as the Language of Emancipation," *Live Mint*, March 8, 2010, https://www.livemint.com/Politics/ItCo2HSpKjf98VvW8X4yAO/Dalits-look-upon-English-as-the-language-of-emancipation.html.

16. Meena Kandasamy, *Touch* (Mumbai: Peacock Books, 2006), 21. See also "Once My Silence Held You Spellbound," in Meena Kandasamy, *Ms. Militancy* (New Delhi: Navayana, 2010), 39–40.

17. Brueck, *Writing Resistance*, 126.

18. Jotirao Phule, "Slavery" (1873), in *Selected Writings of Jotirao Phule*, ed. G. P. Deshpande (Delhi: LeftWord Books, 2002), 24.

19. Tanya Agathocleous, "Jyoti Rao Phule's Slavery," *b2o*, https://www.boundary2.org/2016/10/jyotirao-phule-slavery/.

20. Nico Slate, *Colored Cosmopolitanism: The Shared Struggle for Freedom in the United States and India* (Cambridge, MA: Harvard University Press, 2017), 13.

21. Phule, "Slavery," 25.

22. Ibid.

23. Ibid.

24. Phule in S. Anand, "Jai Angrezi Devi Maiyya Ki" (Praise Be to Mother English), *Open: The Magazine*, May 8, 2010.

25. "Sanskrit, English, and the Dalits," *Economic and Political Weekly*, July 24, 1999, 2056.

26. Ibid., 2054.

27. Merrill and Brueck, "Beyond Untouchability."

28. Kancha Ilaiah, *Why I Am Not a Hindu: A Sudra Critique of Hindutva* (1996; repr., Calcutta: Samya, 2005), 13.

29. Ibid., 56.

30. Kancha Ilaiah Shepherd, *From a Shepherd Boy to an Intellectual—My Memoirs* (New Delhi: Sage, 2019), 31.

31. See Shepherd, *From a Shepherd Boy to an Intellectual*.

32. Kancha Ilaiah Shepherd, "Do English Educated Become Christians?," Countercurrents.org, https://countercurrents.org/2019/12/do-english-educated-become-christians.

33. Ibid.

34. Kancha Ilaiah, "Dalit and English," *Anveshi Broadsheet on Contemporary Politics: Language, Region and Community* (English version) 2, nos. 4 and 5, https://www.anveshi.org.in/wp-content/uploads/2015/01/Language-Region-and-Community-English.pdf.

35. Chandrabhan Prasad, "The Impure Milk of Macaulay" (2000), in *Dalit Diary, 1999–2003: Reflections on Apartheid in India* (New Delhi: Navayana, 2004).

36. See Akshya Saxena, "Purchasing Power, Stolen Power, and the Limits of Capitalist Form: Dalit Capitalists and the Caste Question in the Indian Anglophone Novel," *ariel: A Review of International English Literature* 52, no. 1 (2021): 61–90.

37. Macaulay in Lynn Zastoupil and Martin Moir, eds., *The Great Indian Education Debate: Documents relating to the Orientalist-Anglicist Controversy, 1781–1843* (London: Curzon Press, 1999), 171, my italics.

38. Anand, "Jai Angrezi Devi Maiyya Ki" (Praise Be to Mother English).

39. Sumathi Ramaswamy, "The Work of Goddesses in the Age of Mass Reproduction," in *Transcultural Turbulences: Towards a Multi-Sited Reading of Image Flows*, ed. Christiane Brosius and Roland Wenzlhuemer (London: Springer, 2011), 206.

40. Prasad in Shivam Vij, "Dalit Intellectualizing and Other Backward Classes," *Himal South Asian*, September 2006, http://old.himalmag.com/component/content/article/1548-Dalit-intellectualising-and-the-Other-Backward-Classes.html.

41. Prasad in Anand, "Jai Angrezi Devi Maiyya Ki."

42. Ramaswamy, "Work of Goddesses," 195.

43. Chandrabhan Prasad, "Hail English, the Dalit Goddess," *Daily News and Analysis*, October 28, 2006, https://www.dnaindia.com/analysis/comment-hail-english-the-dalit-goddess-1060755.

44. Chandramohan Sathyanathan, *Love after Babel, and Other Poems* (Ottawa: Daraja Press, 2019).

45. Ibid.

46. Yogesh Maitreya, *The Bridge of Migration* (Mumbai: Panther's Paw Publications, 2017).

47. Ibid., 68.

48. Patel in Kothari, "Caste in a Casteless Language," 65.

49. Maitreya, "Recollecting an Old Self," in *Bridge of Migration*, 58.

50. Sathyanathan, "Killing the Shambuka," in *Letters to Namdeo Dhasal* (Vadodra: DesirePaths Publishers, 2016), 1.

51. Henry Louis Gates, Jr., *The Signifying Monkey: A Theory of African-American Criticism* (New York: Oxford University Press, 1988).

52. "Namantar," https://www.edexlive.com/people/2020/jan/31/how-yogesh-maitreya-set-up-a-publishing-house-to-develop-an-anti-caste-sensibility-among-indias-you-10082.html.

53. Ibid.

54. Maitreya in Shekhar, Hansda Sowvendra, "The Indian Publishing House That's Become a Movement," *The Hindu*, March 15, 2020, https://www.thehindu.com/books/the-publishing-house-thats-become-a-movement/article31058534.ece.

55. Yogesh Maitreya, "My English Isn't Broken, Your English Is Brahmin," BuzzFeed, January 4, 2018, https://www.buzzfeed.com/yogeshmaitreya/does-the-subaltern-speak-in-correct-grammar.

56. Ibid.

57. Maitreya, *Bridge of Migration*, 90.

58. Cynthia Stephen, "A Poem for Today's India," Countercurrents.org, October 10, 2017, https://countercurrents.org/2017/10/a-poem-for-todays-india/; Aruna Gogulamanda, "A Dalit Woman in the Land of Goddesses," Firstpost.com, https://www.firstpost.com/long-reads/a-dalit-woman-in-the-land-of-goddesses-3919861.html.

59. Namdeo Dhasal, "Cruelty," in *A Current of Blood*, trans. Dilip Chitre (New Delhi: Navayana, 2011).

60. Ibid.

61. Laurie Hovell, "Namdeo Dhasal: Poet and Panther," in "Miscellany," *Journal of South Asian Literature* 24, no. 2 (Summer, Fall 1989): 65–82.

62. Brueck, *Writing Resistance*, 121.

63. Ajay Navaria, *Yes, Sir* (New Delhi: Samayik Prakashan, 2012), 182.

64. Ibid., 181, my emphasis.

65. Ibid., 182, my emphasis.

66. B. R. Ambedkar, *Waiting for a Visa* (1935–36), http://www.columbia.edu/itc/mealac/pritchett/00ambedkar/txt_ambedkar_waiting.html.

67. Navaria, *Yes, Sir*, 52, my emphasis.

68. Ibid.

69. Patel in Kothari, "Caste in a Casteless Language," 65.

70. Navaria, *Yes, Sir*, 52.

71. Selma Sonntag, "Ideology and Policy in the Politics of the English Language in North India," in *Ideology, Politics, and Language Policies: Focus on English*, ed. Thomas Ricento (Amsterdam: John Benjamins, 2000), 133–49.

72. Agrawal in Sonntag, "Ideology and Policy," 68.

Chapter 3. Text: A Desire Called English in Indian Anglophone Literature

1. Mulk Raj Anand, *The King Emperor's English; or, the Role of the English Language in the Free India*, afterward by Maulana Abul Kalam Azad (Bombay: Hind Kitabs, 1948).

2. Kristen Bluemel, "Mulk Raj Anand's Passage through Bloomsbury," in *George Orwell and the Radical Eccentrics: Intermodernism in Literary London* (New York: Palgrave MacMillan, 2004), 94.

3. Rashmi Sadana, *English Heart, Hindi Heartland: The Political Life of Literature in India* (Berkeley: University of California Press, 2012), 14.

4. Stuart Jeffries begins his review of *The White Tiger* by noting the risk taken by Adiga by asking this question, "How do you get the nerve, I ask Aravind Adiga, to write a novel about the experiences of the Indian poor?" See Stuart Jeffries, "Roars of Anger" in *The Guardian*, October 15, 2008.

5. Arundhati Roy, *The God of Small Things* (New York: Random House, 1997), 79.

6. Ibid., 80.

7. Ibid.

8. Subramanian Shankar, "Teaching Mulk Raj Anand's *Untouchable*: Colonial Context, Nationalism, Caste," *Cambridge Journal of Postcolonial Literary Inquiry* 4, no. 2 (April 2017): 332–41.

9. Priyamvada Gopal, *The Indian English Novel: Nation, History, and Narration* (Oxford: Oxford University Press, 2009), 51.

10. Ibid.

11. Nandini Sahu, ed., *The Post-Colonial Space: Writing the Self and the Nation* (New Delhi: Atlantic, 2007), 79.

12. Most scholarship on *Untouchable* has focused on how Anand's membership in the Progressive Writers' Association shaped his imagination of a caste-marked revolutionary subject as India emerged into nationhood. See Ben Conisbee Baer, "Shit Writing: Mulk Raj Anand's *Untouchable*, the Image of Gandhi, and the Progressive Writers' Association," *Modernism/modernity* 16, no. 3 (2009); Ulka Anjaria, *Realism in the Twentieth-Century Indian Novel: Colonial Difference and Literary Form* (New York: Cambridge University Press, 2012); Aamir Mufti, *Enlightenment in the Colony: The Jewish Question and the Crisis of Postcolonial Culture* (Princeton, NJ: Princeton University Press, 2007); Mufti, *Forget English! Orientalisms and World Literatures* (Cambridge, MA: Harvard University Press, 2016); Toral Gajarawala, *Untouchable Fictions: Literary Realism and the Crisis of Caste* (New York: Fordham University Press, 2012); Snehal Shingavi, *The Mahatma Misunderstood: The Politics and Forms of Literary Nationalism in India* (London: Anthem, 2013); Neetu Khanna, *The Visceral Logics of Decolonization* (Durham, NC: Duke University Press, 2020). In *Forget English!* Mufti reads *Untouchable* with Salman Rushdie's *Midnight's Children* (1981) to illuminate the unbridgeable "social distance" between the English of the narrative voice and the subaltern characters of Bakha and Padma respectively. Tracing the discursive suturing between the worlds of the narrator and the subaltern subject, Mufti argues that he finds that Bakha sounds too much like the narrator. On the other hand, in *Midnight's Children*, the character of Padma sounds nothing like the narrator. Mufti writes that Gandhi's comment about Bakha as a Bloomsbury intellectual is "more than just an amusing throwaway remark . . . for it identifies a central tension of the Indian (and world) Anglophone novel as a form" (161). However, in his reading, Mufti situates Bakha as a national subject on par with Clarissa Dalloway, and does not investigate the specificity of Bakha as a Dalit, indeed the titular "untouchable" subject who might have a different relationship to the English language.

13. Tom Rice, "Listening," in *Keywords in Sound*, ed. David Novak and Matt Sakakeeny (Durham, NC: Duke University Press, 2015), 99–111.

14. Mulk Raj Anand, *Untouchable* (1935; London: Penguin, 1940), 130, 132, 132, 135.

15. Ibid., 8.

16. Gilles Deleuze and Felix Guattari, *A Thousand Plateaus: Capitalism and Schizophrenia*, trans. and foreword by Brian Massumi (Minneapolis: University of Minnesota Press, 1987), 80.

17. Baer, "Shit Writing," 579.

18. Ibid., 581.

19. Marjorie Garber, *Vested Interests: Cross-Dressing and Cultural Anxiety* (New York: Routledge, 1991), 390.

20. Anand, *Untouchable*, 3.

21. Ambedkar and Muhammed Ali Jinnah were two leaders who dressed in English-style clothes. Faisal Devji has discussed the different rhetorical and linguistic styles of some of these leaders. See Faisal Devji, "Jinnah and the Theater of Politics," *Asiatische Studien: Études asiatiques* 67, no. 4 (2013): 1179–1204.

22. Ambedkar in Masoodi, "The Changing Fabric of Dalit Life." This poem is routinely recited by the Cultural Squad of the Bahujan Samaj Party (Majority People's Party), a national-level political party of caste and religious minorities in India, in order to generate awareness among Dalits about the injustices perpetrated on them by the upper castes and to mobilize them. See Ashwaq Masoodi, "The Changing Fabric of Dalit Life," *Live Mint*, April 21, 2007, https://www.livemint.com/Leisure/avsrwntNuBHG3THdAb5aMP/The-changing-fabric-of-Dalit-life.html. In the context of the discussion on clothes, it is also telling that in the account provided by Anand, Gandhi's criticism of Bakha's language is preceded by his critique of Anand's outfit. Anand reports, "Gandhi looked at my thick corduroy suit and said: 'Why do you want to look like a monkey?' I answered, 'You looked like a monkey at one time with your frock coat and top-hat.' He smiled at my brazen answer and asked his secretary Mahadev Desai to lend me *Kurta Pyjama*" (Anand in Sahu, *Post-Colonial Space*, 79).

23. Anand, *Untouchable*, 113.

24. It is important to note that caste discrimination exists beyond Hinduism. For instance, Christian and Muslim communities discriminate against Dalit converts by maintaining separate caste-marked graveyards.

25. Ibid., 115.

26. Ibid., 112.

27. Ibid., 113.

28. Ibid., 121.

29. Ibid., 113.

30. Baer, "Shit Writing," 580.

31. Ibid.

32. Anand, *Untouchable*, 11.

33. Ibid., 87.

34. Rey Chow and James Steintrager, eds., *Sound Objects* (Durham, NC: Duke University Press, 2019).

35. Anand, *Untouchable*, 8.

36. Ibid., 30.

37. Ibid., 44, 42.

38. Baer, "Shit Writing," 579.

39. Anand, *King Emperor's English*, 16.

40. Ibid., 17.

41. Anand, *Untouchable*, 128, parentheses original; my emphasis.

42. Ibid., 136.

43. Ibid., 141.

44. Ibid., 146.

45. Forster in ibid., viii.

46. Aravind Adiga, *The White Tiger* (London: HarperCollins Publishers, 2008), 3.

47. Ibid., 4–5, my italics.

48. Ibid., 3.

49. Ibid., 295.
50. Ibid., 247, 176, 47.
51. Ibid., 152.
52. See Betty Joseph, "Neoliberalism and Allegory," *Cultural Critique* 82 (Fall 2012): 68–94.
53. Adiga, *White Tiger*, 150, my italics.
54. Ibid., 283.
55. Ibid., 40.
56. Ibid., 147.
57. Ibid.
58. Ibid., 160.

Chapter 4. Sound: The Mother's Voice and Anglophonic Soundscapes in Northeast India

1. Since her attention to literacy in *Born Translated*, Rebecca Walkowitz has continued exploring the way different kinds of literacies shape linguistic knowledge. See "Less Than One Language: Typographic Multilingualism and Post-Anglophone Fiction," *SubStance* 50, no. 1 (2021): 95–115.

2. Friedrich Kittler, *Discourse Networks 1800/1900*, trans. Michael Metteer (Stanford, CA: Stanford University Press, 1990), 34.

3. Ibid., 25.

4. *Census of India*. Office of the Registrar General and Census Commissioner, Ministry of Home Affairs, Government of India, 2011. http://censusindia.gov.in/.

5. Ibid.

6. G. N. Devy, "Indigenous Languages," *Seminar*, no. 601 (Republic of Ideas) (September 2009).

7. See Shefali Chandra, *The Sexual Life of English: Languages of Caste and Desire in Colonial India* (Durham, NC: Duke University Press, 2012).

8. Mladen Dolar, *A Voice and Nothing More* (Cambridge, MA: MIT Press, 2006), 19.

9. Ibid.

10. Yasemin Yildiz, *Beyond the Mother Tongue: The Postmonolingual Condition* (New York: Fordham University Press, 2012), 2.

11. There are numerous easily available reports of Manorama's murder. I do not want to describe the details here because there is a casualness with which such instances of torture and murder circulate in India today. That said, the brutality of the act is important for gauging the impunity with which the Armed Forces act in the region.

12. Adriana Cavarero, "Towards a Theory of Sexual Difference," in *The Lonely Mirror: Italian Perspectives on Feminist Theory*, ed. Sandra Kemp and Paola Bono (New York: Routledge, 1993), 200.

13. Naoki Sakai, *Translation and Subjectivity: On "Japan" and Cultural Nationalism* (Minneapolis: University of Minnesota Press, 1997), 4.

14. See more in Papori Bora, "Speech of the Nation and Conversations at the Margins of the Nation-State," *Interventions* 17, no. 5 (2015): 669–85, and Sanjib Baruah, *Durable Disorder: Understanding the Politics of Northeast India* (Oxford: Oxford University Press, 2007).

15. Baruah, *Durable Disorder*, 13.

16. See Papori Bora, "The Problem without a Name: Comments on Cultural Difference (Racism) in India," *South Asia: Journal of South Asian Studies* 42, no. 5 (2019): 845–60.

17. Bora, "Speech of the Nation," 683.

18. Bora writes, "This inequality emerges from the fact that India as a political and cultural category is always already given in nationalist thought. In this imagination, the Northeast is an afterthought. To speak to India, the Northeast has to accept the terms set by nationalism. When it tries to speak autonomously, in a way that does not regurgitate the lines provided to it by nationalism, it is deemed the speech of an outsider" (Ibid., 671).

19. Northeast Network, *Tailoring Peace: Citizens Roundtable in Manipur and Beyond* (2005), 33–34.

20. Giorgio Agamben, *Remnants of Auschwitz: The Witness and the Archive* (London: MIT Press, 1999), 115.

21. *The Quint*, "On this Mother's Day, the Quint Salutes the Brave Mothers of Manipur," May 7, 2016, YouTube video.

22. Laura Kunreuther, "Sounds of Democracy: Performance, Protest, and Political Subjectivity," *Cultural Anthropology* 33, no. 1 (2018): 1–31.

23. Nandana Dutta, "Northeast India: A New Literary Region for Indian Writing in English," September 18, 2018, Oxford University Press Blog, https://blog.oup.com/2018/09/northeast-india-new-literary-region/.

24. Arkotong Longkumer, "'Along Kingdom's Highway': The Proliferation of Christianity, Education, and Print amongst the Nagas in Northeast India," *Contemporary South Asia* 27, no. 2 (2019): 160–78.

25. Pooja Rangan, *Immediations: The Humanitarian Impulse in Documentary* (Durham, NC: Duke University Press, 2017), 108.

26. Ibid.

27. Anubha Bhonsle, *Mother, Where's My Country? Looking for Light in the Darkness of Manipur* (New Delhi: Speaking Tree Books, 2016), 105.

28. Teresa Rehman, *The Mothers of Manipur: Twelve Women Who Made History* (New Delhi: Zubaan Books, 2017), xxxii.

29. Deepti Misri, "'Are You a Man': Performing Naked Protest in India," in *Signs* 36, no. 3 (Spring, 2011): 609.

30. Devi in Gayatri Chakravorty Spivak, "'Draupadi' by Mahasveta Devi," in "Writing and Sexual Difference," *Critical Inquiry* 8, no. 2 (Winter, 1981): 393.

31. Ibid., 402.

32. Ibid., 390.

33. Ibid.

34. Arundhati Roy, "What Is the Morally Appropriate Language in Which to Think and Write?," *Literary Hub*, July 25, 2018, https://lithub.com/what-is-the-morally-appropriate-language-in-which-to-think-and-write/.

35. Amit R. Baishya, *Contemporary Literature from Northeast India: Deathworlds, Terror and Survival* (London: Routledge, 2019), 8.

36. Yumlembam Ibomcha, "Nightmare," in *The Oxford Anthology of Writings from North-East India*, Volume I: Fiction, ed. Tilottoma Mishra (New Delhi: Oxford University Press, 2011), 173–77.

37. See Marianne Hirsch, *The Generation of Postmemory: Writing and Visual Culture after the Holocaust* (New York: Columbia University Press, 2012).

38. Temsula Ao, *These Hills Called Home: Stories from a War Zone* (New Delhi: Zubaan, 2014), x.

39. Ibid.

40. Ibid., 9.

41. Ibid.

42. Ibid., 10.

43. Rangan, *Immediations*, 2017.

44. Ao, *These Hills Called Home*, 27.

45. Ibid., 28.

46. Ibid., 29.

47. Ibid., 32.

48. Ibid., 33.

49. Baishya, *Contemporary Literature from Northeast India*, 150.

Chapter 5. Sight: Cinematic English and the Pleasures of Not Reading

1. Vikram Seth, *A Suitable Boy* (New Delhi: Penguin Books, 1994), 45.

2. Rita Raley, "Machine Translation and Global English," *The Yale Journal of Criticism* 16, no. 2 (Fall 2003): 291–313; Michael Allan, "Picturing Other Languages," *College Literature* 82, no. 1 (September 2019): 96–114; Lydia Liu, *The Freudian Robot: Digital Media and the Future of the Unconscious* (Chicago: University of Chicago Press, 2011).

3. See Minae Mizumura, *The Fall of Language in the Age of English* (New York: Columbia University Press, 2015).

4. Sangeeta Gopal and Sujata Moorti, eds., *Global Bollywood: Travels of Hindi Song and Dance* (Minneapolis: University of Minnesota Press, 2008), 9.

5. In addition to Swarup's original novel *Q & A*, the film was also inspired by Indian cinema. Simon Beaufoy (script writer) drew on films like *Deewar* (1975), *Satya* (1998), and *D-Company* (2002). Boyle has also stated that the chase in one of the opening scenes of *Slumdog Millionaire* was based on a chase scene in another mainstream Hindi film *Black Friday* (2007).

6. These actors from the Mumbai slums were not compensated adequately or on par with the other "professional" actors. Ajay Gehlawat, introduction to *The Slumdog Phenomenon: A Critical Anthology*, ed. Ajay Gehlawat (New York: Anthem Press, 2013), 166.

7. Ian Garwood, "The Songless Bollywood Film," *South Asian Popular Culture* 4, no. 2 (2006): 175.

8. Rachel Beckman, "An Out-of-Character Role for Subtitles," *The Washington Post*, November 16, 2008, https://www.washingtonpost.com/wp-dyn/content/article/2008/11/14/AR2008111400700.html.

9. Simon Beaufoy, Danny Boyle, and Rob Feld, *The Shooting Script: Slumdog Millionaire* (New York: New Market Press, 2008), 141.

10. David Norman Rodowick, *Reading the Figural or, Philosophy after New Media* (Durham, NC: Duke University Press, 2001), xiii.

11. Garwood, "Songless Bollywood Film," 176.

12. See Tejaswini Ganti, *Producing Bollywood: Inside the Contemporary Hindi Film Industry* (Durham, NC: Duke University Press, 2012), 99.

13. Ranjani Mazumdar, *Bombay Cinema: An Archive of a City* (Minneapolis: University of Minnesota Press, 2007), 78.

14. Mukul Kesavan, "Lost in Translation," *The Telegraph*, February 5, 2009.

15. Rey Chow, *Not Like a Native Speaker: On Languaging as a Postcolonial Experience* (New York: Columbia University Press, 2014), 10.

16. Swati Chattopadhyay, *Unlearning the City: Infrastructure in a New Optical Field* (Minneapolis: University of Minnesota Press, 2012), xxii.

17. Bobby Friction, "Can Indian Hip Hop Take Over the World," https://www.bbc.co.uk/programmes/articles/1XmwgT9wFx8QTfnWpttjFxf/can-indian-hip-hop-take-over-the-world.

18. Cyrus Oshidar in Gauri Sharma, "Hip-Hop Homeland: India's Underground Rap Scene," *Al Jazeera*, July 8, 2016, https://www.aljazeera.com/indepth/features/2016/05/hip-hop-homeland-india-underground-rap-scene-160531093658178.html.

19. Friction in Michael Hann, "Divine and Prabh Deep Leading India's Hip Hop Revolution," *Financial Times*, August 29, 2019, https://www.ft.com/content/c087c7ce-c8db-11e9-af46-b09e8bfe60c0.

20. Ashish Rajadhyaksha, "Bollywoodization of Indian Cinema: Cultural Nationalism in a Global Arena," *Inter-Asia Cultural Studies* 4, no. 1 (2003): 29.

21. Ravi Vasudevan, "The Meanings of 'Bollywood,'" *Journal of the Moving Image* 7 (2008): 339.

22. M. Madhava Prasad, "This Thing Called Bollywood," *India-Seminar Unsettling Cinema: A Symposium on the Place of Cinema in India* #525, May 2003, http://www.india-seminar.com/2003/525/525%20madhava%20prasad.htm.

23. Ibid.

24. Budhaditya Chattopadhya, "The Auditory Spectacle: Design Sound for the Dubbing Era of Indian Cinema," *The New Soundtrack* 5, no. 1 (March 2015): 55–68.

25. *The Report of the Working Group on National Film Policy*, 3.

26. Ibid.

27. Monika Mehta, *Censorship and Sexuality in Bombay Cinema* (Dallas: University of Texas Press, 2011), 33.

28. Maithili Rao, "*Kama Sutra*: Passionless!," *Screen Weekly*, February 13, 1998, 8.

29. Ingrid Piller, "Iconicity in Brand Names," in *Form Miming Meaning*, ed. Max Nänny and Olga Fischer (Amsterdam: John Benjamins, 1999), 327.

30. Mehta, *Censorship and Sexuality*, 75.

31. Ibid.

32. Krishna R. Mohan, "Censorship Is Every Filmmaker's Fear, Admits Shakti Samanta," *Screen Weekly*, February 27, 1998, 4.

33. Tom Conley, *Film Hieroglyphs: Ruptures in Classical Cinema* (Minneapolis: University of Minnesota Press, 1991), xxiv.

Coda. Radical Anglophony, or The Ethics of Attunement

1. Lisbeth Lipari, *Listening, Thinking, Being: Towards an Ethic of Attunement* (University Park, PA: Penn State University Press, 2014), 206.

INDEX

accents, 23, 85, 131–32, 163. *See also* pronunciation
Achebe, Chinua, 10, 14, 24
Adejunmobi, Moradewun, 5
Adichie, Chimamanda Ngozi, 24
Adiga, Aravind, 27, 100, 102, 113–21, 148
African-American literary tradition, 8, 11, 13, 71, 84, 93, 95
Agathocleous, Tanya, 71
Ahmad, Aijaz, 32
Akhtar, Zoya, 27, 153
Akkarmashi (Limbale), 66
Alighieri, Dante, 12–13, 146
Allan, Michael, 152
Ambedkar, Bhim Rao, xiii, xvi, 17–18, 26, 40, 63–73, 81, 86, 91, 96–99, 106, 181n1, 185n51, 188n24, 194n21
Anand, Mulk Raj, 27, 91, 99, 101–13, 121, 193n12, 194n22
Ananthamurthy, U. R., 101
Andhra Pradesh, 37, 60
Anglophone, as a term, 20, 25, 28, 122, 161, 178, 180
Anglophone world, xvii, 5, 8–9, 21, 98, 177, 179–80
Anjaria, Ulka, 15
Anveshi Broadsheet, 74
Anzaldúa, Gloria, 147
Ao, Temsula, 27, 128, 142–47
Ao Naga tribe, 142
aporia, 2
Aquil, Raziuddin, 9–10
Arac, Jonathan, 5
Aravumadan, Srinivas, 5
Armed Forces Special Powers Act (AFSPA), 128–29
autism, 143–44
Awadhi, 49. *See also* Hindi; Hindustani
Azad, Maulana Abdul Kalam, 19, 47

Babu Fictions (Khair), 104
Baer, Ben, 105, 107, 110–12
Baggs, Amanda, 135

Baishya, Amit R., 140, 146
Baishya, Anirban, 10
Baker, Houston, 12–13
Baluta (Pawar), 66
Bambaiyya, 163
Bartholdi, Frédéric-Auguste, 80
Baudh, Shanti Swarup, 78, 80
bearing witness, 27, 70, 73, 83–84, 127–28, 134, 140
Beecroft, Alexander, 8
Bengali, 10, 137
Bhabha, Homi, 41
Bhattacharya, Bhabhani, 101, 122
Bhavan, Bhartiya Vidya, 42
Bhoomkar, Sanjay, 66
bilingualism, 17, 26, 31, 70, 87, 162, 171, 176. *See also* language
Biography, 63
biopolitics, 178
Black vernacular tradition, 13, 84
Blues music, 13
Bollywood, 135, 153–54, 170–71, 173
book vendors, 148–51, 153
Bora, Papori, 133
Born Translated (Walkowitz), 195n1
Bose, Aparna Lanjewar, 60
Botterill, Steve, 13
Boyle, Danny, 27, 153, 160
Brahminical hegemony, 63, 69–71, 85, 90, 106. *See also* caste
brand names, 89–90, 151. *See also* names
British East India Company, 17
British Empire: administrators of, 11; and caste, 63, 70, 92; critiques of, 107; and education, 71, 75; and English, 17, 39, 44, 53, 56, 85, 151, 187n14; legacy of, 55; symbols of, 9, 109–10, 160. *See also* colonialism
Brueck, Laura, 67, 69, 73, 87, 186n61
Buddhism, 49
bureaucratese, 30–31, 48, 89, 93
Burning from Both the Ends (Patel), 64
Byapari, Manoranjan, 62

call centers, 5, 21–23, 163, 179, 182n8
caste: and colonialism, 1, 12, 92; critiques of, 70, 74, 79, 86, 92, 102, 112, 122; and education, 6, 163; and embodiment, 26, 65, 81, 89, 95, 104–5; and English, 27, 40–41, 55, 61–76, 78, 84–99, 111, 123, 149, 179, 189n3; hierarchies of, 17, 22, 34, 41, 50, 63, 84, 90–96, 110, 181n1, 185n51; influence of, xiii, 26, 64; justification of, xv–xvi; and language, 49, 92; and literature, 64, 69, 101–2; pervasiveness of, 62, 65, 88; preservation of, 62, 80; and race, 71, 83–84; resistance to, 72, 74, 82, 84; symbols of, 83, 193n12; and violence, 74, 90, 98, 181n6. *See also* Brahminical hegemony; class; Dalits
Caste Question, The (Rao), 62
Castes of Mind (Dirks), 92
censorship, 173–76
Census of India, 6, 126
Chakraborty, Dipesh, 14
Chandra, Shefali, 41
Chandra, Vikram, 10
Changkija, Monalisa, 142
Chatterjee, Partha, 9–10
Chatterjee, Upamanyu, 26, 45–46, 54
Chattopadhyay, Budhaditya, 173
Chattopadhyay, Swati, 166
Chaucer, Geoffrey, 12
Chaudhuri, Amit, 10
"Cheers" (Navaria), 88, 93–96
Chitre, Dilip, 66
Chow, Rey, 5, 14–15, 58, 108, 164, 182n8
Christianity, 17, 134
cinema, 27–28, 152–54, 158, 166, 170, 173–75, 177
Clash of Empires (Liu), 37
class: conflicts of, 166; and English, 40, 55, 163, 171, 179; hierarchy of, 17, 22, 24, 74, 100–101, 111, 116; influence of, 26; and marginality, 22–23; policing of, 149; and power, 41; and privilege, 6, 50; symbols of, 119, 169; and violence, 98. *See also* caste; social mobility
clothing, xv, 105–9, 119, 172, 185n51, 194n21–194n22
Cohn, Bernard, 11
colonialism: and caste, 92; and English, xiii, 8, 33, 39, 96, 178–79; language of, 5, 49, 51; legacies of, 1, 6–7, 20, 36–38, 55, 75, 125, 160, 178; and literary studies, 25; and modernity, 9–11; and race, 133; and shame, 44; strategies of, 11, 15, 17. *See also* British Empire; Orientalism
Colored Cosmopolitanism (Slate), 71
Commission for Scientific and Technical Terminology, 29–30, 139
Constitution of India, 17–20, 26, 36, 40, 47–48, 70–75, 119, 132, 139, 171–72, 188n24
cosmopolitanism, 24, 65, 100. *See also* globalization
Creole, 8

"Dalit and English" (Shepherd), 74
Dalit Anglophone literature, 26, 66, 69, 98
Dalit Bhagvati Jagran, 78
Dalit Goddess English, 17, 75–80, 126–27, 166
Dalit Panthers, 64, 66, 86
Dalits: and denial of English, 61; and education, xvi, 73–74; and global capital, 79; key leaders, 26; oral culture, 86; as a political subject, 86; representation of, 27, 83–85; restrictions on, xvi, 60, 90–91, 106, 110; as a term, 181n1; writing by, 60–61, 63–64, 66, 69, 83, 86–96, 189n1. *See also* caste; Harijan
Damrosch, David, 24, 152
Dasgupta, Sandipto, 36
De, Rohit, 20
Deccan Herald, 44
decolonization, 14
Defoe, Daniel, 15
dehumanization, 140–41
Deleuze, Gilles, 57–58, 105
democracy, xiii, 19, 26, 31–40, 47, 50–53, 62, 87, 100, 117, 129–35
Department of Education, 29
Derrida, Jacques, 2, 58
Desai, Gaurav, 5
desi literary traditions, 147
De Souza, Eunice, 86
devanagari script, 17, 19, 30, 32–33, 36, 94–95, 141, 164, 171. *See also* Hindi
Devi, Mahasweta, 45, 128, 136, 147
De vulgari eloquentia (Dante), 146
Devy, G. N., 127
DeWispelare, Daniel, 9
Dhasal, Namdeo, 66, 86
Dickens, Charles, 85

dictionaries, 29–31, 35, 37, 139–40.
   See also translation
"Dilemma" (Maitreya), 82
Dirks, Nicholas, 92
disability, 140
Discourse Networks 1800/1900 (Kittler), 125
Disparately Yours (Dube), 2
Doshi, Tishani, 168
Draupadi (Devi), 45, 136
Dreamers (Poonam), 21, 186n60
Dube, Anita, 2–4, 21
Dutt, Michael Madhusudan, 68
Dutt, Toru, 68
Dutta, Yashica, 66

education: access to, xvi, 6, 29, 62, 116, 123, 181n6, 182n2; and the British Empire, 71; and caste, 6, 70, 73–75, 116–17, 163; and cinema, 177; and democratic society, 19; and English, 21–22, 49, 96; failures of, 69; and Hindi, 50; language of, 31; and missionaries, 134; perceptions of, 34, 77; spending on, 17, 75; teaching strategies, 37, 124
8 Mile (Eminem), 154
Elam, Daniel, 25
English: access to, 66–67, 74, 88, 114, 182n2; in Africa, 24–25; appearances of, 185n51; and the body, 138–39; and Bollywood, 171, 173; as a brand, 94, 162; and British cultural values, 16; and bureaucracy, 48, 88; and caste, 1, 17, 26–27, 40–41, 55, 61–78, 84–99, 111, 123, 149, 179, 189n3; and class, 40; and clothing, 105–7, 194n21–194n22; and colonialism, xiii, 2–17, 28, 33, 39, 44–51, 57, 63, 76, 97–102, 112, 145, 151, 178; as a commodity, 119; and democracy, 19, 21, 31, 40, 62, 100, 129, 134–35; desire for, 69, 80, 110; education of, 21–22; and elitism, 40–41, 100; failures of, 53, 69; foreignness of, 18, 107; as a global language, xvii, 4, 7, 10, 14, 24–25, 34, 42, 67, 150–51, 168; and Hindi, 7, 18–20, 26–38, 45, 87, 92, 108, 162, 175–76; and identity, 49, 61, 113–14; inability to speak, 27, 102, 115, 122; as a machine, 46, 56, 112–13; and missionaries, 134–35; and modernity, 19, 35, 37–38, 42–43, 47–48, 52, 77; as mother figure, 72; as mother tongue, 79, 93, 126–27;

noncomprehension of, 23, 33–34, 36, 45, 53, 56, 117, 151, 160, 164, 169; nonreading of, 28, 31, 148–49, 154–56; as an object, 27, 43; as an official language, xiv, 6–7, 17, 20, 35–38, 46, 132, 135, 172, 174; and other languages, 7, 15–16, 152; personification of, 54–55; power of, 14, 17, 26, 70; and privilege, 138, 169, 179; and progress, xiii, xvi–xvii, 22, 42–43, 74–75, 78, 91–93, 121, 127, 155, 163, 168; promotion of, 35, 55, 73, 79, 96, 99–100, 106, 112; and protest, 115–16, 119, 131; as a sound object, 23, 27, 136; spread of, 9, 12, 31, 50, 61–62, 116–17, 161, 173; strategic use of, xv, 61, 72, 74, 81–83, 85–87, 92, 123, 128, 138, 187n14; as a technology, 166; and translation, 23–24, 29, 109; and Urdu, 140; value of, 31, 33–34, 48, 118–19, 177; as vernacular, 7–8, 12, 15–17, 19, 23, 98; versions of, 8, 102, 139, 186n60.
   See also Hindi; language; vernacular
English, August (Chatterjee), 26, 45–46, 54–55
English Heart, Hindi Heartland (Sadana), 31, 99, 150
Enlightenment, 63
Enlightenment in the Colony (Mufti), 33, 35
etiology of turpitude, 16
Eurocentrism, 14–15
Ezekiel, Nissim, 86

Facts of Resonance (Napolin), 186n63
Fall of Language in the Age of English, The (Mizumura), 152
Fanon, Frantz, 13, 15
Fine Balance, A (Mistry), 101
First War of Indian Independence, 71
Flesh and Fish Blood (Shankar), 9, 92
Florentine dialect, 12
foreignness, 18, 39, 58, 97, 109
Forget English! (Mufti), 20, 193n12
Forster, E. M., 113
From a Shepherd Boy to an Intellectual (Shepherd), 73–74
"From Mumbai" (Maitreya), 85–86

Gajarawala, Toral, 104
Gandhi, Indira, 166
Gandhi, Mohandas, 32–36, 42–45, 63, 73, 103–4, 106, 109–12, 121, 181n1, 187n14, 193n12, 194n22

Ganti, Tejaswini, 162
Garber, Marjorie, 105
Garwood, Ian, 160
Gates Jr., Henry Louis, 12–13, 84
Gehlawat, Ajay, 155
gender, 6, 79, 127–28, 130, 134
Ghalib, Mirza, 120
Ghose, Manmohan, 68
Ghosh, Amitav, 11, 17, 101
Ghubar-e-Khatir (Azad), 47
Gidla, Sujatha, 66
Gikandi, Simon, 5, 14–15
Gilchrist, John Borthwick, 16–17
Gitelman, Lisa, 31
Glass Palace, The (Ghosh), 11
globalization, xiii, 4, 20, 24, 61, 63, 79, 123, 154, 162, 164, 178. *See also* cosmopolitanism
God of Small Things, The (Roy), 100–101, 115, 140
Godwin, William, 71
Gogulamanda, Aruna, 60
Gopal, Priyamvada, 103
Gopinath, Praseeda, xiii
Government of India Act (1935), 20
Gower, John, 12
Goyal, Yogita, 182n1
grammar, 85, 112, 116. *See also* language
Great Expectations (Dickens), 85
Growing Up Untouchable in India (Pawar), 66
Guattari, Felix, 57–58, 105
Guide (Narayan), 122
Gujarat, 64
Gujarati, xiii, 82
Gulamgiri (Phule), 70
Gully Boy (Akhtar), 27, 116, 153–54, 164, 166–70
Gupta, Akhil, 31, 41
Gupta, Charu, 10, 63
Gurjars, 96
Guru, Gopal, 66
Gyaneshwari, 136

Haitian Creole, 8
Hakala, Walter, 30
Hally, Colonel G. J., 71
Harijan, 103, 181n1, 187n14. *See also* Dalits
Harry Potter, 149
Haryanvi, 169
Hazaar Chaurasir Ma (Devi), 45

He Who Rides the Tiger (Bhattacharya), 101, 122
Hindi: and caste, 34, 88, 91; in cinema, 170; and class, 169; compatibility with other languages, 108; development of, 37, 51; dialects of, 49, 79, 92; and English, 7, 18–20, 26–38, 45, 87, 92, 108, 162, 175–76; fetishization of, 170; as Indian language, xiv, 32–33; limits of, 36, 39, 41, 43–44, 51, 53, 56; and modernity, 35; as mother tongue, 126–27; and nationalism, 18, 37, 42; as an official language, 17, 36, 132; promotion of, 29, 33, 37, 49–50, 79, 94, 126; and religion, 19; as scientific, 30–31; as sentimental, 43; sounds of, 125, 165. *See also* devanagari script; English; language
Hinduism, 4, 18–19, 79, 84, 112
Hindu nationalism, xiv, xvi, 18, 170. *See also* nationalism
Hindustani, 16, 32–33, 42, 47, 49, 73, 79, 94, 100, 107–8, 165, 170–71
Hindustan Times, 44
hip-hop, 165–68
Hirsch, Marianne, 142
His Footsteps, through Darkness and Light (Mondal), 66
History in the Vernacular (Aquil and Chatterjee), 9
History of the Commonwealth (Godwin), 71
Hobson, Will, 66
Holmstrom, Lakshmi, 66

Ibis Trilogy, The (Ghosh), 17, 102
Ibomcha, Yumlembam, 27, 128, 141, 146–47
Igbo, 25
Ilaiah, Kancha, 26, 68, 73, 81, 89
illiteracy, 52–53, 117, 148. *See also* literacy
imperialism, 80
India: bureaucracy of, 2, 29; caste hierarchies in, 111; conflict zones in, 146; and democracy, 35–36, 62, 100, 115, 134–35; diversity of, 38–39, 60; education in, 17; global power of, 42; Hindu majority culture, 121; independence of, 17, 33, 112; and modernization, 166; as a mother figure, 79; national identity of, 18, 21, 26, 32–35, 40, 53–54, 113–14, 136, 171; national languages of, 6–7, 17, 33; place of English in, 6, 8, 10, 46, 116–17; and

postcolonialism, 19; separatist movements, 18, 128, 143; variety of languages in, 5–6, 10, 16, 26, 32, 42, 51, 96, 126, 169, 171; welfare state policies, 46, 61
India Demands English (Mathai), 26, 40–42, 45–48, 58, 80, 96, 100, 106, 126
Indian Constituent Assembly, 17, 36
Indian Express, 44
Indian National Congress, 47, 71
indigeneity, 13, 37, 79
Internet, 69, 74, 152, 166, 168. *See also* social media
Iqbal, 120
Islamicate culture, 175–76. *See also* Urdu
Ismail, Mirza, 44
Italian, 12

Jadhav, Narendra, 66
Jaipur Literary Festival, 189n1
Japanese literary culture, 152
Jim Crow, 83–84
Jinnah, Muhammed Ali, 185n51, 194n21
Jnanpith Award, 46
Johnson, Samuel, 15
Jones, William, 16
Joothan (Valmiki), 66
Joseph, Betty, 118
Joseph, Manu, 122
Joseph, Pothan, 44

Kafka, Franz, 2–3
Kama Sutra (Nair), 174–76
Kandasamy, Meena, 66–67, 89
Kanhailal, Oja Heisnam, 136
Kannada, 66
Kanthapura (Rao), 101
Karnataka, 37
Karukku (Bama), 66
Kashmir, 128, 139
Kashmiri, 139, 169
Katyal, Akhil, 168
Kaur, Rupi, 68
Keeling, Kara, 152
Kesavan, Mukul, 163
Khair, Tabish, 104
Khan, Moin, 22, 24, 84, 116
"Killing the Shambuka" (Sathyanathan), 83
King Emperor's English, The (Anand), 99, 110–11
Kire, Easterine, 142
Kittler, Friedrich, 125, 127, 129

Koshy, Susan, 9
Kothari, Rita, 93
Kumar, Ravish, 168
Kunreuther, Laura, 134

Lahiri, Madhumita, 21
language: and cinema, 153; and difference, 59, 186n63, 193n12; education of, 37; as infrastructure, 43, 46, 48, 71, 84; limits of, 143; and literature, 35; lived experiences of, 30, 48, 58, 67, 89, 104–5, 139; as a machine, 58; and national identity, 32, 44; and non-verbal sounds, 143; as an object, 2–3, 26, 42–43, 57, 103, 108, 118–19, 122–23, 159, 173; ownership of, 36, 58, 67, 144; as performance, 116; pictograms and hieroglyphs, 151–52; and power, 30–31, 49, 134, 138–39; respect for, 33; and rights, 41, 82; as a site for struggle, 125–26; as a sound object, 27, 108; standardization of, 33; theories of, 124–25; and violence, 145; visibility of, 105–6, 108. *See also* bilingualism; English; grammar; Hindi; pronunciation; translation; vernacular; *specific languages*
"Last Song, The" (Ao), 143–45
Latin, 8, 12
"Learning to Speak in English" (Maitreya), 81
Leima, Momon Soibom, 134
Leinau, Annette Damayanti, 14
Liberty Enlightening the World (Bartholdi), 80
Limbale, Sharankumar, 66
linguistic color line, 6
linguistic determination, 43
linguistic exceptionalism, 4–5
linguistic pluralism, 60
Lipari, Lisbeth, 180
literacy, 6, 98, 112, 120, 124, 148, 150–51, 153, 156, 158. *See also* illiteracy
literary studies, 1, 4–5, 9–15, 24–25, 28, 84, 93, 114
Liu, Lydia, 37, 152
Lok Foundation-Oxford University survey, 6
Lorde, Audre, 13
Luminescent Threads (Mondal), 66

Macaulay, Thomas Babington, 16–17, 71–72, 75–76, 91, 100, 164
Maharashtra, 82–83

Maitreya, Yogesh, 61, 67, 81, 83, 85–86, 88
Malayalam, 67, 100–101
Malviya, Madan Mohan, 39
Mammaries of the Welfare State (Chatterjee), 26, 45–46, 54, 56
Mandal, Prasad Bindeshwari, 61–62
Mandal Commission Report, 61–62, 88–89, 95
Mani, B. Venkat, 17
Manipur, 27, 127–28, 130–36, 141
Manorama, Thangjam, 131, 133, 195n11
Marathi, 66, 70, 82, 126, 162–63
margi literary tradition, 147
Masks of Conquest (Viswanathan), 41, 187n71
Mathai, Isaac, 40, 67, 96, 100
Mead, Henry, 72
Meeropol, Abel, 83
Mehta, Monika, 175
Meira Paibis, 130–40, 147, 177, 179
Meitelon, 128, 142
memory, 38, 142, 145, 158, 171
Mercatus Institute, 75
Merrill, Christi, 67, 69, 73, 87
Midnight's Children (Rushdie), 193n12
Mini, Darshana, 10
Ministry of Utmost Happiness, The (Roy), 139–40
"Minute on Indian Education" (Macaulay), 17, 71–72, 76, 100, 164
Mir, Farina, 12
Misra, Tilottama, 136
Misri, Deepti, 136
missionaries, 17, 71, 134
Mistry, Rohinton, 101
Mizumura, Minae, 5, 152
modernity, 19, 35, 42–43, 50–52, 62, 112–13, 122
Modi, Narendra, xiii, xiv, xv, 42, 151, 162, 179, 181n2
Mondal, Monidipa, 66
Monolingualism of the Other (Derrida), 58
Moon, Vasant, 66
Moos, S. N., 41, 43
Moraes, Dom, 86
"Mother English" (Phule), 72
motherhood, 125, 127, 130, 133, 136
Mothers of Manipur, The (Rehman), 136
mother tongue, 43–44, 65, 77, 79, 82, 126, 129, 136
Mowitt, John, 69

Mufti, Aamir, 9, 20, 33, 35, 39, 47, 193n12
Mukherjee, Arun Prabha, 66
"Mulligatawny Dreams" (Kandasamy), 67
Mumbai, 27, 153–54, 160, 164
Munshi, K. M., 41–42
Murakami, Haruki, 149
Muslims, xiii, 18, 33, 47, 121, 139–40, 165, 168. *See also* Urdu

Nagaland, 143
Naga National Council, 128
Nagaraj, D. R., 66
Nair, Mira, 174–75
names, 64–65, 74, 83, 89, 92–95, 112, 116, 118, 144, 149, 156. *See also* brand names
Napolin, Julie Beth, 186n63
Narayan, R. K., 122
nastaliq script, 19, 32, 171
national identity, 18, 32–34, 37, 40, 171
nationalism, 37, 42, 49, 102, 107, 133, 196n18. *See also* Hindu nationalism
Navaria, Ajay, 69, 87–88
Naxalite movement, 137
Nehru, Jawaharlal, 17–18, 40, 42, 46–47, 56–58, 113–14
neoimperialism, 80
neoliberalism, xiii, 102, 118, 169
newspapers, 44
Ngambi, Ima Lourembam, 131–32
Ngangom, Robin, 141
Nigeria, 5, 25
"Nightmare" (Ibomcha), 141
noncomprehension, 23, 33–34, 45, 53
nonreading, 56, 148–49
non-verbal sounds, 143
Northeast India, 27, 128, 146
Noudelmann, François, 23–24

Obama, Barack, xiv
Official Language Act of 1963, 37, 94
"On the Need of Common Language" (Sathyanathan), 81
orality, 125, 128, 142, 145–46
Orientalism, 5, 8, 11, 15, 110, 183n15. *See also* colonialism
Orientalist philology, 11, 15–16

Pakistan, 33, 185n51
Panther's Paw, 67
Patel, Geeta, 16
Patel, Neerav, 64, 67, 74, 82, 93

paternalism, 100
Pawar, Daya, 66
Peasants' Revolt (1381), 12
Persian, 16, 32–33
Peters, John Durham, 32
Phanishwarnath Renu, 46
Phule, Jotiba, 26, 66, 68–72, 81
Phule, Savitribai, 68, 70, 72, 86, 126
"Picturing Other Languages" (Allan), 152
Pinto, Jerry, 66
Place of English in India, The (Moos), 41
Planning Commission, 48
Poetry in a Global Age (Ramazani), 68
Poonam, Snigdha, 21–22, 186n60
postcolonial India, xiii, 18–20, 35, 44, 142, 148
postcolonial studies, 2, 9, 24
poverty, 46, 103, 115, 162, 181n2
Prasad, Chandrabhan, 17, 68, 73–76, 80–81, 90, 126, 166
Prasad, M. Madhava, 171
Premchand, 46, 87
Probyn, Elspeth, 44
pronunciation, 22, 67, 116–17, 124–25, 172, 179. *See also* accents; language
protests, 115–16, 119, 127, 131, 136–38, 147
psychoanalytic feminist criticism, 130
public sphere, 62, 112, 129
Punjabi, 12, 67, 108, 169
Purab Aur Paschim (Kumar), 172, 174
Puri, Anjali, 181n6

Raag Darbari (Sukla), 26, 45–55, 58, 67, 96, 116, 132, 151
race, 71, 83–84, 93, 133
Racine, Jean-Luc, 66
Racine, Josiane, 66
radio broadcasting, 50, 67
Rajagopalachari, C., 42–43, 79, 171
Raley, Rita, 9, 16, 151
Ramaswamy, Sumathi, 79
Ramayana (Valmiki), 84
Ramazani, Jahan, 17, 68
Rangan, Pooja, 135, 144
Rao, Anupama, 62
Rao, Raja, 101
Reading the Figural (Rodowick), 153
"Recollecting an Old Self" (Maitreya), 83
Rehman, Teresa, 136
religious rituals, 79
"Remains of the Name, The" (Patel), 64

Rodowick, D. N., 153, 161
Roman script, xvii, 16, 19, 23, 94–95, 134, 139, 151–53, 161, 164–66
Roy, Arundhati, 100, 128, 139–40, 147
Rumi, 120
Rushdie, Salman, 10, 193n12

Sadana, Rashmi, 5, 18, 31, 99, 150
Sahitya Akademi, 46, 60, 88, 189n3
Samanta, Shakti, 175
Samskara (Ananthamurthy), 101
Sanskrit, xiv, 16, 26, 32, 34, 37, 42, 47, 50, 72, 104
Saraswati, 74, 79
Sathyanathan, Chandramohan, 60, 81, 83–84, 86, 88–89
satire, 45–46
Satyashodhak Samaj, 70
savarna Hindus, 61, 65, 73, 81, 84, 87, 90
Screen Weekly, 170–71, 174
separatism, 43
Sepoy Revolt (Mead), 72
Serious Men (Joseph), 102
Seth, Vikram, 150
Sevasadan, 87
17th Assam Rifles, 131
Sexual Life of English, The (Chandra), 41, 190n10
shahirs, 86
shame, 44, 82, 99, 135, 137
Shankar, Subramanian, 9–10, 12, 63, 92
Shepherd, Kancha Ilaiah, 26, 68, 73, 81, 89
shit narrative, 155, 162
Shivdas, Parmar Kalidas, 91
Short Stories by Kafka (Dube), 3
shudras, 72–73, 104, 181n1
Signifying Monkey, The (Gates), 84
"Signs Taken for Wonders" (Bhabha), 41
silence, 27, 63, 141
Slate, Nico, 71
slavery, 11, 13, 70–71
Slumdog Millionaire (Boyle and Thadani), 27, 153–59, 161–64, 169–70, 197n5
"Soaba" (Ao), 143–44
social media, xv, 19, 27, 60, 68–69. *See also* Internet
social mobility, 22–23, 88, 127, 154. *See also* class
Somerset, Fiona, 7–8
songs, 145–46, 154–55, 167, 172
Sonic Color Line, The (Stoever), 152

Sorenson, Janet, 183n15
sound, 108–10, 125, 127, 136, 140–44, 173, 176
Spivak, Gayatri Chakravorty, 137–38
Spoken English, 21–22, 186n60
Srinivasan, Ragini Tharoor, 182n8, 184n36
Steintrager, James A., 108
Stephen, Cynthia, 60
Stoever, Jennifer, 152
Stowe, Harriet Beecher, 71
"Strange Fruit" (Meeropol), 83
Strike (Dube), 3–4
Subaltern Studies collective, 9–10
subtitles, 160–61, 176
Suitable Boy, A (Seth), 150
Sukla, Srilal, 26, 45–46
super-signs, 37–39, 53, 172. *See also* translation
Swadeshi movement, 33
Swarup, 197n5

Tabassum, Wajidah, 174
Tageldin, Shaden, 9, 11
Tagore, Rabindranath, 33, 35, 44
Tamil, 66–67
Tamil Nadu, 37
tapori, 162
Taseer, Aatish, 6
technology industry, 24
tekhne, 28, 178
Telangana, 73
Teltumbde, Anand, 66
Telugu, 66, 73–74, 126
Thadani, Loveleen, 153
These Hills Called Home (Ao), 142–43
Thiong'o wa, Ngũgĩ, 10, 14, 24
Thoughts on Linguistic States (Ambedkar), 40
Three-Language Formula, 37
Torch Bearers, 130–40, 147, 177, 179
touch, 26, 81, 84, 87–89, 94–95, 159
Tran, Ben, 9
translation, 20–23, 30, 36, 47, 55, 66–67, 87–92, 108–9, 128, 137–40, 160–69, 175–76. *See also* dictionaries; language; super-signs; transliteration
transliteration, 103, 108–9, 137, 140, 152, 165. *See also* translation
transvestism, 105
trauma, 132, 136, 139, 141–47
Trevelyan, Charles, 16
Trump, Donald, xiv
Tukaram, 86

Uncle Tom's Cabin (Stowe), 71
United States, 5, 13, 70–71, 75, 80, 83
Unlearning the City (Chattopadhyay), 166
Untouchable (Anand), 27, 91, 99, 101–13, 121, 193n12
Untouchable Fictions (Gajarawala), 104
Urdu, 10–12, 18–19, 32–35, 39, 42, 47, 120, 139–40, 168–71, 174, 185n51. *See also* Islamicate culture; Muslims
"Uttaran" (Tabassum), 174
Uttar Pradesh, 46, 49–50, 75

Valmiki, Omprakash, 66
Varhadi, 82
Vasudevan, Ravi, 171
Vemula, Rohith, xiii, xvi, xvii, 69, 83–84, 86
vernacular, 6–7, 10–13, 16–17, 28, 84. *See also* English; language
Vested Interests (Garber), 105
villages, 46, 48, 52
Viramma (Racine and Racine), 66
Viswanathan, Gauri, 41, 50, 187n71
voice, 26–27, 115, 125–30, 132, 134–36, 142–45, 165–69, 178–80

Wade, Cleo, 68
Waiting for a Visa (Ambedkar), 73, 91, 99
Walkowitz, Rebecca, 9, 20, 23, 114, 195n1
Wanjari, Yogesh Maitreya, 60
Warner, Tobias, 5
Watson, Nicholas, 7–8
West Bengal, 37, 137
What Did I Do to Be So Black and Blue? (Patel), 64
What Is World Literature? (Damrosch), 152
White Tiger, The (Adiga), 27, 100–102, 113–22, 148–51, 163, 168, 177–79, 181n2, 192n4
"Witnessing" (Maitreya), 86
Wood, Charles, 16
Words without Borders, 69, 87
Wright, Gillian, 47
writing: and destiny, 155; as a haptic act, 64; as images, 154; and intimacy, 82; motivations for, 83, 165; styles of, 21, 66, 68, 70, 110, 141; visibility of, 165

Yengde, Suraj, 66
Yes, Sir (Navaria), 69, 90–91

Translation / Transnation
SERIES EDITOR EMILY APTER

Writing Outside the Nation by Azade Seyhan

Ambassadors of Culture: The Transamerican Origins of Latino Writing by Kirsten Silva Gruesz

The Literary Channel: The Inter-National Invention of the Novel edited by Margaret Cohen and Carolyn Dever

Experimental Nations: Or, the Invention of the Maghreb by Réda Bensmaïa

What Is World Literature? by David Damrosch

We, the People of Europe?: Reflections on Transnational Citizenship by Étienne Balibar

The Portable Bunyan: A Transnational History of "The Pilgrim's Progress" by Isabel Hofmeyr

Nation, Language, and the Ethics of Translation edited by Sandra Bermann and Michael Wood

Utopian Generations: The Political Horizon of Twentieth-Century Literature by Nicholas Brown

Guru English: South Asian Religion in a Cosmopolitan Language by Srinivas Aravamudan

Poetry of the Revolution: Marx, Manifestos, and the Avant-Gardes by Martin Puchner

The Translation Zone: A New Comparative Literature by Emily Apter

In Spite of Partition: Jews, Arabs, and the Limits of Separatist Imagination by Gil Z. Hochberg

The Princeton Sourcebook in Comparative Literature: From the European Enlightenment to the Global Present edited by David Damrosch, Natalie Melas, and Mbongiseni Buthelezi

The Spread of Novels: Translation and Prose Fiction in the Eighteenth Century by Mary Helen McMurran

The Novel and the Sea by Margaret Cohen

The Event of Postcolonial Shame by Timothy Bewes

Hamlet's Arab Journey: Shakespeare's Prince and Nasser's Ghost by Margaret Litvin

Archives of Authority: Empire, Culture, and the Cold War by
    Andrew N. Rubin

Security: Politics, Humanity, and the Philology of Care by John T.
    Hamilton

Dictionary of Untranslatables: A Philosophical Lexicon edited by
    Barbara Cassin

Learning Zulu: A Secret History of Language in South Africa by
    Mark Sanders

*In the Shadow of World Literature: Sites of Reading in Colonial
    Egypt* by Michael Allan

Leaks, Hacks, and Scandals: Arab Culture in the Digital Age by Tarek
    El-Ariss

City of Beginnings: Poetic Modernism in Beirut by Robyn Creswell

Vernacular English: Reading the Anglophone in Postcolonial India
    by Akshya Saxena

A NOTE ON THE TYPE

{~~~~}

THIS BOOK has been composed in Miller, a Scotch Roman typeface designed by Matthew Carter and first released by Font Bureau in 1997. It resembles Monticello, the typeface developed for The Papers of Thomas Jefferson in the 1940s by C. H. Griffith and P. J. Conkwright and reinterpreted in digital form by Carter in 2003.

Pleasant Jefferson ("P. J.") Conkwright (1905-1986) was Typographer at Princeton University Press from 1939 to 1970. He was an acclaimed book designer and AIGA Medalist.

The ornament used throughout this book was designed by Pierre Simon Fournier (1712-1768) and was a favorite of Conkwright's, used in his design of the *Princeton University Library Chronicle*.

GPSR Authorized Representative: Easy Access System Europe - Mustamäe tee
50, 10621 Tallinn, Estonia, gpsr.requests@easproject.com

www.ingramcontent.com/pod-product-compliance
Lightning Source LLC
Chambersburg PA
CBHW021705230426
43668CB00008B/733